**DATE DUE**

Supporters of Stali wn
supporters saw hin ian
Revolution, Geoffrey he
Russian Revolution. sts
that:

- In the years betw er
  than Lenin, whic for
  the overthrow of
- During the autu an
  insurrection car for
  a Party-orchestra
- During the Russ hat
  the only way to in
  the Tsar's army.

As well as examinir his
volume probes deeper to explore the ideas which drove Trotsky forward during his years of influence over Russia's revolutionary politics, discussing such key concepts as how to construct a revolutionary party, how to stage a successful insurrection, how to fight a revolutionary war, and how to build a socialist state.

**Geoffrey Swain** is the Alec Nove Chair in Russian and East European Studies at the University of Glasgow, UK. He has written extensively on the modern history of Russia and Eastern Europe, including biographies of the dissident communists *Trotsky* (2006) and *Tito* (2011).

# Introduction to the series

History is the narrative constructed by historians from traces left by the past. Historical enquiry is often driven by contemporary issues and, in consequence, historical narratives are constantly reconsidered, reconstructed and reshaped. The fact that different historians have different perspectives on issues means that there is often controversy and no universally agreed version of past events. *Seminar Studies* was designed to bridge the gap between current research and debate, and the broad, popular general surveys that often date rapidly.

The volumes in the series are written by historians who are not only familiar with the latest research and current debates concerning their topic, but who have themselves contributed to our understanding of the subject. The books are intended to provide the reader with a clear introduction to a major topic in history. They provide both a narrative of events and a critical analysis of contemporary interpretations. They include the kinds of tools generally omitted from specialist monographs: a chronology of events, a glossary of terms and brief biographies of 'who's who'. They also include bibliographical essays in order to guide students to the literature on various aspects of the subject. Students and teachers alike will find that the selection of documents will stimulate the discussion and offer insight into the raw materials used by historians in their attempt to understand the past.

**Clive Emsley and Gordon Martel**
Series Editors

# Trotsky and the Russian Revolution

Geoffrey Swain

Routledge
Taylor & Francis Group

LONDON AND NEW YORK

First published 2014
by Routledge
2 Park Square, Milton Park, Abingdon, Oxon OX14 4RN

and by Routledge
711 Third Avenue, New York, NY 10017

*Routledge is an imprint of the Taylor & Francis Group, an informa business*

British Library Cataloguing in Publication Data
A catalogue record for this book is available from the British Library

Library of Congress Cataloging in Publication Data
Swain, Geoff, author.
  Trotsky and the Russian revolution / Geoffrey Swain.
    pages; cm. – (Seminar studies in history)
  Includes bibliographical references.
  1. Trotsky, Leon, 1879–1940.  2. Soviet Union – History – Revolution, 1917–21.
3. Rossiiskaia kommunisticheskaia partiia (bol?shevikov)  I. Title.  II. Series: Seminar studies in history.
  DK254.T6S935 2014
  947.084092–dc23
[B]
                                                                          2013031878

ISBN: 978-0-415-73667-1 (hbk)
ISBN: 978-1-447-90144-0 (pbk)
ISBN: 978-1-315-81715-6 (ebk)

Typeset in 10/13.5pt ITC Berkeley
by Graphicraft Limited, Hong Kong

Printed and bound in Great Britain by
TJ International Ltd, Padstow, Cornwall

# Contents

# DOCUMENTS

# List of plates

# Chronology

**1920**

*February*  In Ekaterinburg, developing Labour Armies

*summer*  At the front during the Russo-Polish War

*autumn*  Campaigning for the militarisation of labour

**1921**

*March*  The Kronstadt Uprising; the Tenth Party Congress bans factions

**1922**

*April*  Speaks at Eleventh Party Congress on importance of Gosplan

*December*  Lenin 'meets Trotsky half way' on powers of Gosplan

**1923**

*April*  Twelfth Party Congress backs Trotsky on planning

*October*  Failure of attempt by German Communist Party to seize power

*December*  Trotsky agrees to the resolution 'On Building the Party'

**1924**

*January*  Trotsky writes *The New Course*; condemned as a deviationist

*November*  Uses the book *Lessons of October* to attack Zinoviev and Kamenev

**1925**

*January*  Resigns as Commissar of War

*May*  Starts work on Dnieper Dam project

**1926**

*April*  Ceases work on Dnieper Dam project; joins Zinoviev's and Kamenev's opposition to Stalin

*July*  Trotsky and Zinoviev issue *Declaration of 13*

*October*  Removed from Politburo

**1927**

*April*  In China Chiang Kai-shek massacres members of the Chinese Communist Party; Trotsky sees parallel with the danger of Thermidor

*October*  Removed from the Central Committee

*November*  Expelled from the Bolshevik Party

**1928**

*January*  Exiled to Alma Ata, Kazakhstan

**1929**  Deported to Turkey

**1934**  Moves from Turkey to France

**1935**  Moves from France to Norway

**1936**  Leaves Norway for final exile in Mexico

**1940**  Assassinated by Stalin's agent in Mexico

# Who's who

**Akselrod, Pavel** (1850–1928): First active alongside Plekhanov in the late 1870s, he became one of the editors of *Iskra* and was a firm believer in the idea that workers did not need the guidance of any political party in order to gain political consciousness.

**Chernyshevskii, Nikolai** (1828–89): The most influential of the social revolutionaries of the 1860s, and in many ways the founder of Populism.

**Chiang Kai-shek** (1887–1975): See Kuomintang (Glossary). For Trotsky, Chiang Kai-shek's assault on the Chinese communists epitomised the Thermidor danger inherent in Stalin's rule.

**Kamenev, Lev** (1883–1936): Although at one time married to Trotsky's sister, Kamenev was one of Lenin's most loyal supporters in the pre-revolutionary years when Lenin's disagreement with Trotsky on organisational matters was at its height. However, in October 1917 Kamenev joined with Zinoviev in opposing Bolshevik plans for an insurrection, arguing that an insurrection was unnecessary since the Bolsheviks were likely to emerge as the controlling force in post-revolutionary Russian politics by constitutional means. In the early 1920s, Kamenev was one of the triumvirate, alongside Stalin and Zinoviev, which ruled Soviet Russia after Lenin's death and progressively marginalised Trotsky. However, in 1925 Kamenev turned against Stalin and was joined in this struggle by Trotsky in 1926.

**Kamenev, Sergei** (1881–1936): Initially commander of Red forces on the Eastern Front, in July 1919 he became Commander-in-Chief of the Red Army and retained that position until 1924.

**Krylenko, Nikolai** (1885–1938): A leading member of the Military Revolutionary Committee, he spoke in favour of Trotsky's concept of insurrection at the crucial meeting of the Bolshevik Central Committee on 16 October 1917. Later he became the Soviet Union's Commissar of Justice, before falling victim to Stalin's purges.

**Lockhart, Robert Bruce** (1887–1970): British Vice-Consul in Moscow during the First World War and Acting Consul during the Revolution, Bruce Lockhart returned home just before the Bolshevik seizure of power, but was then sent back to Moscow in January 1918 on a mission to see if anything could be done to keep fighting going on the Eastern Front. He briefly established a good working relationship with Trotsky.

**Martov, Yulii** (1873–1923): One of the leaders of the Mensheviks, but a close associate of Lenin on the editorial board of *Iskra* until the split of the Russian Social Democratic Labour Party into its Bolshevik and Menshevik factions in 1903.

**Plekhanov, Georgii** (1856–1918): Always referred to as the founder of Russian Marxism, he was until the late 1870s a Populist, albeit a Populist who denounced the use of terror. However, the investigation he carried out into rural life during the second half of the 1870s convinced Plekhanov that the traditional communal lifestyle of the Russian peasantry was essentially a Populist myth, that capitalist economic relationships were coming to Russia, just as they were to every European country, and that therefore revolutionaries should accept, as Marx did, that the only revolutionary class in Russia was the urban proletariat. Plekhanov's orthodox Marxism insisted that in the course of Russia's capitalist development, its only ally could be the liberal middle class, something with which Trotsky vehemently disagreed.

**Robespierre, Maximilien** (1758–94): A leading protagonist in the French Revolution, who during the period 1793–94 headed the Committee of Public Safety and was virtual dictator of France, responsible for a reign of terror which sent thousands to the guillotine on the mere suspicion of engaging in counter-revolutionary activities. When Robespierre was overthrown and himself guillotined on 28 July 1794, that date – 10 Thermidor according to the revolutionary calendar then in operation – was considered the start of the French Revolution turning towards reaction and the start of the process through which Napoleon eventually emerged as Emperor of France.

**Sedova, Natalia (Natasha)** (1882–1962): Trotsky's partner from 1904 and ultimately his second wife until his death.

**Sokolovskaya, Aleksandra** (1872–1938): Trotsky's first wife. Like most radicals of their era, neither Trotsky nor Sokolovskaya believed in marriage as an institution, but in order to ensure that they were exiled to the same place, they went through a wedding ceremony. Sokolovskaya was arrested in 1935 for keeping up a correspondence with the exiled Trotsky and died in Stalin's purges.

**Voroshilov, Kliment** (1881–1969): Together with Stalin, Voroshilov was responsible for preventing the Whites take control of Tsaritsyn over the summer and autumn of 1918. Despite limited military training, he had a flare for military affairs and went on to head the First Cavalry Army during the Russian Civil War and the 1920 Polish War. Under Stalin he became Commissar for Defence, and under Khrushchev President of the Soviet Union.

**Zinoviev, Grigorii** (1883–1936): One of Lenin's most loyal supporters in the pre-revolutionary years when Lenin's disagreement with Trotsky on organisational matters was at its height. However, in October 1917 Zinoviev joined with Kamenev in opposing Bolshevik plans for an insurrection, arguing that an insurrection was unnecessary since the Bolsheviks were likely to emerge as the controlling force in post-revolutionary Russian politics by constitutional means. During the civil war, Zinoviev clashed with Trotsky over the question of how much control the Party should have over the Red Army, and during the trade union controversy of 1920–21 he again clashed with Trotsky. In the early 1920s, Zinoviev was one of the triumvirate, alongside Stalin and Kamenev, which ruled Soviet Russia after Lenin's death and progressively marginalised Trotsky. However, in 1925 Zinoviev turned against Stalin and was joined in this struggle by Trotsky in 1926.

# Glossary

*Balkan Wars*: The First Balkan War began on 8 October 1912 when Bulgaria, Greece, Montenegro and Serbia declared war on Ottoman Turkey in order to bring an end to Turkish rule in the Balkans. The war culminated in the Treaty of London, 30 May 1913. The Second Balkan War began on 16 June 1913 because Bulgaria did not receive in that treaty all the territory in Macedonia that it had been promised by Serbia and Greece in a secret agreement before the first war began. It ended with the Treaty of Bucharest on 10 August 1913.

*Cheka*: The name given to the Extraordinary Commission for Combating Counter-Revolution and Speculation, established in December 1917, which became the Bolshevik secret police.

*Constituent Assembly*: Long promised by the Provisional Government, the elections to the Constituent Assembly took place on 12 November 1917. This gave 52.3 per cent of the votes to the Socialist Revolutionary Party, and 23.6 per cent to the Bolsheviks. However, the allocation of Socialist Revolutionary Party candidates took place before the split in the SR Party and the formation in late October of the Left Socialist Revolutionaries as a separate party. The victory of the Left SRs at the Extraordinary Congress of Peasant Soviets and the Second Congress of Peasant Soviets, both held in November, suggested that they would have secured a large number of seats if able to stand in the Constituent Assembly elections. The Bolshevik–Left Socialist Revolutionary Coalition Government requested that the Constituent Assembly should recognise what it termed the 'right of recall' and allow local soviets to call by-elections where the local SR deputy was not felt to represent the popular will. When the Constituent Assembly met on 5 January 1918 it refused point blank to agree to this, and so was forcibly dissolved.

*Duma*: More accurately the Imperial State Duma. Between 1906 and 1917 there were four elected Dumas. The first lasted from April to July 1906 and was dissolved by the Tsar when it tried to press ahead with radical land reform. The second met from February to June 1907 and was also dissolved when it tried to press ahead with radical land reform. On 3 June 1907 the Tsar carried out a 'coup': the constitutional law he himself had drawn up stated that the electoral system could be changed only with the consent of the Duma; however, he changed the electoral franchise unilaterally so that in future elections there would be fewer worker and peasant deputies and thus less pressure for radical reform. Under this revised electoral franchise the third Duma met from November 1907 to July 1912, and the fourth from September 1912 to February 1917.

*German October*: The events in Germany of October 1923 when the German Communist Party made a rather half-hearted attempt to take advantage of the country's hyper-inflationary economic crisis and seize power.

*Gosplan*: The state planning commission first established in February 1921 and later the instrument of Stalin's forced industrialisation policies. Trotsky pressed consistently from 1921 until his exile for this body, and the economists who ran it, to be given more power.

*Interdistrict Group*: Sometimes known by its the Russian title, *Mezhraionka*, this was one of the most active underground social democratic groups operating between 1905 and 1917. Active from 1913 to 1917, its direct antecedents go back to 1911. Because it both rejected the decisions of the Prague and Vienna conferences and looked back to the unity which had existed in the Russian Social Democratic Labour Party between 1906 and 1910, it was close to Trotsky's non-faction stance. Thus Trotsky increasingly identified with it and became one of its leaders on his return to Russia in 1917.

*July Days*: The events of 3–4 July 1917 in Petrograd. The first government to be formed after the February Revolution of 1917 had, with one exception, been composed of liberals. After its lack of popular support became evident, a coalition of moderate socialists and liberals formed a coalition government in early May. That coalition fell apart on 2 July, when the liberals resigned. Thus the moderate socialists were faced with the dilemma of trying to patch up their relationship with the liberals, or form a government based only on the political parties represented in the Soviet. The dilemma, a Soviet Government or a Coalition Government, was made more acute because the Bolsheviks had linked the slogan of a 'Soviet Government' to the conduct of the war. In June the Provisional Government had launched an offensive on the Eastern Front. This had not gone well, and on the eve of the coalition falling apart determined efforts had been made to deploy reserve units based in Petrograd and Kronstadt to the battlefield. Those units were unwilling to be deployed to the front, not because of cowardice but because they accepted the Bolshevik view that this was an imperialist war and it was their primary duty to defend the revolution, not fight against Germany. The mood of the soldiers and sailors demonstrating on 3 and 4 July for a Soviet Government was such that Lenin and Trotsky toyed with the idea of starting an insurrection, but they quickly realised that the ground had not been sufficiently well prepared. After the July Days, the Provisional Government denounced the Bolsheviks as German agents and arrested most of their leaders.

*Kronstadt Naval Base*: Situated on an island in the Gulf of Finland from where access to St Petersburg could be controlled, the sailors of the naval base played a key role in the events of revolutionary Russia. In 1905 it was the site of a mutiny, during the July Days of 1917 sailors from Kronstadt demonstrated in the capital, urging the Bolsheviks to seize power, and in March 1921 it was the centre of one of the most extensive rebellions against the Soviet regime.

*Kulak*: The Russian word for 'fist' and therefore figuratively the person who 'squeezed' the peasants. Kulaks, including Trotsky's father David Bronstein, were usually peasants who, because of their relative wealth, were able to acquire equipment, such as Bronstein's mill or a number of large carts. This meant that other peasants often had to market their grain and other produce through a kulak intermediary, who could dictate the terms of trade. For Bolsheviks the kulak became a demonised concept and a term of abuse, used to describe the actions of any peasant who resisted the policies imposed by the Soviet regime.

*Kuomintang* (Guomindang or KMT): The Chinese Nationalist Party founded shortly after the overthrow of the Chinese Emperor in the 1911 Revolution. By the mid-1920s it was led by Chiang Kai-shek, who was unhappy with the party's close alliance with the Chinese Communist Party. When the KMT gained control of Shanghai, and the local communists began to talk ever more openly of the need for revolution, Chiang felt the time had come to break the alliance with the communists and in April 1927 he organised a brutal massacre of communist activists.

*Military Opposition*: Formed in the run-up to the Eighth Party Congress in March 1919, the Military Opposition argued that Trotsky made too much use of 'military specialists', officers from the old Imperial Army, and did not allow sufficient Party control over military matters. Although defeated at the congress, Trotsky always felt that the Bolshevik leadership, Stalin and Zinoviev in particular, never really abandoned this view.

*Military Revolutionary Committee (MRC)*: A sub-committee of the Petrograd Soviet, established initially to resist any plans Kerensky might have to redeploy troops from Petrograd or even evacuate the then capital, this was the natural body to resist Kerensky's attempt to remove the commissars the MRC had appointed to oversee troop movement, and thus begin the process of insurrection. It thus carried out the Bolshevik seizure of power and remained the only source of power for the first few weeks of Bolshevik rule, until a properly constituted government was formed at the end of November.

*New Economic Policy* (NEP): Introduced at the Tenth Party Congress in March 1921 to put an end to the almost endemic peasant uprisings which had broken out as Russia's Civil War came to a conclusion. Under it the peasants were allowed to sell their grain surplus in a free market after a certain amount of tax had been paid, initially in kind. To provide peasants with goods for purchase, light industry was denationalised and, while the state retained control of heavy industry, the banks and foreign trade, much of light industry was restored to private ownership.

*October Manifesto*: The high point of the 1905 Revolution, when on 17 October, under pressure from the widespread general strike organised that month by the Petersburg Soviet, the Tsar agreed that in future he would rule in collaboration with an elected legislative assembly. At this stage he did not spell out how the assembly would be elected or precisely what its powers would be.

*Panteleev Affair*: During the desperate struggle in August 1918 to retain control over the bridge across the Volga at Sviyazhsk, a Red Army unit fled the battlefield and tried to hijack a boat to take them to safety. The military commissar of this unit was a certain Panteleev, a member of the Bolshevik Party. Trotsky ordered the execution of all involved, including Panteleev. This action was used repeatedly by his opponents as evidence that Trotsky put more trust in military specialists, officers from the old Imperial Army, than communists.

*Petersburg Soviet*: Established by Mensheviks to lead the general strike of October 1905, it soon controlled much of the capital and briefly acted as a parallel city administration. Until its closure and the arrest of its leaders, including Trotsky in early December 1905, it acted as both the parliament and the executive of the labour movement.

*Petrograd Soviet*: On 27 February 1917, at the height of the revolution which ended the rule of the Tsar, the Soviet was reconstituted on the model of the earlier Petersburg Soviet. Initially its leadership was politically cautious, seeing itself as the critical friend of the Provisional Government; from May 1917 Soviet members participated in government. Both Trotsky and Lenin argued that the Soviet was the embryo of a new form of workers' government and that it should challenge rather than support the Provisional Government, advancing instead the demand for a Soviet Government.

*Politburo*: The first Political Bureau of the Central Committee of the Bolshevik Party (Politburo) was established during the October insurrection. However, it was only during the Civil War that it emerged as the predominant executive body of the Bolshevik Party.

*Poor Peasant Committees*: Established by decree on 11 June 1918, these committees were supposed to take class war into the countryside. The assumption was that kulaks were organising resistance to the Bolsheviks' policy of paying a low fixed price for grain, and so, to ensure grain expropriation could take place, poor peasants were to mobilise opinion against the kulaks; where this failed, the committees could turn to special armed units for support. By November 1918 Lenin had realised that these committees did not target the kulaks, but in fact turned the bulk of the peasantry, the middle peasants, against the Bolsheviks. In December 1918 the Poor Peasant Committees were abolished in Russia, but they continued to operate in Ukraine and elsewhere. The Eighth Party Congress in March 1919 endorsed Lenin's policy in favour of the middle peasants, but even thereafter many Bolsheviks were resistant to the change in policy.

*Revolutionary Military Council (RVS)*: At the end of August 1918 Trotsky |abolished the Supreme Military Council and brought all military formations – those preparing for a resumption of hostilities against Imperial Germany and those engaged in fighting counter-revolution – under the control of this single body.

*Russian Social Democratic Labour Party (RSDLP)*: Founded in 1898, the RSDLP split into two factions at its Second Congress in 1903. The split into the Bolshevik and Menshevik factions took place over the issue of organisation: the Bolsheviks wanted a highly centralised and disciplined organisation; the Mensheviks wanted to ensure that excessive centralism did not exclude from the party those working-class militants who needed to be at its core. The party was reunited in 1906, and remained so until the January 1910 Plenum of the Central Committee. That plenum resolved to call a party conference, but disagreements about how best to do this and who should take part re-opened divisions with the result that two conferences were held in 1912, a Bolshevik conference in Prague and a Menshevik one in Vienna, with Trotsky playing the leading role in organising the latter. There was also a second issue that divided Bolsheviks and Mensheviks, which emerged in the aftermath of the 1905 Revolution. Duma politics meant that a forum existed for open political activity, which in turn raised the question of political alliances. Most Mensheviks followed Plekhanov and favoured an alliance in the Duma with liberal groups; most Bolsheviks followed Lenin and favoured an alliance with the peasantry. Trotsky was a Menshevik in that he supported them on the question of organisation, but a Bolshevik in that he opposed joint political activity with the liberals and favoured working with the peasantry.

*South Russia Workers' Union*: The underground workers' organisation that Trotsky, Aleksandra Sokolovskaya and their friends ran in 1897–98. Although its base was Nikolaev (today Mikolaiv), it also had contacts in Odessa. The fact that 200 people were arrested when it was closed down by the police is testament to Trotsky's success as an underground organiser.

*Supreme Military Council*: Established by Trotsky in March 1918 to restructure Russia's military forces after the Treaty of Brest-Litovsk. The council operated on the assumption that a resumption of war with Imperial Germany was likely at any moment, and so concentrated on drafting plans for this eventuality. It had no authority over the troops operating against internal counter-revolution.

*Thermidor*: See Robespierre (Who's who).

*Treaty of Brest-Litovsk*: Signed on 3 March 1918. Under the terms of this treaty, the new Soviet Russia lost large swathes of the territory of Imperial Russia to German occupation. The three Baltic States of Estonia, Latvia and Lithuania, along with Belarus and Ukraine, were lost and occupied by German and Austro-Hungarian troops.

# Introduction

## TROTSKY IN HISTORY

The classic biography of Trotsky remains that written by Isaac Deutscher in 1954, the trilogy *The Prophet Armed, The Prophet Unarmed, The Prophet Outcast*.[1] Deutscher went along with, and indeed helped to foster, the Trotsky myth – the idea that he was 'the best Bolshevik'. Together, Lenin and Trotsky carried out the October Revolution and, with Lenin's support, Trotsky consistently challenged Stalin from the end of 1922 onwards to save the revolution from its bureaucratic degeneration. In this version of events Trotsky was Lenin's true heir, only to be removed from that position by the manipulative Stalin. This approach shapes the structure of Deutscher's trilogy. He devotes a whole volume to the years of exile when Trotsky sniped at Stalin from afar, and most of another volume to the years after Lenin's death when the factional struggle between Stalin and Trotsky was at its height.

This view has been challenged repeatedly in the 60 years since Deutscher's trilogy appeared. In a reconsideration of the events of October 1917, James White has completely reassessed the Lenin–Trotsky relationship at the height of the insurrection, showing that the two men's visions of the mechanics of seizing power were entirely different.[2] As to the notion that Lenin made Trotsky his heir, Eric van Ree has thoroughly debunked this myth.[3] Richard Day, writing more than 30 years ago, argued convincingly that Trotsky, far from being the most internationalist Bolshevik, was firmly convinced of the possibility of building socialism in one country, if only his own policies had been adopted.[4] More controversially, Nikolai Valentinov suggested not long after Deutscher's trilogy first appeared that in 1925, far from opposing Stalin, Trotsky was in alliance with him.[5] Although Valentinov's suggestion of a pact sealed at a secret meeting has not stood the test of time, other evidence confirms a period of testy collaboration between the two men into the mid-1920s.

If Trotsky was Lenin's true heir, he must have been a serious Marxist scholar. That was the approach taken by Baruch Knei-Paz in his great 1978 study *The Social and Political Thought of Leon Trotsky*.[6] Knei-Paz collected Trotsky's writing under certain themes, bringing together early and later essays into a coherent exposition; but this approach makes Trotsky a far greater thinker than he was in reality. Trotsky wrote an enormous amount and, as a journalist, he was always happy to write on subjects about which he knew very little. He could also write beautifully, but he was no philosopher. Knei-Paz does a better job than Trotsky himself in synthesising his ideas. Trotsky was a jobbing journalist and revolutionary activist and his writings cannot be divorced from their immediate context. His first revolutionary comrade, Grigorii Ziv, doubted that Trotsky had the patience to engage fully with Marxism as an analytical tool. A similar verdict came from Anatolii Lunacharskii, a close comrade in 1917. He concluded that Trotsky was a very orthodox Marxist: 'he takes revolutionary Marxism and draws from it the conclusions applicable to a given situation; he is bold as can be in opposing liberalism and semi-socialism, but he is no innovator'.[7]

Thereafter, roughly once a decade, a new biography of Trotsky appeared. In 1988 Pierre Broué, a convinced Trotskyist, wrote a sympathetic yet scholarly account, which concentrated on the years of anti-Stalin struggle.[8] In 1997 an English-language version of Dmitrii Volkogonov's biography appeared.[9] This was as anti-Trotsky as Broué's had been pro-Trotsky; although interesting as the first post-Soviet biography, the author was so hostile to his subject that he added little to a scholarly appreciation of one of the great revolutionary leaders of the twentieth century. Over the past ten years several more balanced accounts have appeared, written by those putting scholarship above political standpoints. The first was by Ian Thatcher.[10] This was a meticulous work of scholarship which concentrated on the evolution of Trotsky's ideas and his writing on historical events. It was also an avowedly political biography, and deliberately ignored Trotsky's private life. Thatcher, while sympathetic to his subject, was determined to demolish some of the myths of Trotsky's own making, in particular the idea that he was the 'best' Leninist. Of the many strengths of this study, it is worth singling out the detailed treatment given to the early years of exile, 1929–33, when Trotsky became increasingly concerned about the rise of Hitler in Germany and the negative role played by the Communist International under Stalin's leadership in the affairs of the German Communist Party.

In 2009 Robert Service, who had already written biographies of Lenin and Stalin, completed what his publishers called the 'first full-length biography of Trotsky written by someone outside Russia who is not a Trotskyist'.[11] It provided some useful personal insights – the Jewishness of his early upbringing, the revolutionary activities of Natalia, his romantic partner for most of his life, and the trauma of his life in exile – but it tended to underplay the differences between Trotsky and Lenin, thus inadvertently reverting to the Deutscher model. Their differing understanding of the peasantry and the centrality of Trotsky's fear of a Thermidor reaction are issues that are skated over, and the tension between them at the time of Brest-Litovsk is deliberately played down. Nor does Service bring out the important differences between the two men on the eve of Lenin's death on the issue of Party 'interference' in the economy.

Service's biography was quickly followed by two more. Bertrand Patanaude published *Trotsky: Downfall of a Revolutionary* later in 2009.[12] As the title implied, it concentrated on Trotsky's years in Mexico, but to help the reader understand some of the issues which confronted him in the second half of the 1930s, Patanaude provided a series of flashbacks to earlier events in Trotsky's life. Unfortunately, these flashbacks relied on an uncritical reading of Trotsky's own version of his life. The reader learns things of essentially ephemeral interest, such as how Natalia's poor cooking irritated his guards in Mexico. In 2011 Joshua Rubinstein published *Leon Trotsky: A Revolutionary's Life* as part of Yale University Press's 'Jewish Lives' series.[13] Writing a 'Jewish Life' of a man who consistently rejected the significance of his Jewish origins was no easy task, but Rubinstein did unearth some previously ignored material written by Trotsky while a correspondent during the Balkan Wars. However, ultimately the 'Jewish Life' prism revealed little new about the man. Rubinstein's biography is particularly weak on the realm of ideas, particularly the nature of Trotsky's disagreements with Lenin.

One of the most difficult periods of Trotsky's life for biographers has been his time as Commissar of War during the Russian Civil War. Deutscher covered this only superficially and Thatcher confessed that 'the exact course of the battles of the Civil War, with the various twists in fate and fortune, are too complicated to go into in any detail'.[14] The Civil War period is covered most extensively by the current author in his own biography of Trotsky,[15] which set out deliberately to stand Deutscher's trilogy on its head and focus not only on Trotsky's early years but equally on the Civil War period. There was a reason for this. Getting to grips with the Civil War years enables the historian to see much more clearly the continuities in Trotsky's thought, particularly on the two key issues of the theory of Party organisation and the question of the peasantry, the two issues which repeatedly brought Trotsky into conflict with other Bolsheviks.

At first glance the pre-revolutionary Trotsky seems very different from the post-revolutionary Trotsky. Before the revolution he favoured the self-organisation of workers and after the revolution his talk was always of labour discipline. The Civil War years help connect the two. Trotsky believed the Party could not presume to be all knowing, but had to involve people on the ground. During his lifetime the people on the ground changed from the

Petersburg Soviet, to leaders of the legal labour movement, to the Petrograd Soviet, to former Tsarist generals, to economic managers and planners; but Trotsky believed consistently that the Party had to involve these people in its affairs and not dictate to them. A study of the Civil War helps bring this out, and also brings out the centrality of what might be termed Trotsky's peasant obsession. In 1906 he predicted the danger of a peasant insurgency against proletarian power in his pamphlet *Results and Prospects*; in the 1920s he anticipated Thermidor, a peasant-sponsored counter-revolution; but during the Civil War, particularly its first months, Trotsky successfully defeated a peasant-inspired rebellion. He knew the potential of peasant power under arms.

## WHAT IS LENINISM, WHAT IS TROTSKYISM?

The two fundamental issues on which Lenin and Trotsky disagreed were Party organisation and the peasantry. Trotsky's disagreement with Lenin about how the political party of the working class should be structured before the revolution is the subject of the first two chapters of this study and several of the documents. Put most simply, Trotsky believed that workers could achieve political consciousness without the need for a political party to lead and direct them; he therefore opposed Lenin's ideas for a highly centralised and disciplined political party. In 1917, when in his view the workers had showed their political consciousness by overthrowing the Tsar without the political party of the working class playing a significant leading role, the climate of revolution made his disagreement with Lenin a thing of the past and he could join the Bolshevik Party. Hints of differences on this matter continued: Lenin felt the October seizure of power needed to be the work of the Party; Trotsky insisted it was better left to the Soviet. But this tactical divergence never led to any serious disagreement.

Where the question of Party organisation began to resurface as an issue between Lenin and Trotsky was the aftermath of the trade union controversy. In autumn 1920 Trotsky's campaigning within the Party for the militarisation of the trade unions led to the formation of rival factions and prompted Lenin to ban such factions at the Tenth Party Congress. Trotsky found that ban difficult to accept. Both in 1924 and in 1926, his determination to continue campaigning within the Party for the ideas he felt were essential for its salvation meant that he engaged in factional activity, and the language he used to denounce Stalin in the 1920s as the centralist enforcer was similar to the language he had used to criticise Lenin's centralising tendencies two decades earlier.

The place of the peasantry in the Russian Revolution was also a crucial difference between Trotsky and Lenin that evolved over time. Even before the 1905 Revolution, Trotsky had come to the conclusion that the dominant force in the Russian Revolution was going to be the proletariat; and his experience of 1905 convinced him of this. His seminal work, *Results and Prospects*, made clear in 1906 that the Russian Revolution would be led by the working class, and that initially the peasantry would follow its lead. However, Trotsky predicted that this community of interest would not last long and soon the worker and the peasant would come into conflict. The inherent danger to the revolution of this made it essential to try to internationalise the Russian Revolution as quickly as possible, hence Trotsky's interest even in *Results and Prospects* to explore how a revolution in Russia could break out of its isolation.

Lenin dismissed as a distortion of Marxism the idea that the 1905 Revolution could result in the establishment of a workers' government. Although, like Trotsky, Lenin had no time for the liberals and thought the peasants were the only worthy allies of the workers in the overthrow of Tsardom, he was too orthodox a Marxist to accept that Russia was ripe for a socialist revolution. However, because Lenin argued that a possible outcome of the 1905 Revolution was 'the democratic dictatorship of the proletariat and peasantry', even in 1905 he had a less pessimistic attitude towards the peasantry than Trotsky. In his writings during and after 1905, Lenin suggested that some peasants could be won over by the workers and would remain loyal to them. Moreover, when, in 1917, Lenin changed his mind and decided that Trotsky was right after all, and the Russian Revolution would succeed only if the workers took the lead, he nevertheless retained his slightly more flexible vision of the peasantry. Although both men would make utterances that were on occasion identical, by and large Trotsky remained uncertain about the alliance with the peasantry and always feared that middle peasants would fall under the influence of the rich kulaks. Lenin stressed much more clearly and consistently the possibility of the working class forming a permanent alliance with the middle peasantry.

It was because of Trotsky's fear of the unreliability of the peasantry that he was so keen to internationalise the Russian Revolution. In early 1918, to Lenin's fury, he almost sacrificed the survival of the revolution to the hope that the German and Austro-Hungarian proletariats might overthrow their imperial governments. Yet, this was the most extreme example of Trotsky's much-vaunted internationalism. Trotsky believed in world revolution, possibly more than Lenin, but not significantly more than every other Bolshevik. In 1920, as the Red Army approached the border with Poland, it was Lenin who believed that revolution would quickly spread to that country, while Trotsky was extremely sceptical. As with all Bolsheviks, a lot of the talk about world revolution was largely rhetorical. While Trotsky was in power, he had no qualms about talking about building socialism in the absence of a worldwide revolution, and even when he was only on the fringes of power he objected to Stalin's theory of socialism in one country not because such an ambition was impossible but because Stalin's approach implied too many concessions to the peasantry and therefore threatened the restoration of capitalism. Building socialism in the isolated Soviet Union was possible if the correct – that is, Trotsky's own – policies were adopted.

Trotsky wrote at great length about the failings of the German October Revolution of 1923, but this critique was simply camouflage for an attack on his domestic opponents at the time, Zinoviev and Kamenev. It was the same with his writings on China in 1927. Here too his focus was essentially domestic: Chiang Kai-shek's destruction of the Chinese Communist Party was simply a metaphor for Thermidor, for what would happen in Russia if the kulaks ever found a general willing to act on their behalf. China offered a warning of great relevance for the domestic policies of the Soviet Union.

## NOTES

1  I. Deutscher, *The Prophet Armed, The Prophet Unarmed, The Prophet Outcast* (Oxford: Oxford University Press, 1970).

2  J. White, 'Lenin, Trotsky and the Arts of Insurrection: The Congress of Soviets of the Northern Region 11–13 October 1917', *Slavonic and East European Review* no. 1, 1999.

3  E. van Ree, '"Lenin's Last Struggle" Revisited', *Revolutionary Russia* no. 2, 2001.

4  R. B. Day, *Leon Trotsky and the Politics of Economic Isolation* (Cambridge: Cambridge University Press, 1973).

5  N. Valentinov, 'Dopolnenie k "Dnevniku" L. Trotskogo', *Sotsialisticheskii vestnik* nos. 2–3, 1959.

6  B. Knei-Paz, *The Social and Political Thought of Leon Trotsky* (Oxford: Clarendon Press, 1978).

7  G. Ziv, *Trotskii: kharakteristika po lichnym vospominaniem* (New York: Narondnopravstvo, 1921); A. Lunacharskii, *Revolutionary Silhouettes* (Harmondsworth: Penguin, 1967), pp. 66–67.

8  Pierre Broué, *Trotsky* (Paris: Fayard, 1988).

9  Dimitrii Volkogonov, *Trotsky: The Eternal Revolutionary* (London: HarperCollins, 1997).

10  Ian D. Thatcher, *Trotsky* (London: Routledge, 2003).

11  Robert Service, *Trotsky: A Biography* (Basingstoke: Pan, 2009).

12  Bertrand Patanaude, *Trotsky: Downfall of a Revolutionary* (New York: HarperCollins, 2009).

13  Joshua Rubinstein, *Leon Trotsky: A Revolutionary's Life* (New Haven: Yale University Press, 2011).

14  Thatcher, *Trotsky*, p. 100.

15  Geoffrey Swain, *Trotsky* (Harlow: Pearson Longman, 2006).

# 1

# Developing a world view

## UPBRINGING: FROM REBEL TO MARXIST

Given his later idealisation of the working class and fear of peasant reaction, it is ironic that Trotsky was the son of a rich peasant, what the Russians term a 'kulak'. However, his father, David Bronstein, was no usual kulak: he was a Jew and stemmed from one of the relatively few Jewish families which, early in the nineteenth century, had been allowed to buy land in what was then termed 'New Russia' and is now southern Ukraine. He grew up at Yanovka, the small estate purchased by the Bronsteins in spring 1879. It was an isolated spot. The nearest post office was 15 miles away, the nearest railway station 25. Although the farm had seen better days, it was well equipped, with three barns and open sheds, as well as a machine shop, stables and a cow shed. Most important of all for a kulak, there was an engine-powered mill; Trotsky's father could not only store his grain until the market price was right, but hire out his mill to his neighbours. Wheat made David Bronstein rich and the young Trotsky wanted for little. He was, he recalled, 'the son of a prosperous landowner [and] belonged to the privileged class rather than to the oppressed'.[1]

Trotsky's father was ambitious for his son's education, and when Trotsky did not settle at the local school he arranged for him to live with a married elder cousin and study at the St Paul's *Realschule* in Odessa. At the age of nine Trotsky started seven years of education in Odessa and was a model student for most of that time. At the end of the preparatory year he scored maximum marks in every subject, and that was to be the pattern for the rest of his time at the *Realschule*. He later described his time in Odessa as 'becoming an urbanite' and part of this process of urbanisation was to shed all aspects of his Jewishness and assimilate completely into the world of Russian culture. However, 'becoming an urbanite' not only meant for Trotsky a break with Jewishness, but a break with his father and his father's values. Returning to Yanovka after his first year at school, Trotsky noted his gradual distancing from the country:

> Our house looked terribly small to me now; the homemade wheat bread seemed grey, and the whole routine of country life seemed at once familiar and strange . . . Something new had grown up like a wall between myself and the things bound up with my childhood. Everything seemed the same and yet quite different. Objects and people looked like counterfeits of themselves.

Sometimes the issues that divided him from his father were trivial – Trotsky's father considered his glasses an urban affectation, while Trotsky felt they gave him a sense of added importance – but increasingly Trotsky was disturbed by his father's kulak attitudes. In the summer breaks from schooling in Odessa, he would often help his father calculate the wages of labourers, and always interpreted the payment due far more generously than his father did; the labourers soon sensed he was on their side, which understandably infuriated his father. It was not just classic kulak tight-fistedness. Trotsky recalled:

> While the Yanovka people were spending many weary hours trying to measure the area of a field which had the shape of a trapezoid, I would apply Euclid and get my answer in a couple of minutes. But my computation did not tally with the one obtained by 'practical' methods and they refused to believe it. I would bring out my geometry text-book and swear in the name of science; I would get all excited and use harsh words – and all to no purpose. People refused to see the light of reason and this drove me to despair.[2]

What brought matters to a head was Trotsky's father's decision that Trotsky should move to study in Nikolaev in order to prepare for university entrance. Comfortable lodgings had been arranged and in autumn 1895 Trotsky arrived in a nicely pressed tan suit and stylish hat; within weeks these clothes of the swell bourgeois would be exchanged for those of a worker. In Odessa Trotsky had shown no interest in politics. He had rebelled against some of the more authoritarian aspects of his school regime, but that was no more than bravado. In Nikolaev, Trotsky discovered politics. Nikolaev was one of the towns where former political prisoners were allowed to take up residence, and it had been favoured by some of the veterans of the 1880s **People's Will Party**. Unfortunately for Trotsky's father, he had chosen to lodge his son with a respectable family whose own sons were captivated by revolutionary politics. After a month or so of dismissive banter about 'socialist utopias', Trotsky became hooked and was introduced to Franz Shvigovskii, the key figure in a commune of revolutionary youngsters which owed its ideological allegiance to the ideas of Nikolai Chernyshevskii, the radical

**People's Will Party:** Operating between roughly 1879 and 1883, this was the terrorist organisation which successfully assassinated Tsar Alexander II in 1881. Its social programme was a commitment to the old Populist slogan 'Land and Liberty' and the belief that peasants, once masters of all the land, would farm it according to the traditional communal practices of the Russian village.

peasant socialist – or Populist – of the 1860s. This link was reinforced by the fact that Shvigovskii's younger brother was also a pupil at Trotsky's school. Trotsky soon began to neglect his studies and his father came down to sort things out: he was keen to expand his business and diversify into profitable sugar-beet production and brewing; for this he needed a fully qualified engineer, and he expected that to be his own son. He told Trotsky to mend his ways or else. Trotsky responded in kind, and with great vehemence. So Trotsky's father cut off his allowance, forcing him to move into the revolutionary commune. Henceforth he dressed in a blue worker's shirt and refused to use 'bourgeois' bed linen. His only source of income was some private tutoring.[3]

Teenage rebellion was soon followed by teenage love. The only woman associated with the commune was Aleksandra Sokolovskaya, the sister of one of Trotsky's school friends. Trotsky was 17, Aleksandra was 22 and had already completed a course in midwifery at Odessa University. While in Odessa she had studied the writings of Plekhanov, the founder of Russian Marxism, and was a self-declared Marxist. This made her unique among the members of the commune, who all based themselves on the **Populism** of Chernyshevskii and the People's Will. Baiting Aleksandra about her Marxism was a regular pastime of the group – along with writing her love poetry – and she recalled that when she first met Trotsky she had been told by her brother that at last they had found someone who would be able to defeat her in argument.[4]

In spring 1896 Trotsky suddenly fainted. These fits were to occur throughout his life, but the worried young revolutionaries quickly informed the family and Trotsky's father was soon back on the scene, greeting the earnest revolutionaries with a cheerful 'Hello, have you run away from your father, too?' Trotsky, unwilling to patch up his quarrel with his father completely, agreed to return to Yanovka over the summer as a 'guest' rather than a son. At Yanovka a compromise was hammered out. Another Odessa relative, an uncle, was visiting the farm at the time; he owned a small engineering plant and was happy to look after Trotsky for a while. So it was agreed Trotsky would return to Odessa and start attending some mathematics lectures at the university there to see if such a career suited him. However, he remained financially independent from his father, again earning money from giving private lessons.

The call of revolutionary politics, however, was too strong. By December 1896 he was back in the Nikolaev commune and back in the company of Aleksandra Sokolovskaya.[5] Within weeks the two were lovers, brought together by their joint involvement in the revolutionary cause. By February 1897 the revolutionary commune had made the acquaintance of a 'real' worker and, using this contact, a workers' cell was established which

**Populism:** The term used to describe the revolutionary groups of the 1870s and 1880s, who shared the belief that peasants, once masters of all the land, would farm it according to the traditional communal practices of the Russian village. Nikolai Chernyshevskii was the best-known theorist of the Populists.

adopted the rather grandiose name 'South Russia Workers' Union' in honour of a similarly named organisation of the 1870s. Soon about 20 workers were gathering for secret meetings and discussions, with Trotsky producing revolutionary literature, writing proclamations and duplicating them on a hectograph. It was not long before Trotsky had moved from proclamations to a newspaper, *Our Cause*. The paper was edited by Trotsky and he wrote most of the articles, too. His inexhaustible energy kept this tiny show afloat. It was a happy time for him. 'Never in my later life did I come into such intimate contact with the plain workers as in Nikolaev . . . The principal types of the Russian proletariat impressed themselves on my consciousness forever.' However, the authorities pounced on 28 January 1898 and made over 200 arrests – such had been the growth of the organisation in the course of the year.[6]

There then followed nearly two years in prison and subsequently a trial and exile to Siberia. It was in prison that Trotsky's gradual evolution towards Marxism came to fruition. Populism as a body of ideas focused on the peasantry; the South Russia Workers' Union sought to organise industrial workers. Populists had always looked to contact the peasantry through those peasants working as factory workers, but in Nikolaev Trotsky's group was most successful among skilled shipbuilders with few links to the country-side. As the group spread its influence to Odessa, Aleksandra's Marxist contacts became increasingly involved and the group would eventually describe itself as 'social democratic'. Trotsky himself said that it was during his first days in prison that this conversion occurred, but that he clung to his old views simply from stubbornness. His first public statement on the matter to other revolutionaries came while in Odessa prison. He was, he always stressed, a bit of a self-taught Marxist at first, not having read any Marxist classics.

In November 1899, after being sentenced to four years' exile, he was held in Moscow transit prison for six months and it was there that he read Lenin's *The Development of Capitalism in Russia*.[7] That prison was also the scene of his marriage to Aleksandra. Since he was still only 20 he should have needed his father's permission to marry. His father had always refused to grant this, which had led to the final rift between Trotsky and his parents, a rift that was not resolved even after his mother had visited Trotsky in Odessa prison. However, in the transit prison, at the start of the journey into exile, the authorities turned a blind eye to Trotsky's under-age status and allowed him to marry Aleksandra.

Life in Ust-Kut on the River Lena was difficult to bear. It was freezing in the winter, while in the summer mosquitoes made life miserable. Trotsky took the opportunity to read some Marx and later recalled that he had to brush the cockroaches off the page as he ploughed through the first volume of *Capital*. He also studied the details of the **Bernstein–Kautsky controversy** within the German Social Democratic Party over the question of whether Marxism implied reform or revolution.

Trotsky and Aleksandra did not stay long in Ust-Kut. They were granted permission to move further east for a while to the River Ilim, where Trotsky was given a job as a clerk. But he did not take this work seriously and was soon sacked for incompetence. The couple then moved further south to Verkholensk. From the very start of his exile Trotsky had been writing articles for the *Eastern Review*, a legal newspaper started by Populist exiles. These articles were not political. Many focused on literature, although those on the peasantry had a social edge. After two years of exile, a social democratic organisation called the Siberian Union was established in Siberia, and its members contacted Trotsky for help with their literary ventures; soon he was writing proclamations and leaflets once again. Among the themes he felt obliged to take up was the need for more centralism among the disparate social democratic organisations in Russia. Thus, when in summer 1902 he first heard that Lenin, Yulii Martov and other leading émigré social democrats had launched a new newspaper called *Iskra*, and then read a copy of Lenin's *What is to be Done?*, he knew what he had to do – escape from exile.

While in Siberia, Aleksandra had given birth to two daughters, yet she still encouraged Trotsky to escape. He recalled in his memoirs: 'she was the first to broach the idea of my escape when we realised the great new tasks; she brushed away all my doubts'. Although Aleksandra accepted the separation and Trotsky was essentially right to say in his memoirs, 'life separated us, but nothing could destroy our friendship and our intellectual kinship', it may be presumed that Aleksandra had hoped to reunite with Trotsky once her own escape from exile could be arranged. By the time they did meet up two years later, however, Trotsky had already found a second love.[8]

**Bernstein–Kautsky controversy:** In 1899 the German Social Democrat Edward Bernstein wrote a book which suggested that Marxist 'revolution' could come about by a series of incremental reforms enacted through parliament. Karl Kautsky led the orthodox Marxists among German Social Democrats who denounced such ideas as 'revisionism'. For the impact of this controversy on Russia, see p. 13.

*Iskra*: The underground newspaper founded by Lenin, Martov, Plekhanov, Akselrod and others in 1900. Its mission was to try to bring under more centralised leadership the scattered groups of working-class social democratic organisations operating in Russia since the foundation of the Russian Social Democratic Labour Party in 1898.

## BATTLING WITH LENIN

Trotsky arrived in London in October 1902 and went straight to the house where Lenin was staying. It was the start of a tempestuous relationship that would last over 20 years. After discussions about publishing work and the need for a centralised Party organisation, Lenin found Trotsky a room in the house shared by his fellow *Iskra* editors. After a brief spell reading back issues, Trotsky was put to work. First he wrote short notices, then longer political articles, and finally editorials. Trotsky did not stay in London long, though. He was sent on a short lecture tour of social democratic groups in France and Belgium, all the while promoting the *Iskra* cause. After this he was originally supposed to return to Russia, but the plan was changed and he was ordered to Paris. There, on the stairs of the building in which he had been housed, he met Natasha Sedova, a young social democrat activist who had been deputed first to find him a room and then to act as his guide. Although Trotsky moved on to Switzerland and Germany to repeat his lecture, he and Natasha kept in touch, and by the time the editorial board of *Iskra* had moved to Geneva in April 1903 the couple were living together.[9]

In March 1903 Lenin decided that Trotsky should not return to Russia but stay abroad and be co-opted on to the editorial board of *Iskra*. Plekhanov, the most authoritative of the *Iskra* editors, detected a ruse on Lenin's part to win control of the board and opposed the proposal. In the end Trotsky was brought on to the board as an adviser. However, the issue of the future of the board did not go away, and opened up the first major disagreement between Lenin and Trotsky. All *Iskra*'s efforts were geared towards calling a Second Congress of the Russian Social Democratic Labour Party (RSDLP), which would adopt a new – centralised – organisational structure. Most *Iskra* activists assumed that once this congress had been held, and once the new centralised structure was in place, a new *Iskra* editorial board would be elected by the congress. The self-appointed group who had established the paper would bow out, their principal task achieved. Lenin did not accept this. In his scheme the Central Committee would be concerned only with events in Russia, not with the conduct of the editorial board. In Geneva, Trotsky raised this with Lenin, who responded: 'we are the stable centre, we are stronger in ideas, and we must exercise guidance from here'.

'Then this will mean a complete dictatorship of the editorial board?' Trotsky asked.

'Well, what's wrong with that?' Lenin retorted. 'In the present situation, it must be so.'[10]

Although Trotsky had expressed this concern about Lenin's proposals even before the Second Congress began, like most other delegates he had not anticipated that the Party would split into Bolshevik and Menshevik factions. The Second Congress opened on 30 July and lasted until 23 August. In the early sessions Trotsky and Lenin appeared to be united. One of the first issues to be addressed was whether the RSDLP should have an autonomous Jewish organisation within it. Trotsky had abandoned any sense of Jewish separateness as he became an 'urbanite' and therefore backed Lenin in criticising those Jews who favoured autonomy for a specifically Jewish section in the Party; from the congress floor he explained that not all Jews backed the idea. He also supported Lenin in the debate on the agrarian question. However, behind the scenes tempers were fraying. Matters came to a head over a discussion of the apparently innocuous Rule Number One for Party membership. Lenin's resolution ran: 'a member of the RSDLP is one who accepts its programme and supports the Party both financially and by personal participation in one of the Party organisations'. His opponent Martov's proposal read: 'a member of the RSDLP is one who accepts its programme, supports the Party financially and renders it regular personal assistance under the direction of one of its organisations'. Martov's formulation was broader, and aimed at allowing into the Party all the many workers who were linked to it through such activities as organising strikes and distributing literature, but did not participate in the secret work of the underground cells. Lenin's objections to Martov's proposal were that it would let *all* workers into the Party, including those who could not be relied upon, and would allow opportunist intellectuals to call themselves party members.

In the late 1890s the German Social Democratic Party had been torn apart by a debate between revolutionaries and reformists. The Russian Social Democrats had not been immune from this debate and Lenin argued that the way to resist the growth of reformist ideas was to establish a tightly centralised and disciplined Party organisation. In Lenin's view this would have two consequences: it would enable the Party to exclude 'intellectuals' who preached reformism; and it would guide the proletariat who, left to their own devices, could achieve only 'trade union consciousness' (a realisation of the need for economic struggle) but not 'class political consciousness' (an understanding of the need for revolution). Trotsky, like many of Lenin's critics, argued that his own 'intimate contact with plain workers' had shown him that workers could acquire full consciousness without Party direction, while a centralised Party organisation could be used to expel the Left just as easily as the Right.

At the Second Congress, Trotsky's first contribution to the debate was relatively measured: 'I fear that Lenin's formula will create a fictitious organisation, one which will merely give its members a *qualificiation* but will not serve as a means for party work.' By the next session he had developed what was to be a consistent theme in his critique:

> I did not know that one could exorcise opportunism by means of rules. I think that opportunism is produced by more complex causes. Finally, I did not realise that opportunists are organically incapable of organisation. I know the Jauresist party [in France], which is organised opportunism . . . The point is that Lenin's formula, against intellectuals' individualism, hits quite a different target . . . [I]f statutory definitions are to correspond to actual relations, Comrade Lenin's formula must be rejected. I repeat: it misses the mark.

As the congress first split into Bolshevik and Menshevik factions, and then degenerated into ever more vitriolic accusation and counter-accusation, Trotsky did not hold back. Indeed, his behaviour was almost disruptive. He was one of the delegates who heckled Lenin when the latter proposed giving the *Iskra* board the power to dictate to the Central Committee; he made loud sarcastic comments when the minutes of the crucial debate on the Party rules were being discussed; and he constantly demanded that the voting figures in the Central Committee elections must be made public, so it was clear that the 20 members of what was now the Menshevik faction had deliberately abstained.[11]

After the Second Congress Trotsky played a major role in the Menshevik campaign to subvert its decisions. In two pamphlets, *The Report of the Siberian Delegation* and *Our Political Tasks*, he denounced first Lenin's conduct at the congress, then Lenin's analysis of that congress in his pamphlet *One Step Forward, Two Steps Back*. In the *Report of the Siberian Delegation* [**Document 1**] Trotsky's point was that Lenin's schema made sense on paper, but did not match the reality of Russian cities where there was both an underground Party committee dominated by intellectuals of various schools, and a separate underground workers' organisation. The two needed to be fused, and simply asserting that the underground committee should control the underground organisation would not change the situation on the ground. Martov's formula would mean that the workers' organisation would not be threatened with 'expulsion', but, through mutual co-operation, would gradually move closer to the underground committee and come under first its guidance and then its direction. Asking himself why, when this was so self-evident, Lenin continued to insist on super-centralism, Trotsky could only assume that Lenin had dictatorial ambitions: he must see himself as a latter-day Robespierre, ready to unleash his Terror. But that, the alarmed Trotsky noted, would open the way to a Thermidor reaction – his first use of a term that would be associated with his later ideas.

*Our Political Tasks* [**Document 2**] appeared in August 1904. Summing up the essential difference between the Bolshevik and Menshevik concepts of the Party, Trotsky asserted:

> [I]n the one case we have a party which *thinks for* the proletariat, which substitutes itself politically for it, and in the other we have a party which politically educates and mobilises the proletariat to exercise rational pressure on the will of all political groups and parties.

In his famously prophetic insight Trotsky pointed out the logical outcome of these policies. 'In the internal politics of the party these methods lead to the party organisation substituting itself for the party, the Central Committee substituting itself for the party organisation, and finally the dictator substituting himself for the Central Committee.'

The theme that emerged from the combination of sarcasm and vitriol with which Trotsky assaulted Lenin was this: the working class had to learn for itself through its own activity. There were no short cuts; the working class could be guided but not led.

> It is necessary to understand, gentlemen, that the development of a whole class proceeds surely but slowly, but it is necessary to understand that we have no other basis for political successes, except the standard of the proletarian class consciousness, nor can we find any other. It is necessary once and for all to give up the 'accelerated' methods of political sub-stitutionalism. He who has no patience, he who wants to look for other guarantees – not in the class, but in the top layer engaged in organising conspiracies – might as well leave us today.

Although the main target of Trotsky's attack was Lenin, it was also aimed at Plekhanov and those Mensheviks who looked to the liberals as prospective allies in the struggle against the Tsar. Trotsky, like Lenin, argued that the overthrow of the Tsar would be accompanied by an agrarian revolution which would radicalise the peasantry and make them a potential ally, so cosying up to the liberals was a mistake. Working-class self-activity should be just that – action by and for the working class and not for any other social or political group. Thus he also condemned those committees which, 'instead of organising the proletariat into becoming socially aware, intercede with the bourgeois-democratic movement'.[12]

## LIVING REVOLUTION

By autumn 1904 Trotsky had already elaborated the ideas that would dominate his activity during the 1905 Revolution. Working-class self-activity, under clear social democratic slogans rather than 'liberal petitioning' would be the essence of everything he did during that revolutionary year, and it made his association with Plekhanov even more difficult, since this orthodox Marxist disdained the peasants and saw only the liberals as potential allies. In September 1904 Trotsky wrote an *Open Letter to Comrades* announcing that he had left the Menshevik Bureau; in private he told colleagues that he hoped to reach an understanding with the Bolsheviks.

By autumn 1904 events in Russia were developing quickly. The Tsar had finally agreed that the elected assemblies for local government would be allowed to hold a congress. That congress inevitably raised national political issues and resolved to call on all local assemblies and all public bodies to petition the Tsar to grant an elected national assembly with legislative power. All sorts of public bodies responded and, in imitation of events in France on the eve of the 1848 Revolution, massive banquets were held to get around the ban on public meetings. Trotsky drafted a pamphlet in which he urged the working class to take part in this campaign as an independent entity. Revolution was in the air, 'the incredible becomes real, the impossible becomes probable', so working-class action was needed.

> Tear the workers away from the machines and workshops; lead them through the factory gate out into the street; direct them to neighbouring factories; proclaim a stoppage there; and carry new masses into the street . . . Taking possession of the first suitable buildings for public meetings, entrenching yourself in those buildings, using them for uninterrupted revolutionary meetings with a permanently shifting and changing audience, you shall bring order into the movement of the masses, raise their confidence, explain to them the purpose and sense of events; and thus you shall transform the city into a revolutionary camp.[13]

**Bloody Sunday:** On 9 January 1905 demonstrating workers trying to present the Tsar with a petition calling for both improved labour conditions and radical political change were fired on by soldiers instructed to enforce a ruling which made all public demonstrations illegal. Over a hundred demonstrators were killed and this massacre sparked the months of strikes and unrest during 1905 which became known as the 1905 Revolution.

The Mensheviks were still debating whether this pamphlet should be published when the **Bloody Sunday** massacre occurred on 9 January 1905.

In Geneva Trotsky learned of Bloody Sunday the day after it happened. He and Natasha decided to go back to Russia at once, staying first in Kiev and then moving to Petersburg. He was there on 6 August when the Tsar offered his opponents the right to summon a purely consultative 'parliamentary' assembly, and Trotsky persuaded the Petersburg Mensheviks to have nothing to do with such an assembly, which some liberal leaders were ready to accept. Writing in the safety of Finland at the end of September, he finally formulated his view that while Russia might be experiencing a bourgeois-democratic revolution, this did not mean that the liberal bourgeoisie was bound to come to power. The key in Russia was the attitude of the peasantry, which political grouping could inspire them to rebel. Trotsky was ever more convinced that only the working class could persuade the peasantry to act and that, if it gave a firm lead, Russian social democracy could emerge from the revolution to capture power.[14]

Among the proposals that Trotsky had drafted in Finland was one for an elected non-Party workers' organisation. In his absence this idea was taken up by the Petersburg Mensheviks, who on 10 October issued an appeal for the formation of 'a revolutionary workers' council (soviet) of self-management', to help lead the print workers' strike which had begun a week earlier. After issuing this appeal, the Mensheviks sent 50 agitators into the factories, and on 13 October over 30 delegates attended the first meeting of the General Workers' Committee of Petersburg at the Polytechnic Institute. The gathering resolved to call a general strike and summoned a fuller meeting for the following day. This was attended by over 100 delegates, who still tended to use the term 'council' or 'soviet', rather than 'committee', which explains why that name was formally adopted on 17 October.[15]

Trotsky first attended the Petersburg Soviet on that second meeting of 14 October, and until his arrest on 3 December he devoted every waking hour to its work, attending as one of the agreed number of Party representatives.[16] The October General Strike was so total that the Tsar was forced to act. On the 17th he issued a manifesto in which he agreed to turn the previously proposed consultative assembly into a legislative assembly. Few details of this new assembly emerged until the following day, however. So it was on the morning of the 18th that excited crowds took to the streets and made their way across the River Neva to the university, the traditional venue in the city for public gatherings. Here Trotsky addressed the crowds and demanded an amnesty for political prisoners and the withdrawal of troops from Petersburg. He concluded with a theatrical flourish:

> As for the Tsar's manifesto, look, it's only a scrap of paper. Here it is before you – here it is crumpled in my fist. Today they have issued it, tomorrow they will take it away and tear it into pieces, just as I am now tearing up this paper freedom before your eyes.[17]

It was the amnesty issue that the Soviet leaders took up first. Trotsky and the other Social Democrats involved in the Soviet hoped that continuing the strike might force the Tsar to make further dramatic concessions, and possibly even to abdicate, but they were astute enough politicians not to make such revolutionary demands at this early stage. Instead, they called on the strike to continue until the Tsar granted the amnesty.

This tactic enabled the Soviet leadership to organise an orderly retreat. For all the reservations people had about the Tsar's manifesto, it was clear that a significant concession had been made and a new chapter in Russia's history had opened. Workers began to drift back to work, and on 21 October the Soviet called for a general return to work, but its leaders could still claim a partial victory. There was to be no general amnesty, but on the 22nd the Tsar did issue the decree 'For the Relief of the Fate of Persons who, Prior to the Issuing of the Manifesto, Had Perpetrated Criminal Acts against the State'. Under the terms of this decree a large number of political prisoners were freed.

The Tsar's concession had not come out of the blue. The Soviet had resolved to make 23 October a day of commemoration for all those who had died during the revolutionary struggle. It planned a city-wide demonstration to accompany the funerals of victims. In order to ensure that this passed off peacefully, the Soviet decided on 21 October to send a delegation to meet the Tsar's newly appointed prime minister, Sergei Witte. The prime minister himself was all smiles and did not rule out the Soviet's request that the police should be withdrawn and the demonstration controlled by Soviet-appointed

**Black Hundreds:** Officially the Union of the Russian People, these groups loyal to the Tsar and the established political order emerged during the 1905 Revolution as strike breakers and militants ready to challenge the power of Russia's various socialist parties on the streets. Their counter-demonstrations often turned to violence.

marshals, but he stressed that the security of the city was exclusively the concern of the Petersburg Governor. The latter then informed the delegation that he could not sanction their proposal since he had intelligence to suggest that right-wing populist groups known as **Black Hundreds** planned to disrupt the demonstration. There was a passionate debate when the delegation returned to the Soviet in the early hours of 22 October, led by Trotsky. It was clear to many of those present that the police were in cahoots with the Black Hundreds and that the Police Chief had brought them into the discussion simply to put pressure on the Soviet leaders. But it was equally clear that the demonstration was likely to be marred by violence. So, after much heart-searching, the Soviet voted to call off the demonstration. The Tsar's decision to grant the amnesty later that day was a gesture to encourage the Soviet's moderation.[18]

The Soviet, however, was not interested in moderation but in testing to the limit the Tsar's manifesto. The Tsar had mentioned freedom of speech, but how could there be freedom of speech if censorship continued? The Soviet announced on 19 October that print workers would work only with copy that had not been sent to the censors. To enforce this, the print workers remained on strike and by 22 October the censorship system had been sidelined and freedom of the press effectively won. At the same time the Soviet moved to establish its own newspaper, *Izvestiya*. Since the Soviet had no printing press of its own, workers started to produce it in plants closed down by industrial action. Sympathetic workers would travel to the printing presses of a strike-bound company, get their fellow workers to restore electricity to the plant, and print the necessary copies.[19]

The turning point for the Soviet occurred on 23 October, when the Tsar began to reassert his authority. On that day a campaign began among the sailors of the Kronstadt Naval Base for the civil liberties promised in the manifesto to be extended to military personnel. When, on 26 October, some soldiers stationed at the base presented similar demands to their commanding officers, they were arrested. As the soldiers were marched away to detention some sailors tried to free them, the guards opened fire, and the sailors reached for their own weapons. In the end martial law was declared and troops were brought in from Petersburg to restore order. A total of 1,200 sailors faced court-martial and possible execution.

News of these events spread to Petersburg and by 29 October protest meetings were being held in factories across the city. The events in Kronstadt coincided with other evidence that the Tsar had given with one hand only to take away with the other. In Poland martial law had been declared because of nationalist unrest, while peasant disturbances in Chernigov, Saratov and Tambov had prompted the authorities there to do the same. On 1 November the Soviet resolved to call another general strike, although it did so only after the most heated discussion.

In organisational terms the November strike was a triumph. It had been called because of pressure from below and the workers were solidly behind it; more factories were involved than during October. At once Witte called for a return to work; the Soviet responded by calling on workers to stay out. On 5 November the government made a concession. The Petersburg Press Agency reported that 'we are authorised to state that . . . participants in the Kronstadt events have not been and will not be judged by courts martial'; the same statement also promised that martial law would be lifted in Poland. Should the strike continue? When the Soviet's executive met later that day, Trotsky argued powerfully that the strike had to end since the revolutionary movement throughout the country was on the wane. 'Our strike, real as it is, is in the nature of a demonstration . . . to show the awakening army that the working class is on its side.' This, Trotsky argued, had been achieved:

> If we consider that the purpose of our action is the overthrow of the autocracy, then of course we have not achieved that aim . . . Events are working for us and there is no advantage for us in forcing their progress . . . for tomorrow we shall be stronger than we are today . . . Do not forget that the electoral campaign, which must bring the entire revolutionary proletariat to its feet, lies ahead. And who knows whether this electoral campaign will not end by blowing the existing regime sky high?

Trotsky's eloquence persuaded the Soviet to call for a return to work on 7 November.[20]

Thirty years later, Trotsky was still wondering if he made the right decision in November 1905. At one level the Soviet seemed to be at the peak of its power at the start of that month. It had a total membership of 562 delegates, representing 147 factories, 34 workshops and 16 trade unions; its executive comprised 22 worker deputies and nine Party representatives with an advisory vote – three Bolsheviks, three Mensheviks and three Socialist Revolutionaries (SRs – the name the Populists had adopted in 1901). It still had great authority. All issues discussed were raised first in the localities, then formulated into proposals by the executive, then discussed again in the full Soviet; only two executive decisions were taken without full Soviet approval, and both were endorsed retrospectively.[21] By November, it also had significant funds: on the 15th it voted to donate 2,000 roubles to striking postal and telegraph workers. And on the 23rd it threatened a nationwide railway strike if a telegraph engineer's death sentence were carried out. The government backed down, leaving Trotsky with 'a vivid recollection of the memorable meeting of the Executive Committee at which a plan of action was drawn up while awaiting the government's reply'.[22]

But below the surface the balance of forces had changed. Back on 26 October some delegates from one of the Petersburg districts had voted to introduce the eight-hour working day 'by revolutionary means'. In other words, workers would labour for eight hours and then go home. The Soviet leadership was never keen on this proposal, but the idea caught on and on 31 October the Soviet agreed to endorse it. This campaign was quickly overtaken by the November strike, and after the decision of 5 November to order a return to work the Soviet announced the following day that the campaign for the eight-hour day by revolutionary means was not yet a universal slogan, but rather should be demanded only when there was a chance of success. This attempted clarification had little impact. Employers were determined to retain their right to control the number of hours worked so, instead of returning to work on 7 November, many workers found themselves locked out until, after four hours of passionate debate, the Soviet officially called off the eight-hour day campaign on 12 November.[23]

On 26 November the government decided to act and arrested the Soviet's chairman. This was a blow from which the Soviet struggled to recover. Trotsky drew up the Soviet's official protest against the arrest and promptly took over the role of chairman himself. But he remained in power only a week as he and the other Soviet leaders were themselves arrested on 3 December.[24]

Clearly, then, unlike any of the other revolutionary leaders of 1917, Trotsky was in the thick of the working-class unrest during the 1905 Revolution. Maybe he exaggerated in his autobiography when he declared, 'all the decisions of the Soviet were shaped by me', but many of them certainly were. Trotsky also worked hard to bring the Bolsheviks and the Mensheviks together, encouraging them to form a federative commission. Then there was his journalism. Not only was he involved in *Izvestiya*, of which ten issues appeared, but he was the driving force in the Menshevik paper *Novaya zhizn*, contributing to 16 issues. From mid-November he was also involved in *Russkaya gazeta*, a more radical paper that was openly critical of the liberals. This was a hectic schedule, as he recalled: 'the fifty-two days of the existence of the Soviet were filled to the brim with work – the Soviet, the Executive Committee, endless meetings, and three newspapers'.[25]

## RESULTS AND PROSPECTS

Trotsky's second spell in detention was far easier than his first. After a short time in Kresty prison, he was moved first to solitary confinement in the Peter-Paul Fortress and then to the House of Preliminary Detention, where the regime was positively lax. In April 1906 Russia's new elected assembly, the First State Duma, started its work and the prisoners were suddenly allowed to associate freely and were given access to lawyers, via whom they could smuggle out pamphlets and articles and keep in contact with the Party leadership.

Trotsky would often retreat to cell 462 so that he could study and write. One of his major concerns was how the Soviet leaders should defend themselves. While he was in prison the Russian Social Democratic Labour Party held a congress in Stockholm and elected a new Menshevik-dominated Central Committee. That committee advised the Soviet leaders to base their defence on the premise that they had only acted under the terms of the Tsar's manifesto, which mentioned the right to freedom of assembly. Although the committee's motivation was simply to reduce the sentences likely to be passed by the court, Trotsky was furious. He felt that taking such a line would legitimise the manifesto and mean that, in court, the Soviet leaders would sound like the liberal politicians he so despised. Although some had reservations, all of the accused were convinced by his arguments and resolved to use their trial as a platform for socialist propaganda. The proceedings began on 19 September 1906.[26]

The Soviet leaders were accused of preparing for an armed uprising, and when Trotsky rose to speak on 4 October he tackled this issue head on. The Soviet had never discussed the need for a republic or the need for an insurrection; but it was, in effect, a government in its own right and therefore had the authority to use force and other repressive measures should these be necessary. However, force was not the essence of the insurrection. 'To unite the proletarian masses within a single revolutionary protest action, to oppose them as enemies of the organised power of the state – that, gentleman of the court, is insurrection as the Soviet understood it and I understand it too.'[27]

The trial had some dramatic moments. It was attended by Trotsky's parents, and his mother periodically cried throughout his testimony. During cross-examination Trotsky suffered one of his fainting fits and proceedings had to be suspended. The defence tried to call the Petersburg police chief as a witness, so that he could tell the court about the links between the police and the Black Hundreds, and when this was refused the defendants voted to boycott the trial. In the end, then, the verdict was handed down to an empty court room. That verdict was enforced settlement in exile and the deprivation of all civic rights.[28]

During his time in prison, Trotsky not only prepared for his defence, but reflected on the importance of his time working for the Soviet. It 'underlined the unquestionable and unlimited hegemony of the proletariat in the bourgeois revolution'. Although the Soviet did not attain power, its achievements hinted at what proletarian power would be like.

By the pressure of strikes, the Soviet won the freedom of the press. It organised regular street patrols to ensure the safety of citizens. To a greater or lesser extent, it took the postal and telegraph services and railways into its hands. It intervened authoritatively in economic disputes between workers and capitalists. It made an attempt to introduce the eight-hour day by direct revolutionary pressure . . . If the proletariat, on the one hand, and the reactionary press, on the other, called the Soviet a workers' parliament, that merely reflects that the Soviet did indeed constitute an embryonic organ of revolutionary government.[29]

Trotsky was generalising from what he had seen, but the notion that the proletariat might play a hegemonic role in the bourgeois revolution was not something that orthodox Marxists could easily accept.

His ideas were most clearly formulated in the 1906 essay *Results and Prospects* [**Document 3**], a piece of writing which outlined the views that guided him for the rest of his life. Here he argued that the formation of the Soviet made it impossible to close one's eyes to the following fact:

The chief actor in this bourgeois revolution is the proletariat, which is being impelled towards power by the entire course of the revolution . . . Once the proletariat has taken power in its hands it will not give it up without a desperate resistance, until it is torn from its hands by armed force.[30]

The Social Democrats should therefore consciously work towards forming a working-class government:

The proletariat in power will stand before the peasants . . . [and recognise] all revolutionary changes (expropriations) in land relationships carried out by the peasants. The proletariat will make these changes the starting point for further state measures in agriculture. Under such conditions the Russian peasantry in the first and most difficult period of the revolution will be interested in the maintenance of a proletarian regime.

There was, of course, the possibility that the peasantry would not look to the working class for leadership, but instead form its own political party, but Trotsky dismissed such a danger: 'Historical experience shows that the peasantry are absolutely incapable of taking up an *independent* political role.' They were always forced to choose between the policy of the bourgeoisie and the policy of the proletariat.[31]

Trotsky concluded his analysis of the peasantry by gazing into the revolution's crystal ball and speculating what would happen after the working class's victory.

The proletariat will enter the government as the revolutionary representative of the nation, as the recognised national leader in the struggle against absolutism and feudal barbarism . . . [However,] every passing day will deepen the policy of the proletariat in power, and more and more define its *class character* . . . The abolition of feudalism will meet with support from the *entire* peasantry . . . but any legislation carried through for the purpose of protecting the agricultural proletariat will not only not receive the active sympathy of the majority, but will even meet with the active opposition of a minority of the peasantry. The proletariat will find itself compelled to carry the class struggle into the villages and in this manner destroy that community of interest which is undoubtedly to be found among all peasants, although within comparatively narrow limits . . . The primitiveness of the peasantry turns its hostile face towards the proletariat. The cooling-off of the peasantry, its political passivity, and, more so, active opposition from its upper sections, cannot but have an influence on a section of intellectuals and the petty-bourgeoisie of the towns. Thus the more definite and determined the policy of the proletariat in power becomes, the narrower and more shaky does the ground beneath its feet become.[32]

Having raised the danger that the working class, having established its government in Russia, might end up clashing with that country's peasantry, Trotsky offered a way out: revolution throughout Europe. The triumph of revolution in Russia would mean revolution in Russian Poland, which in turn would spark uprisings in German and Austrian Poland. The German and Austrian emperors would send troops to restore order, revolutionary Russia would respond by declaring war, and that war would lead to revolution in both Germany and Austria.

Left to its own resources, the working class of Russia will inevitably be crushed by the counter-revolution the moment the peasantry turns its back on it. It will have no alternative but to link the fate of its political rule, and, hence, the fate of the whole Russian Revolution, with the fate of the socialist revolution in Europe.[33]

*Results and Prospects* expressed all of Trotsky's key ideas; it was, in essence, a credo for life which never changed. Friend and foe alike would later refer to it as Trotsky's theory of permanent revolution, and friend and foe alike would point to the similarities and differences with Lenin's writings at this time.

Like Trotsky, Lenin had no time for the prospect of liberal rule in Russia. However, Lenin did not believe that the proletariat would be able to form a government alone; he preferred to talk about 'a revolutionary dictatorship of the proletariat and peasantry'. Trotsky was dismissive of the very idea of independent political activity on the part of the peasantry; when a peasant group was formed in the First Duma he went out of his way to stress in a footnote to *Results and Prospects* that this did not disprove his theory. Lenin, on the other hand, welcomed the formation of this group as the nucleus of 'a strong revolutionary peasant party' which would emerge as the revolution progressed. His references to the peasantry during 1905 were quite different to those of Trotsky. When a Peasant Union was established in November he asked himself why serious Marxists had devoted so little time to the peasantry. 'The moment has now come when the peasant has come forward as the conscious creator of a new structure in Russian life.' Marxists had to ask what the peasantry could give the revolution and what the revolution could give the peasantry. His answers were similar to Trotsky's: once land and liberty had been achieved, not all peasants would join in the struggle against capital, but a clash with the proletariat was not inevitable; nor would the peasantry necessarily act as a single block. Lenin stressed that some peasants would 'determinedly and consciously go over to the workers' if the Social Democrats were to explain their policies patiently to them. Thus Lenin sent 'warmest greetings' to the Peasant Union and called its delegates 'true democrats' and 'allies with whom we are united in a common great struggle'. Although Trotsky accepted that the Peasant Union 'embraced some elements of radical democracy' – and he publicly shook the hand of its chairman when he addressed the Soviet on 27 November – he saw little evidence of consciousness at the Peasant Union Congress. 'In a folkloric sense this was one of the revolution's most interesting gatherings,' he wrote. 'One saw many picturesque characters, provincial "naturals", spontaneous revolutionaries who had "thought it all out for themselves", village politicians with passionate temperaments and even more passionate hopes, but with rather confused ideas.'[34]

By the end of 1905 Trotsky had more than served his revolutionary apprenticeship. If, when he had first arrived abroad, he still had a great deal of 'juvenile bumptiousness' about him and nobody took him very seriously, it was accepted that he could write and speak well and that 'this was no chick but an eagle'. Handsome, elegant and nonchalant, his condescending manner could shock observers. However, by 1906, Lunacharskii, a close associate in 1917, could comment:

> His popularity among the Petersburg proletariat at the time of his arrest was tremendous and increased still more as a result of his picaresque and heroic behaviour in court. I must say that of all the social-democratic leaders of 1905–6 Trotsky undoubtedly showed himself, despite his youth, to be the best prepared . . . [He] understood better than all the others what it meant to conduct the political struggle on a broad, national scale.[35]

# FURTHER READING

For Trotsky's youth, the best sources are his own autobiography *My Life*, and the portrait drawn by his long-time American associate, Max Eastman: *Leon Trotsky: Portrait of a Youth*. For those who read Russian, the memories of his fellow teenage rebel Grigorii Ziv are full of insights: *Trotskii: kharakteristika po lichnym vospominaniem*. For the events of 1905, Trotsky's own collection – *1905* – is indispensable. Other first-hand accounts are *Istoriya soveta rabochikh deputatov* (no author) and D. Sverchkov's *Na zare revolyutsii*. A. V. Lunacharksii gives a vivid portrayal of the young Trotsky in his *Revolutionary Silhouettes*.

# NOTES

1 L. Trotsky, *My Life* (London: Pathfinder, 1970), pp. 1, 87.
2 Trotsky, *My Life*, pp. 26, 79, 82, 88.
3 Max Eastman, *Leon Trotsky: Portrait of a Youth* (London: Faber and Gwyer, 1926), pp. 46–48, 51.
4 Eastman, *Portrait*, p. 56.
5 Eastman, *Portrait*, pp. 65–69.
6 Eastman, *Portrait*, pp. 18–40; Trotsky, *My Life*, pp. 105–11, 183.
7 Ziv, *Trotskii*, p. 26; Eastman, *Portrait*, p. 128; Trotsky, *My Life*, pp. 120–22.
8 Trotsky, *My Life*, pp. 131–32.
9 Trotsky, *My Life*, p. 148; Eastman, *Portrait*, pp. 164–68.
10 Trotsky, *My Life*, p. 157.
11 B. Pearce (ed.), *1903: Second Congress of the Russian Social Democratic Labour Party: Minutes* (London: Pluto Press, 1978), pp. 324, 414, 433, 442, 455.
12 L. Trotsky, *Our Political Tasks* (London: New Park Publications, 1979). The passage 'It is necessary to understand . . .' comes from the section 'A Dictatorship over the Proletariat' which is omitted from English editions. An English translation can be found in Geoffrey Swain, *The Bolshevik Seizure of Power* (Southampton: University of Southampton, 1993, line 13098; this is a Historical Document Expert System (HiDES) software package).
13 Cited in I. Deutscher, *The Prophet Armed* (Oxford: Oxford University Press, 1970), p. 110.
14 Trotsky, *My Life*, pp. 168–74.
15 The founding of the Soviet is described in G. D. Surh, *1905 in St Petersburg* (Stanford: Stanford University Press, 1989), p. 328; L. Trotsky, *1905* (Harmondsworth: Penguin, 1973), p. 265; and Kozovlev, 'Kak voznik Sovet', in *Istoriya soveta rabochikh deputatov* (Petersburg, 1906), p. 22.
16 Trotsky, *1905*, p. 126; Deutscher, *Armed*, p. 126.
17 Trotsky, *1905*, p. 135.
18 Trotsky, *1905*, pp. 141–46; Zlydnev, 'U grafa S Yu Witte', in *Istoriya*, p. 267.

19 Trotsky, *1905*, p. 172.

20 Trotsky, *1905*, pp. 185–87.

21 Khrustalev-Nosar, 'Istoriya sovet rabochickh deputatov', in *Istoriya*, p. 152.

22 Trotsky, *1905*, pp. 230–31.

23 Trotsky, *1905*, pp. 195–98.

24 Trotsky, *1905*, p. 233; Zvezdin, 'Poslednyie dni soveta', in *Istoriya*, p. 172, gives details of the negotiations leading to Trotsky's appointment.

25 Trotsky, *1905*, pp. 178, 181.

26 D. Sverchkov, *Na zare revolyutsii* (Leningrad, 1925), p. 205.

27 Trotsky, *1905*, pp. 399–400, 405.

28 Trotsky, *My Life*, 190–91; Ziv, *Trotskii*, p. 33.

29 Trotsky, *My Life*, p. 180; Trotsky, *1905*, pp. 266–67.

30 L. Trotsky, *Results and Prospects* (London: New Park Publications, 1962), pp. 191–92, 199.

31 Trotsky, *Results*, pp. 202–4; see also Document 3.

32 Trotsky, *Results*, pp. 208–9; see also Document 3.

33 Trotsky, *Results*, p. 241; see also Document 3.

34 Trotsky, *Results*, p. 204; V. I. Lenin, 'The Proletariat and the Peasantry' and 'The Aims of the Proletarian Struggle in Our Revolution', in V. I. Lenin, *On the Revolution of 1905* (Moscow, 1955), pp. 363–64, 631.

35 Lunacharskii, *Revolutionary Silhouettes*, p. 61.

# 2

# The triumph of the 'worker intellectual'

## THE PARTY DIVIDED

On 3 January 1907 Trotsky was moved to the Petersburg transit prison before commencing exile, which this time would be for an indefinite period. Even before he left Petersburg, he was determined to escape and hid a passport and gold coins in his boots. He was destined for a village a thousand miles from the nearest railway. The first stage of the journey was under military guard by railway as far as Tyumen, then by sledge along the course of the River Ob to Tobolsk and from there north towards Obdorsk. While en route Trotsky's party stopped at the village of Berezov for a rest, because thereafter the sleighs were to be pulled by reindeer rather than horses. A local land surveyor suggested to Trotsky that, although there were no roads in the area, the River Sosva could be followed towards the Urals, where a narrow-gauge railway serving the local mines led eventually to the main Trans-Siberian Railway at Perm, from where it was a straight journey back to Petersburg. Trotsky feigned sciatica, found a guide willing to take him by deer sled along the Sosva, and set off through the February blizzards.

Back in Finland he was briefly in the company of Lenin again, before travelling with all the other Party leaders to London for the Fifth Party Congress in May 1907 and a second spell of foreign exile.[1] At the Fifth Party Congress Trotsky adopted the stance that he would be known for throughout the next decade, that of conciliator. This meant that he supported the Mensheviks when it came to questions of Party organisation, or, more accurately, how the Party should be reorganised in the aftermath of 1905, but on one issue he made public his support for the Bolsheviks. Trotsky, like the Bolsheviks, identified the peasantry as the proletariat's natural ally, although he did insist that the congress minutes note that he differed from them in one important respect: unlike Lenin, he did not believe that the peasantry could play an independent political role.[2] From London, Trotsky went to Berlin, and then in October 1907 he moved to Vienna, where he earned a living as a journalist, working for the *Eastern Review* and *Kiev Thought*.

While Trotsky and other émigrés were settling abroad, dramatic events were taking place in Russia. In April 1906 the Tsar had allowed the First State Duma to gather as a legislative assembly, but he promptly dissolved it on 21 July that year. The Second State Duma gathered in March 1907 but a fortnight after the Fifth Party Congress ended its work in May that year the Second Duma rejected the government's plans for land reform and the Tsar dissolved it on 3 June. In violation of the Tsar's own constitution, the electoral law was changed in the absence of the Duma and the Third Duma was summoned, to be elected on 1 September by a completely new franchise which drastically reduced the representation of workers, peasants and other oppositional groups. The revolutionary upheaval that had begun in November 1904 was well and truly over.

Although the main ideological dispute between the Bolsheviks and the Mensheviks during the years 1906–07 related to the question of electoral alliances with liberals or peasants, there was a secondary issue which took on greater significance when the Third Duma was summoned: the trade unions.

The Tsar's manifesto had spoken of freedom of assembly, and the government's provisional regulations, under which trade unions were legalised, were made public on 4 March 1906. The workers, who had rallied to the Soviet with such enthusiasm, now put their energies into building up a powerful trade union movement. By mid-May 1907 a total of 245,555 workers had joined a union, 3.5 per cent of the workforce. In the country as a whole 904 unions were registered between March 1906 and December 1907. In 1907 the Social Democratic Duma deputies co-operated closely with the Petersburg Central Bureau of Trade Unions, on which former members of the Soviet were well represented. When the government staged its 3 June coup it also launched an assault on the trade unions. In 1907, 159 unions were closed down; in 1908, the number was 101; then 96 in 1909 and 88 in 1910. Between 1907 and 1911, 604 unions were refused registration and 206 union activists were either imprisoned or exiled.[3]

The impact of the government's dual assault on the Duma and the trade unions served to heighten the divisions within the Party. Despite continuing state persecution, a legal labour movement survived. More than that, as early as January 1908 it became clear that after 1905 there were other 'legal opportunities' for labour activists. In January 1908 the authorities allowed the People's Universities to hold a national congress. A workers' delegation attended this gathering, headed by the leaders of the Petersburg Metal Workers' Union and Petersburg Textile Workers' Union; they found that the congress provided them with a platform for socialist agitation. The Party was ambivalent about this development. By the end of 1907 the Central Committee had fled abroad, leaving behind its Russian Bureau. The latter had been lukewarm about workers attending the Congress of People's Universities, but the success of that event meant it had no hesitation in endorsing the proposal to send a workers' group to the Co-operative Congress in April 1908. The activities of the Russian Bureau at this congress led to its members' arrest, which in turn left the Party in chaos.

In July 1907 the Third Party Conference had voted to take part in the Third Duma elections, despite the narrowing of the franchise. Many Bolsheviks had accepted this decision very reluctantly and then argued that the first weeks of the Duma had proved how ineffective it was in preventing the assault on the labour movement, so the deputies should be recalled. This hard-line stance – known as Recallism – spilled over into trade union work and that of labour representation at legal congresses. Recallists opposed both, just as they had opposed participation in the Third Duma. As one Recallist noted: 'the impossibility of founding legal trade unions puts us almost back in the position we were before the revolution [of 1905], puts back on the shoulders of the party the task of leading economic struggle'. By the summer of 1908 the Recallists had such a grip on the Petersburg Central Committee that it had virtually ceased to work in the trade unions and it tried to disrupt the Congress of Women's Organisations, held in December 1908, where the activities of the trade union-sponsored 'group of working women' were successful in gaining labour concerns high-profile press coverage.

When the members of the Russian Bureau were arrested, some Mensheviks went to the opposite extreme and proposed liquidating the Central Committee and replacing it with an 'information bureau' that would simply co-ordinate the work of labour activists operating within Russia's legal labour movement. These 'Liquidators' met with little support, though; a conference of Petersburg Mensheviks countered that what was needed was not the abolition of the Central Committee and its committee structure, but a mechanism whereby those active in the legal labour movement were given a greater say in Party affairs. Bolshevik legal activists made precisely the same point. Proposals for a joint conference of legal activists and the underground were put to the Fifth Party Conference, held in Paris in December 1908, but were rejected because Lenin believed that those who advanced them were planning to downgrade the position of the underground committees and 'liquidate' the Party through the back door.[4]

## *PRAVDA*, THE VOICE OF THE WORKER INTELLECTUAL

From Vienna, Trotsky surveyed a Party that was no longer just split two ways, but four ways. There were Leninist Bolsheviks and Bolshevik Recallists,

Party Mensheviks and Menshevik Liquidators. To restore the Party to health, Trotsky decided to launch a new workers' newspaper, *Pravda*, a title that was later hijacked by the Bolsheviks for their legal daily paper, launched in 1912. Unlike the other Social Democrat newspapers, each of which had a clear factional line to preach, Trotsky wanted to highlight events within Russia, convinced that just as the dynamic development of the Soviet in 1905 had made factional struggle irrelevant, so a strong labour movement in Russia would help overcome disputes which he felt were accentuated by the difficulties of life abroad.

In *Pravda* Trotsky intended to address himself to 'plain workers' rather than Party men, 'to serve not to lead' his readers. *Pravda*'s plain language and the fact that it preached the unity of the Party made it highly popular. In the editorial of its first issue of 3 October 1908 *Pravda* told its readers 'the workers are taking the place of the intelligentsia'. Workers would have to take on their shoulders the task of reconstructing the Party and the paper's editors were convinced they were ready for the task, for in establishing the Soviet in 1905 and the trade unions thereafter they had shown their capacity for self-organisation. Now, through gritted teeth, they should reconstruct the underground Party. *Pravda*'s task was 'not to split, but to unite'. As to the liberals, the paper's line was abundantly clear: the revolution of 1905 had shown that 'the bourgeoisie has everywhere betrayed the people and done a deal with the government and the ruling classes of the old order'.[5]

Trotsky was convinced that a worker intelligentsia could re-emerge from the defeat of 1905. Issue number two of *Pravda* – which appeared on 17 December 1908 [**Document 4**] – made clear that Social Democrat workers were 'the heart and the brain' of the working class; they, whether active in the Party's underground, or in the trade unions, or in the co-operative societies, would be the people to lead workers' resistance and subsequent advance. *Pravda* put a particularly optimistic gloss on the events at the 1908 Women's Congress held in Petersburg. It marked an important turning point because the majority of those involved in forming the workers' group had resolved that it was now up to workers active in the trade unions and other areas of legal labour activity to take the lead in reviving the Party.

Reviewing its progress in 1910, *Pravda* noted that the first issue of the paper had aroused no interest; there had been some demand for issue two; while issues three, in March 1909, and four, in June 1909, had generated significant attention. By the summer of 1909, the paper argued, the mood had completely changed and trade union activists were pressurising the underground Party to stop squabbling and become active, a clamour that by winter 1909–10 was difficult to ignore. An important milestone in this process was the Congress of Factory Panel Doctors, held in April 1909, which saw the close collaboration between trade unionists and the Social

Democratic faction in the Third State Duma. 'There have never been so many conscious social democrats', the paper crowed over the summer of 1909, but it recognised that most of these workers had never been members of the underground Party and were dubious about joining it now because of the factional in-fighting. 'The leading workers, who are now so active in the trade unions . . . and attend legal congresses are almost all social democrats,' *Pravda* argued, 'but they are not linked to one another through the Party.'[6] Yet *Pravda* was equally keen to suggest in September 1910 that industrial recovery was coming, which meant, by 'relying on the strengthening consciousness of the masses', real agitation could begin to secure labour rights [**Document 5**].

Trotsky's campaign to revitalise the Party by bringing to the fore class-conscious workers was very nearly successful. With Menshevik support, he called for a joint conference of legal activists and committee men, and in September 1909 those legal activists planning to take part in the Temperance Congress, which was due to take place in January 1910, held their own conference to debate the future of the Party. The majority of those present, some 90 per cent, rejected the resolution put forward by those advancing the slogan 'Down with the Central Committee, down with the local committees' and insisted that the way forward was to build an illegal Party around the new core of working-class legal activists. In November 1909 the same legal activists held a second conference, this time with representatives of some of the underground committees, which agreed to unite the new organisations of legal activists with the old underground. It really was as *Pravda* described it:

> Under the burial shroud of the old party, a new one is being formed. And, our task, the task, of all the living healthy elements of Social Democracy, is to put all our forces to this end, to facilitate the birth and growth of the Social Democratic Party on this new, healthy, proletarian base.[7]

The issue of a Party conference was decided at the plenum of the Central Committee held in Paris from 2 to 23 January 1910. The scene of much factional bloodletting, this meeting agreed that a Party conference would be held within six months and that 'Social Democratic groups in the legal sphere, which were prepared to affiliate to the party' and even 'individual activists' would be invited to attend the conference. In preparation, joint conferences of the underground and legal activists, like the one seen in Petersburg in November 1909, were to be encouraged.[8]

Planning for the Sixth Party Conference, which was also intended to bring together underground and legal activists, began at once, but immediately ran into difficulties. A new Russian Bureau of the Central Committee was chosen and empowered to set to work, and its membership reflected an attempt to balance legal activists and the underground. Unfortunately, when the Russian Bureau met in Moscow in May 1910 its members were arrested. A further attempt was made to assemble candidate members in November 1910, but this was unsuccessful, and when they finally did assemble in Tula in February 1911 they too were arrested.[9] According to the Party rules, in these circumstances the Foreign Bureau of the Central Committee had to organise either another Russian Bureau meeting in Russia or a plenum abroad. The Foreign Bureau, while agreeing that the wave of arrests forced it to choose the second option, nevertheless resolved to reconstitute a Russian Bureau and then get it to hold a meeting abroad. Lenin, never happy with the decisions of the January 1910 plenum, interpreted this as a delaying tactic aimed at wrecking the work of the Central Committee and ordered his representative on the Foreign Bureau to walk out, before summoning his own meeting of those members of the Central Committee who felt frustrated by the impasse that had been reached. Lenin's meeting dissolved the Foreign Bureau and established first an Organising Commission and then a Russian Organising Commission to summon the Sixth Party Conference.[10]

Trotsky and Lenin were at loggerheads now, for in November 1910 Trotsky had announced that in Vienna he had established a fund to organise the Sixth Party Conference. So, independent of each other, both men were in the process of organising the conference. In his memoirs Trotsky recalled this as 'the sharpest conflict with Lenin in my whole life'. The situation came to a head when the two men prepared to attend the Copenhagen Congress of the **Socialist International** in 1910. Trotsky was travelling from Vienna and Lenin from Paris, but by chance they ended up at the same German railway station awaiting a connection to Denmark. Their conversation began in a friendly enough manner, but then Trotsky mentioned that he had written an article for the theoretical journal of the German Social Democratic Party *Vorw{au}rts* on 'Russian Social Democracy' and its current state. The article was timed for the Copenhagen Congress and interpreted events from Trotsky's perspective. Lenin reacted with fury and lobbied the Russian delegation to the congress to condemn the article, but they refused to do this. Trotsky recalled that Lenin's temper was not improved by the fact that 'he was suffering from a violent toothache and his head was all bandaged'.[11]

The need for a conference was reinforced by the fact that in 1912 the Third Duma would end its term and a Fourth Duma would be elected. In its first edition of 1911, *Pravda* linked the two issues [**Document 6**]. The elections demanded a restored 'all-Party apparatus'. The plenum of January 1910 had called for a Party conference: the timetable for the Duma elections was set, there was no time to delay and everything to gain from a conference which would 'link together the scattered parts into a new whole', and agree a programme 'acceptable to all tendencies' to be the basis of the slogans for the electoral campaign.

**Socialist International:** The Socialist International was formed in 1889, bringing together all socialist parties. Its key activity was to stage periodic international congresses, eight of which were held before 1914. It fell apart when member parties were unable to adopt a united response to the start of the First World War.

Trotsky strove to be conciliatory as 1911 advanced. He was willing to recognise Lenin's Organising Commission, as long as the Foreign Bureau were reconstituted and agreed to endorse it. But Lenin had no intention of recreating the Foreign Bureau, for it would certainly repeat its insistence on re-establishing a Russian Bureau. Thus Trotsky ended up opposing the work of Lenin's Organising Commission and ignored the Prague Conference which was assembled by Lenin in January 1912 and was designated by the Bolsheviks alone as the Sixth Party Conference. This gathering elected a new Central Committee and expelled the Liquidators from the Party; it also resolved that the Liquidators must be opposed in the Duma elections, scheduled for that autumn. The hegemony of the underground was reasserted when it was resolved that activists in the legal labour movement would be allowed to affiliate their organisations to the Party only if a special conference of underground activists agreed that this could happen.[12]

However, the Foreign Bureau of the Central Committee did not accept that it had been dissolved by Lenin. It met in July 1911 and summoned a conference for the following month which established its own Organising Commission in preparation for a conference in Vienna. Trotsky then took the lead and persuaded the commission to invite both the Petersburg Initiative Group (recently established by leading legal activists in the capital) and the Central Group (the biggest underground organisation in Petersburg, which *Pravda* backed enthusiastically). The Central Group had no truck with the Petersburg Committee set up at the end of October 1911 to elect a delegate to Lenin's Prague Conference. By securing the attendance of both of these organisations, Trotsky hoped the Vienna Conference would be a triumph. In fact, it was the very opposite. The leader of the Central Group was a police agent and the organisation was destroyed by arrests even before delegates could be chosen for Vienna. Thus no representatives of the Petersburg underground were at the conference; only the Initiative Group of legal activists made it to Vienna. What made matters worse was that one of the two representatives from the Initiative Group was another police spy, and he deliberately spread division within the Party.[13]

Trotsky's Vienna Conference of August 1912 did not expel anybody (in contrast to Lenin's Prague Conference), and it presumed only to establish an Organising Committee rather than an all-powerful Central Committee. As planned, it discussed the relationship between legal and illegal activists within the framework of the January 1910 plenum. However, much to Trotsky's disbelief, the conference also decided to make radical changes to the Party programme. Not all developments in Russia were as Trotsky described. Some legal activists really had slipped into 'opportunism'. The right-wing Menshevik editors of *Our Dawn*, a legal journal which had first appeared in Petersburg in January 1910, really were Liquidators and were determined to encourage co-operation between the labour movement and the liberal opposition to the Tsar, something Trotsky, who had no time for the liberals, had always opposed.

During the first months of 1911 *Our Dawn* came up with the notion of a 'petition campaign'. On 4 March, precisely five years would have elapsed since the passing of the legislation which allowed the formation of trade unions. This therefore seemed a suitable date on which to petition the Duma for a genuine law on freedom of assembly, a campaign which the liberals within the Duma could support. Although the Petersburg Initiative Group of legal activists took up this campaign, the Central Group and other underground groups in the capital condemned it, as did the Social Democratic Duma faction and *Pravda*. The campaign seemed to imply that the Duma had the power to pass radical legislation on social issues, which was patently untrue; if the petitions had gone to the Social Democratic Duma deputies rather than the Duma President, the campaign might have been better focused.

These issues resurfaced in Vienna, where there were no representatives of the underground to resist them. The conference decided to revise the Party's electoral programme to make it more amenable to the liberals. Thus, in future, there would be no mention of the democratic republic, only 'sovereign popular representation', while land confiscation became 'a revision of the agrarian legislation of the Third Duma'. Trotsky was appalled. All he had worked for since 1905 stood in ruins.[14]

## HOPE ABANDONED, HOPE RESTORED

Disillusioned with the politics of Russian labour, Trotsky took up the offer of becoming a war correspondent for *Kievan Thought*. In autumn 1912 the longstanding tension in the Balkans had finally exploded. The independent Balkan states had presented Turkey with an ultimatum threatening war unless certain conditions were met. When, at the end of September, the King of Montenegro declared war even before the ultimatum had expired, Trotsky hurried from Vienna to Belgrade, where he witnessed hastily mobilised troops marching to the front with sprigs of green in their hats. From there he went to the Bulgarian capital Sofia, arriving on 6 October. For the next year he would devote himself almost exclusively to war reporting, basing himself mostly in Bulgaria but also returning to Belgrade.

The First Balkan War ended with the Treaty of London on 30 May 1913, but Trotsky stayed on to cover the Second Balkan War, which began when Bulgaria launched a surprise attack on Serbia and Greece. This conflict ended with the Peace of Bucharest on 10 August 1913. His last articles, written in September, were more travelogues than war reports, as he toured the Black

Sea coast and described the isolated communities of Russian religious sects that had settled in the region. Only occasionally would he cover military issues, but two of these would have particular relevance for his later role as Commissar for War:

> The war offered the masses of Bulgarian people the prospect of finishing at last with both the Turkish past and the Turkish present. This is why the Bulgarian soldiers marching to the front put flowers in their caps; this is why regiments go into attack with such enthusiasm under savage artillery bombardment; this is why detached units of cavalry carry out so successfully the tasks of partisan warfare assigned to them; and this is why many wounded soldiers apply, as soon as they have recovered, to go back to the front line. The Turkish army presents a quite different picture. It had no general aims in this war that could have inspired the masses willing sacrifice.[15]

Later, Trotsky would always insist that each and every Red Army soldier must understand why he was fighting.

The other issue related to the supply of troops:

> The medical and also (especially) the victualling services of the Bulgarian army are organised very badly indeed. Carried away by the easy capture of Kirk-Kilissa, Radko Dmitriev thought only of conducting the entire remaining part of the campaign as a sort of cavalry charge; he simply failed to take steps to ensure correspondence between the army's offensive and the movements of its supply columns.[16]

The same problem would haunt Trotsky throughout the Russian Civil War.

Trotsky might well have continued to devote himself to journalism if events in Russia had not, rather belatedly, moved in the direction he had always anticipated. In April 1912 striking miners had been massacred on the **Lena Gold Fields** in Siberia. This was a signal to the working class that little had changed since Bloody Sunday. From then on, Russia experienced a strike wave that ebbed and flowed, but never disappeared until the general strike in Petersburg on the eve of the First World War in July 1914. Against this background, workers became increasingly militant, and those Mensheviks governed by a desire to maintain some sort of dialogue with the liberals were cautious about the apparent willingness of workers to go on strike at the drop of a hat. They began to urge them to think of the consequences before they walked out. The result was that members of the reformist Initiative Group found themselves removed from the leadership of the major trade unions in Petersburg in late 1912 and early 1913 and replaced by more militant figures. By 1914, the victory of the militants was complete.

**Lena Gold Fields Massacre:** On 4 April 1912 workers on the Lena Gold Fields, who had received no pay for several weeks, went on strike. When the strike leaders were arrested, the workers organised a demonstration, which was fired on by troops brought in to restore order. The number of casualties has been disputed, but as on Bloody Sunday, certainly over one hundred people were killed. The massacre prompted an outburst of protest strikes, and subsequent debates in the Duma meant that strikes and demonstrations continued throughout Russia for the next two years.

What was just as pleasing for Trotsky, however, was that the Russian labour movement, while clearly hostile to the reformism of the Petersburg Initiative Group, was equally hostile to Lenin's attempts to bring it under his control. At the end of 1913 Lenin made repeated attempts to bind the new militant trade union leadership to the coat-tails of his Central Committee, but he was rebuffed. Indeed, between 1912 and 1914 no Bolshevik-sponsored Petersburg Committee existed in the city, despite all Lenin's efforts to establish one. The biggest underground organisation in the capital was the Interdistrict Group, formed by some of those who had cut their teeth with the Central Group a few years earlier and continued to advance the programme of Trotsky's *Pravda*.

As Trotsky had always predicted, the workers were pressing ahead on their own path to revolution without the need for leadership from Lenin's disciplined and ultra-centralist Party. To accelerate that process, Trotsky founded the theoretical journal *Bor'ba*. The argument advanced by *Bor'ba* was essentially that of *Pravda*. Russia was now entering a new stage in which advanced workers were deciding issues for themselves. For this, they no longer needed a workers' newspaper but a journal for the emerging class of literate labour activists. Thus armed, a workers' intelligentsia could liberate the workers' movement from 'the vice of factionalism'.[17]

Trotsky was equally optimistic about the new radicalism of the working class as its opposition to the First World War developed. Trotsky had left Vienna as soon as the fighting had started, and by mid-November 1914 he had settled in France. (*Kievan Thought* had asked him to work as a war correspondent on the Western Front.) The émigré community in Paris produced a thriving newspaper, *Our Word*, which Trotsky was soon helping to edit.[18] Initially, factional issues were his chief concern. It was in the pages of *Our Word* that on 14 February 1915 he announced that he could no longer associate himself with the Organising Commission set up by his own Vienna Conference because of the decision of most of the groups associated with it to support Russia's war effort. Trotsky's commitment to opposing the war was total, but this did not bring him any closer to Lenin, for the latter felt Trotsky had still not done enough to distance himself from the Vienna Conference.[19]

In the summer of 1915 Trotsky and Lenin disagreed about how best to oppose the war. Trotsky supported the 'struggle for peace', which he argued could not be dismissed as a version of pacifism. Lenin, by contrast, insisted on 'revolutionary defeatism', arguing that 'defeatism should be the axiom of a revolutionary class during a reactionary war' and that 'wartime revolutionary action against one's own government indubitably means not only desiring its defeat but really facilitating such a defeat'. Although Lenin stressed that revolutionary defeatism did not mean sabotage, he did not explain precisely what it *did* mean. Trotsky responded in articles published in *Our Word* in August and September 1915, again stressing that defeat implied victory and that 'we do not know of any European social and state organism which it would be in the interest of the European proletariat to strengthen'. War was not something revolutionaries could control; it might lead to revolution, but there was no certainty that revolution would stop the war.[20]

And yet, despite the intensity of this arcane disagreement, by the start of 1916 Trotsky had decided to work towards a rapprochement with Lenin and the Bolsheviks. He chose to do this because of the way the labour movement was developing in Russia. *Our Word* declared on 19 January 1916:

> one ought not to and one need not share the sectarian narrow-mindedness of Lenin's group, but it cannot be denied that in Russia, in the thick of political action, so-called Leninism is freeing itself from its sectarian features, and that workers connected with [Lenin's] *Social Democrat* are now in Russia the only active and consistently internationalist force.[21]

Trotsky was referring to developments that had taken place in autumn 1915 and early 1916. As part of the overall war effort, the Tsar had agreed that local chambers of commerce could establish War Industries Committees to help factories adapt to the demands of total war. Soon a hierarchical network of these committees existed all over Russia. Some of the liberals involved in establishing them were keen to include patriotic workers in their activities, so permission was obtained to hold elections to 'workers' groups' within the War Industries Committees.

In Petrograd – as Petersburg was now known, having been renamed to avoid any German connotations – these elections were held in September 1915 and comprised two stages: first a vote at factory level to choose 'electors', then a vote among the electors to choose representatives. Pro- and anti-war Social Democrats took part, and when it came to the second stage of the elections the anti-war faction, led by prominent Bolsheviks, won a famous victory. At the same time, the Interdistrict Group had re-emerged as the dominant underground group in the capital. Early in 1916 both the Bolsheviks and the Interdistrict Group tried to organise a Party conference in the capital which would take as its point of authority the January 1910 Central Committee plenum in Paris, the last Party gathering before the Prague–Vienna debacle.[22] During 1916 the Russian working class was doing precisely what Trotsky had always counselled it should do, and on the basis of active revolutionary politics a rapprochement with Lenin was now quite possible.

Trotsky's close involvement with these events came to a sudden end in September 1916 when he was expelled from France because some mutinous

French soldiers had allegedly been reading *Our Word*. He was deported to Spain and told to board a boat for Cuba. After a protest, the Spanish authorities agreed he could go to New York instead. There he found journalistic work with the Russian-language paper *New World* and for a few weeks it was the usual round of writing articles and addressing labour meetings. Then news came of the abdication of the Tsar and Russia's February Revolution.

On 27 March Trotsky set sail on a Norwegian boat, but at Halifax, Nova Scotia, the boat was stopped and the British authorities interrogated all the Russians on board. On 3 April Trotsky was taken ashore and held in a German PoW camp at Amherst. However, after protests from Russia's new democratic government, he was released on 29 April, put on a Danish boat and this time completed his journey back to Russia, where the re-established Soviet had already been arguing and debating for more than two months.[23] He was optimistic when he arrived. His experience of the Petersburg Soviet had taught him that the best way to revive the Party after the defeat of 1905 was to bring on board the legal worker intellectuals, while the events of 1916 had suggested that these very people had themselves put the Party on a revolutionary footing.

## FURTHER READING

For the intricacies of factional in-fighting within the Social Democratic Party at this time, see G. R. Swain, *Russian Social Democracy and the Legal Labour Movement, 1906–14*. Trotsky's *My Life* is essential reading, and Ziv again provides some insights. Ian Thatcher's *Leon Trotsky and World War One* is excellent on the war years, and incorporates material from his '*Bor'ba*: A Workers' Journal in St Petersburg on the Eve of the First World War'. His study of the Interdistrict Group – 'The St Petersburg/Petrograd Mezhraionka, 1913–17: The Rise and Fall of a Russian Social Democratic Workers' Party Unity Faction' – provides invaluable information on the state of the labour movement on the eve of 1917. Trotsky's Balkan Wars writings have been published as *The War Correspondence of Leon Trotsky: The Balkan Wars, 1912–13*.

## NOTES

1 Trotsky, *My Life*, pp. 193–200; V. Serge and N. Sedova-Trotsky, *The Life and Death of Leon Trotsky* (London: Wildwood House, 1975), p. 20.

2 Cited by Ian Thatcher in *Trotsky*, p. 50.

3  G. R. Swain, 'Freedom of Association and the Trade Unions, 1906–14', in O. Crisp and L. Edmondson (eds), *Civil Rights in Imperial Russia* (Oxford: Oxford University Press, 1989), p. 177.

4  G. R. Swain, *Russian Social Democracy and the Legal Labour Movement, 1906–14* (Basingstoke: Macmillan, 1983), pp. 38–54.

5  *Pravda* (Vienna), 5 November 1909.

6  *Pravda* (Vienna), 14 June 1909 and 8 December 1909.

7  Cited in Swain, *Russian Social Democracy*, p. 89, from where this summary of events is taken.

8  Swain, *Russian Social Democracy*, p. 93.

9  Swain, *Russian Social Democracy*, pp. 96, 104.

10  Swain, *Russian Social Democracy*, pp. 110–14.

11  Trotsky, *My Life*, pp. 218–19.

12  Swain, *Russian Social Democracy*, pp. 141–43.

13  Swain, *Russian Social Democracy*, pp. 146–49.

14  Swain, *Russian Social Democracy*, pp. 119–23.

15  L. Trotsky, *The War Correspondence of Leon Trotsky: The Balkan Wars, 1912–13* (New York: Monad Press, 1980), p. 195.

16  Trotsky, *Balkan*, p. 273.

17  I. Thatcher, '*Bor'ba*: A Workers' Journal in St Petersburg on the Eve of the First World War', *English Historical Review* no. 113, 1998, pp. 100–04.

18  Serge and Sedova, *Life and Death*, p. 28.

19  I. Thatcher, *Leon Trotsky and World War One* (Basingstoke: Palgrave Macmillan, 2000), pp. 46–47, 50–53.

20  B. Pearce, 'Lenin versus Trotsky on "Revolutionary Defeatism"', *Sbornik* no. 7, 1987, p. 18.

21  Pearce, 'Revolutionary Defeatism', p. 18; Deutscher, *Armed*, pp. 233–35.

22  I. Yurenev, 'Mezhraionka, 1911–17', *Proletarskaya revolyutsiya* no. 1, 1924, p. 116. See also G. R. Swain, 'Late Imperial Revolutionaries', in I. Thatcher (ed.), *Late Imperial Russia: Problems and Prospects* (Manchester: Manchester University Press, 2005), pp. 163–64.

23  Trotsky, *My Life*, pp. 277–85.

# 3

# Living the revolution

## ENDING THE QUARREL WITH LENIN

Trotsky arrived in Petrograd on 4 May 1917 and made straight for the Smolny Institute, the home of the Petrograd Soviet. For Trotsky, the prospects for the revolution were quite straightforward: workers should take up where they had left off in 1905 and use the power they exercised via the Soviet to establish a working-class government. As he understood it, during February it had been the workers who had ensured the success of the revolution by seizing control of the postal and telegraph services, the wireless office, all the railway stations and the printing works; if they were prepared to act in this way again, political power could be theirs. He was therefore delighted to discover that Lenin also favoured the principle of the Soviet taking power, and had abandoned the wariness that had marred their co-operation in 1905.

Trotsky's late arrival in Petrograd meant he had a poor understanding of events within the Bolshevik Party during March and April 1917, when the issue of Soviet power had first been raised. When the Tsar was overthrown, the first Bolsheviks to emerge from underground to establish a temporary Bureau of the Central Committee opposed the Provisional Government then being established by the liberals and demanded 'a revolutionary provisional government'. When Kamenev and Stalin returned from exile in Siberia in mid-March they pulled the Central Committee away from this radical stance and called for a dual strategy of close supervision of the Provisional Government combined with moves gradually to develop the Petrograd Soviet into 'the beginnings of a revolutionary power'. When Lenin returned to Petrograd on 3 April, he condemned this caution and called for all Bolsheviks to campaign for a Soviet government. However, events soon convinced him that it was premature to launch such a programme. In mid-April the Provisional Government and the Soviet clashed over the liberal Foreign Minister's determination to continue pursuing the war aims of the Tsar.

Soviet protest demonstrations were called, and the Bolshevik Petrograd Committee, echoing Lenin's radicalism, issued leaflets calling for the over-throw of the Provisional Government and the immediate establishment of Soviet power. On 24 April, during the Seventh Party Conference, Lenin condemned this as 'adventurist': 'we cannot now overthrow the government', he stressed. Thus, just as Stalin had moved to discipline those Bolsheviks keen to seize power in March, Lenin criticised those calling for insurrection in April.[1]

Trotsky's reception on his arrival was rather lukewarm. The leadership of the Soviet had fallen into the hands of pro-war Mensheviks who, far from urging the Soviet to seize power, were negotiating with the liberals about forming a coalition government. Because of his role in 1905, Trotsky was given a non-voting seat on the Soviet Executive, but his views were com-pletely out of tune with the rest of the Soviet leadership. Thus his first political act of 1917, on 5 May, was to join with the Bolsheviks and vote in the Soviet against the formation of a coalition government. His message was simple: do not trust the bourgeoisie, control your own leaders and rely on your own force. This stance did not go down well. To quote his own *History of the Russian Revolution*, he 'left the hall amid far less applause than had greeted [his] entrance' and for the next few weeks Trotsky showed little interest in attending the Soviet Executive.

Trotsky believed that the anti-war opposition in the Soviet was the home of the worker intellectuals, whose revolutionary consciousness was now such that factional disagreements with Lenin over the organisational principles of the underground struggle were firmly in the past. Trotsky immediately re-established contact with the Interdistrict Group, which had survived its wartime persecution more or less intact and retained a good following in the factories, and urged them to consider uniting with the Bolsheviks.[2] Talks between the two groups about a possible merger began almost at once. On 7 May they hosted a joint meeting to mark Trotsky's return and the talks proper began three days later. Trotsky found himself face to face with his old protagonist and was wrong-footed by Lenin's determination to be con-ciliatory: Lenin had wanted to make Trotsky editor of *Pravda*, but his Central Committee colleagues vetoed this; nevertheless, Trotsky and his sup-porters were offered seats on the paper's editorial board as well as on the Central Committee. However, the talks stalled because of fears that, despite Lenin's apparent generosity, the Interdistrict Group was being taken over rather than offered a genuine merger. For a while, therefore, the merger was put on hold.

Trotsky had always argued that Bolshevik sectarianism was a product of the backwardness of the Russian working-class movement; practical activity among the grassroots by worker intellectuals would end this backwardness.

Events of May–June 1917 seemed to bear this out, for increasingly, irrespective of the issues that still divided them, the Interdistrict Group and the Bolsheviks co-operated closely in co-ordinating their opposition to the Provisional Government and its policy of supporting the war. Moreover, when the First Congress of Soviets assembled at the start of June, this co-operation increased. On 4 June the Bolshevik faction at the congress read out a statement on the Provisional Government's planned military offensive which had been written by Trotsky. When called upon to speak, he took the same line as Lenin, predicting that the offensive would end in disaster and urging the Soviet to establish a government that was able and willing to spread revolution to Europe. As the congress proceeded so did the Interdistrict Group–Bolshevik co-operation. Although Lenin faced opposition from within his own Central Committee and Trotsky faced opposition from more cautious colleagues, the two organisations agreed to organise a massive demonstration on 10 June under the slogan 'Down with the ten capitalist ministers'. However, the Provisional Government banned this demonstration and both organisations accepted that they had no choice but to cancel it, which left them with the problem of trying to explain this retreat to their supporters without losing face. Lenin drafted a statement, but both he and the other Bolshevik leaders were unhappy with it. Trotsky, who had delivered a similar speech in 1905, submitted an alternative which the Bolsheviks accepted and this was read out in the name of the whole opposition.[3]

Very little now separated Lenin and Trotsky, but nuances could still be detected. During the First Congress of Soviets, stung by a Menshevik challenge that no socialist party was ready to assume power, Lenin had asserted that the Bolsheviks were just such a party. Trotsky's emphasis was different: he always referred to a 'Soviet government', with the implication that this might have a non-Bolshevik composition; and, given the composition of the Soviet at the time, he seemed to accept that the formation of such a government was some way off.

Such differences would be important in the future, but the rank and file of the Interdistrict Group were already ignoring them and calling for a full merger with the Bolsheviks. On 2 July a special conference of the Interdistrict Group took place and the result was a foregone conclusion. Trotsky still faced some opposition from leading figures within the organisation but decided to pre-empt them by publishing a statement in *Pravda* to the effect that 'there are in my opinion at the present time no differences either in principle or tactics between the Interdistrict and Bolshevik organisations; accordingly there are no motives which justify the separate existence of these organisations'.[4]

# CHECKING ADVENTURISM, COMBATING REACTION

As Trotsky had predicted, the Provisional Government's **June Offensive** had been a disaster. Preparations for the offensive had been the one thing that had kept the unstable government together but, as it faltered, the liberal ministers decided to bring it down by resigning. In the absence of a secure government, Trotsky and the Bolsheviks resolved to organise mass demonstrations under the slogan 'All power to the Soviets'. Although in the Petrograd Soviet as a whole the Bolsheviks were still in a minority, the Soviet had both Workers' and Soldiers' sections and in the former Trotsky and the Bolsheviks had a clear majority by July. The Workers' Section thus supported the idea of a demonstration which would lobby the meeting of the Soviet Executive called to decide how the Soviet should respond to the collapse of the government. Crowds rallied outside the Tauride Palace as, in the early hours of 4 July, the Executive held preliminary discussions, resolving that any decision taken should be binding on all members, something which prompted Trotsky and his supporters to walk out. Many workers wanted to protest with Trotsky at the way the Executive planned to force through a motion in favour of forming a second coalition government, but this anger soon intermingled with a separate but related issue.

Throughout the June Offensive the First Machine Gun Regiment, stationed in Petrograd, had resisted orders that it was to move to the front. By the end of June rumours were rife that the whole regiment would either be sent to the front or disbanded, and activists were determined to rebel rather than suffer either fate. Some offered the **Bolshevik Military Organisation** enough machine guns to seize power, but the Central Committee stamped on such a wild scheme. However, the Bolshevik Military Organisation did encourage the gunners to take part in the planned demonstration, and by the evening of 3 July some had taken control of strategic positions in the capital. Trotsky learned that the regiment had joined the demonstration only around that time. The news took him by surprise, particularly when it became clear that the Kronstadt sailors were also determined to join in. When the Bolsheviks and the Interdistrict Group met before dawn on 4 July they had to decide whether to try to cancel the demonstration, which already seemed to be getting out of hand, or stand at its head and try to keep it within bounds. They opted for the latter. Trotsky played a key role during these 'July Days'.

The Kronstadt sailors arrived at about ten in the morning and marched straight to the Bolshevik headquarters at the Kshesinskaya Mansion. Lenin addressed them from the balcony, but, for all his revolutionary rhetoric, he

**June Offensive:** In mid-June 1917 (the start of July by the western calendar) Russia's Provisional Government launched a long-planned offensive, hoping to hasten victory in the First World War. Despite detailed preparation, and some early success, within ten days it was clear that the offensive had fizzled out. Since it was the policy of the Provisional Government to delay major reforms in Russia until victory had been secured, the collapse of the offensive did much to radicalise those who felt immediate social reform was essential.

**Bolshevik Military Organisation:** The Bolshevik Military Organisation was founded in April 1917 to organise disenchanted soldiers. By mid-July it had over 30,000 members and held a conference representing some 500 military units. Thereafter it played a key role in all preparations for an insurrection.

did not urge them to seize power. Instead the demonstrators were led to the city centre, to link up with workers who had marched in from the industrial suburbs. The angry demonstrators then marched along the main thorough-fare, Nevskii Prospekt, and on to the Field of Mars. En route there was some shooting, but a heavy downpour of rain calmed the mood a little. After this tour of the city the demonstrators arrived at the Tauride Palace at about five in the afternoon, where they were joined by more workers.[5] When the Kronstadt sailors arrived at the palace they demanded to speak to one of the socialist ministers who had been in the government. The most left-wing of their number, the leader of the SR Party, Victor Chernov, agreed to talk to them. He made a short speech, blaming the liberals for precipitating the crisis, but when a voice from the crowd called for the nationalisation of the land the crowd surged forward and angry demonstrators grabbed Chernov and pushed him into a nearby car, declaring he was under arrest. Trotsky was quickly on the scene. Pushing people aside, he rushed to Chernov's rescue and eventually persuaded the sailors to release their captive.[6]

Notwithstanding Trotsky's swift action to defuse the situation, the violence displayed on that day played into the hands of the Provisional Government. During the night of 4–5 July, units loyal to the Soviet Executive and the Provisional Government began to arrive and by midday on the 5th these troops were in full control of the capital. At the same time the Provisional Government announced that it had evidence that Lenin and the Bolsheviks were funded by the Germans and their plans to seize power and surrender the country had barely been thwarted.

That morning, Trotsky had met Lenin. The latter was in a gloomy mood: 'now they will shoot us down, one by one', he said. A warrant had been issued for his arrest, and Lenin felt he had no choice but to go into hiding. Several other leading Bolsheviks were detained at this time, leaving the Bolshevik group in the Soviet leaderless, so Trotsky was approached to take over as leader, even though, strictly speaking, he was not yet even a member of the Bolshevik faction. On 10 July he defended the action of the Bolsheviks during the July Days both on the floor of the Soviet and in the Executive, and published an open letter to the Provisional Government in which he stressed that the Interdistrict Group had supported the Bolsheviks fully. With a rhet-orical flourish he ended: 'you can have no grounds for exempting me from the action of the decree by virtue of which Lenin . . . [was] subjected to arrest'. The Provisional Government called his bluff and did indeed arrest him on 23 July.[7]

He was released on 2 September.[8] By then, the political situation in revo-lutionary Russia had changed completely. A second coalition government had been formed, but it was even less stable than the first. The new prime minister, Alexander Kerensky, appointed as Commander-in-Chief of the

Army General Lavr Kornilov, whose troops on the South-West Front had achieved some success during the ill-starred June Offensive. Kornilov, however, was an inveterate plotter against the revolution and his summer campaign for the restoration of discipline in the rapidly disintegrating army through the reintroduction of the death penalty made him the rallying point for all counter-revolutionary forces. By mid-August plans were already well advanced for Kornilov to seize power and arrest the Soviet. Kerensky discovered this threat to his position on 26 August, but he could resist Kornilov only by appealing to the Soviet to mobilise its forces. This he did and the Soviet saved both the prime minister and the revolution.

Trotsky went straight from the Kresty prison to a meeting of the Committee for the Defence of the Revolution, which had been established by the Soviet. Within the Soviet itself Kornilov's attempted putsch had prompted a radical turn to the left, particularly among the soldier delegates. Indeed, the day before Trotsky's release, on 1 September, the Soviet had supported a Bolshevik resolution for the first time. The Menshevik and SR leaders of the Soviet decided to test whether this had been a 'one-off' or marked a complete change of direction, so they called a second vote on the Bolshevik resolution for 9 September. This was Trotsky's first public appearance at the Soviet since his release and the vote was won; two days later there was an even more convincing Bolshevik victory after another display of Trotsky's oratory.[9] With Lenin still in hiding and Trotsky's oratorical skills plain for all to see, he was set to dominate the public face of Bolshevism for the next six weeks.

The issue facing the country in the aftermath of Kornilov's attempted putsch was whether to support Kerensky's bid to form a third coalition government with the liberals, or to favour a Soviet government – the policy of the Bolsheviks. To win popular backing for his proposal for a third coalition government, Kerensky summoned an assembly known as the Democratic Conference made up not only of the various soviets that now existed throughout Russia but also of other democratically elected organisations, such as trade unions, co-operatives and local town and provincial councils. The conference opened on 14 September and Trotsky read out the Bolshevik Party's official statement. After a series of rather contradictory votes, Kerensky won support for his proposal; however, the majority of delegates insisted that his new government should be held responsible to a temporary popular assembly so that it and its policies could be monitored until elections to a national Constituent Assembly could be held in mid-November. This temporary assembly was given the name 'Preparliament', and the key debate at the Democratic Conference then became: would all political parties be willing to take part in the work of the Preparliament, which would comprise not only those social groups represented at the Democratic Conference but also representatives of property owners and their organisations?

The Bolsheviks discussed the issue of participation in the Preparliament on 20 September at a conference which included delegates to the Democratic Conference, members of the Petrograd Committee and members of the Central Committee. Trotsky called for the Preparliament to be boycotted; however, the majority of those present did not agree that the parliamentary struggle should be abandoned. No agreement could be reached in the Central Committee, so it was left to the Democratic Conference delegates to decide, and they voted to participate. Consequently, on 22 September, the Bolsheviks informed the Democratic Conference that they would take part in the Preparliament.[10]

Trotsky's call for a boycott meant that he and Lenin were now on exactly the same wavelength. Although, very briefly, Lenin had toyed with the idea of what might be termed the parliamentary way forward, he was soon bombarding the Bolshevik Central Committee with a series of letters ever more urgently urging them to prepare to seize power through an armed uprising. When he heard of Trotsky's stance on the Preparliament, he sent him the message, 'Bravo Comrade Trotsky!'[11] However, while Lenin and Trotsky were both calling for an armed uprising to establish a workers' government, their visions of how this was to be achieved were far from identical. Lenin favoured a coup staged by the Bolshevik Party and its Military Organisation of radicalised soldiers. Trotsky favoured action through the soviets.

At the very close of the Democratic Conference it had been decided to summon a Second Congress of Soviets to take place in Petrograd on 20 October. Trotsky assumed that this would be the occasion for action, so in the interim he acted quickly to gain control of the Soviet, formally taking over as chairman of the Executive on 25 September. The very first resolution passed under his chairmanship set Trotsky's agenda: it called for the new coalition government to resign and announced that the forthcoming Second Congress of Soviets would create a genuinely revolutionary government.[12]

As a result of Lenin's interventions, the Bolshevik Central Committee reopened the question of participating in the work of the Preparliament. On 5 October it was decided that the Bolsheviks would stage a demonstrative walkout on the first day. Thus Trotsky denounced the Preparliament during its opening session on 7 October, after which the Bolshevik delegates made their exit.[13]

# INSURRECTION

Although Trotsky was committed to a Soviet insurrection against Kerensky's government, the precise agent of that insurrection was still unclear to him at the beginning of October. However, he was sure that it could not be the

Bolshevik Party (meaning he had diverged yet again from Lenin's view). Ironically, it was the Mensheviks who resolved the conundrum for him. With the Imperial German Army apparently preparing to march on the capital, and the government drafting plans to evacuate the seat of government to Moscow, on 9 October the Mensheviks introduced into the Soviet a proposal that a Committee of Revolutionary Defence be formed to help defend the capital. Trotsky backed this proposal, seeing a military committee of the Soviet, rather than the Military Organisation of the Bolshevik Party, as the perfect instrument to carry out an insurrection.[14] Not all Bolsheviks agreed, however. On 10 October the Bolshevik Central Committee met to debate the issue. Lenin put the case for an immediate putsch, while Kamenev and Zinoviev argued against.[15] Neither Lenin's views nor those of Zinoviev and Kamenev were accepted. The Central Committee voted in favour of the *principle* of insurrection, but appeared to do little more.

Nevertheless, Trotsky busied himself with preparations. He wrote very little during 1917, apart from the ephemera of short inflammatory speeches. It was only later, in exile, when he wrote his *History of the Russian Revolution*, that he explained some of the tensions that existed between himself and Lenin during October. As he made clear in his account [**Document 7**], no practical plan for insurrection was adopted on 10 October, but since it was supposed to occur before the opening of the Second Congress of Soviets, originally planned for 20 October, the target date for insurrection had to be around the 15th. On 12 October he guided through the Soviet a draft resolution establishing the Military Revolutionary Committee (MRC), as the Committee for Revolutionary Defence had been rechristened; the next day this was endorsed by the Soldiers' Section of the Soviet. Also on the 13th, Trotsky attended the Congress of Soviets of the Northern Region, where the resolution he proposed was, in his words, 'an almost undisguised summons to insurrection' on 20 October.[16]

However, when the Bolshevik Central Committee next met – on 16 October – those opposed to insurrection, including Kamenev, could rightly point out that almost a week had passed since 10 October and the Party had done nothing of consequence to prepare for an uprising. This expanded meeting of the Central Committee, which included representatives of the Petrograd Party Committee and the Military Organisation as well as members of the Soviet, tried to work out a consensus on the issue. Again Kamenev and Zinoviev called for the policy to be dropped, and again Lenin wanted an immediate insurrection. Lenin therefore interpreted the statement made by the MRC representative Trotsky had sent to the meeting, Krylenko, as shilly-shallying on Trotsky's part. Krylenko argued, 'the water is boiling hard enough' and there could be no question of withdrawing the resolution of 10 October. However, he (and therefore Trotsky) disagreed with Lenin 'on the question of who shall begin it and how it shall begin'. A Party-led insurrection on a fixed date would not work, Krylenko argued; what would work was exploiting the growing opposition to Kerensky's movement of troops from the capital to the front. In this sense, Kerensky's determination to transfer the troops, and the Soviet's determination to resist this, meant that 'the thing is already begun'. As Trotsky made clear some 15 years after the event, 'within the general frame of Lenin's formula' – the resolution in favour of insurrection backed by the Central Committee – 'there arose subordinate, but very important questions'.[17]

Lenin wanted the Bolsheviks to seize power before the Second Congress of Soviets assembled. Trotsky believed that defending the congress from possible government attack was likely to present an opportunity for a seizure of power. He would be proved right, even though the opening of the congress was postponed from 20 October to the 26th. In any event, the idea of the Bolsheviks staging a coup on their own behalf had been moved off the agenda by Kamenev's decision to resign from the Central Committee and publish in the Menshevik press an explanation of why he and Zinoviev opposed insurrection. By 18 October, the press was full of articles on Bolshevik plans for an uprising. Trotsky understood that Lenin's idea of unilateral action by the Bolsheviks was so unpopular that rumours of it had to be denied. As he recalled later, alarm 'penetrated even the workers' sections and still more the regiments; to them, too, it began to seem as though a coming-out were being prepared without them'. So he resolved to make a statement both to the Soviet and on its behalf in which he outlined his strategy for revolution. This made clear that

> we have not set a date for the attack. But the opposing side has, evidently, already set it. We will meet it, we will repel it duly, and we will declare that at the first counter-revolutionary attempt to hamper the work of the Congress [of Soviets] we will answer with a counter-offensive which will be ruthless and which we will carry out to the end.

To Trotsky's fury, Kamenev, sitting next to him, jumped to his feet and stated that he endorsed Trotsky's statement fully, implying that the statement was a rejection of the insurrection rather than a rather tortuous explanation of how the insurrection would take place.[18] When the Bolshevik Central Committee met on 20 October it was not planning insurrection, but squabbling about the behaviour of Kamenev.[19]

Despite Lenin's concern and Bolshevik infighting, below the surface Trotsky's strategy was beginning to bear fruit. Not only had he got the Soviet to establish the MRC, but it had agreed to call a conference of the Petrograd garrison, which took place on 18–21 October. This made clear that the garrison had no confidence in the Provisional Government and would be prepared to take armed action in defence of the revolution if called to do so by the Petrograd Soviet or the Congress of Soviets. With garrison support for the policy of the MRC, late in the night of the 21st Trotsky sent three of the MRC Bureau members to talk to the command of the Petrograd Military District and ask them to accept that, henceforth, all orders would have to be counter-signed by the MRC. The proposal was turned down and the MRC reported to the Soviet that it had broken with the command. A gauntlet had been thrown down, but it was still unclear how things would develop.

Sunday 22 October had been designated 'Soviet Day', a day of peaceful meetings and demonstrations, and Trotsky spent the day addressing public meetings and working the crowds, heating the mood. By the 23rd the MRC had got down to drafting a detailed plan of operations. As Trotsky recalled, it was basically very simple: chosen detachments were allocated to seize strategic points of the capital when a signal was given. The key to success was to win over as many garrison units to support the MRC, or at least to ensure that they remained neutral in any struggle. A key moment came on the afternoon of the 23rd, when Trotsky addressed the garrison of the Peter-Paul Fortress, at the very heart of the capital, and persuaded its members to follow the MRC. Later in the day the troops responsible for the arsenal also came out in support of the MRC.

Lenin, though, was concerned that all this activity was being undertaken not in the name of a seizure of power but in order to defend the Second Congress of Soviets from possible government attack. As Trotsky recalled, 'that word "insurrection" was not spoken by any one of the leaders'. When the MRC reported to the Soviet on the evening of the 23rd it listed those units which had now stated that they would obey the orders of the MRC rather than the untrustworthy government, but the logic that crowding out the government implied its overthrow was never spelled out. The Soviet backed the actions of the MRC in the spirit that they were measures to defend the Congress of Soviets, and it was up to Kerensky to attack – and attack he did.[20]

On the morning of the 24th he closed down the Bolshevik and Soviet press; at the same time he cut the Smolny telephone lines, resolved to prosecute members of the MRC and demanded the removal of all MRC commissars. Trotsky sent troops to reopen the Bolshevik press, and by doing so he had effectively embarked on an insurrection. As he noted later: 'although an insurrection can win on the offensive, it develops better the more it looks like self-defence'.[21]

When the Central Committee met on the 24th its task was to try to give organisational form to a process that was already under way. Yet the central ambiguity of what was taking place remained. Was power actually being

seized or was all this military activity simply intended to ensure the Second
Congress of Soviets met and had the opportunity to resolve the political
future of the country? Trotsky dared not come clean, even with the Bolshevik
caucus gathering for the opening of the Second Congress of Soviets: 'it was
still impossible to throw off the defensive envelope of the attack without
creating confusion in the minds of certain units of the garrison'. He reassured
a delegation from the Petrograd City Council that 'the question of power is
to be decided by the Congress of Soviets . . . if the congress declines power,
the Petrograd Soviet will submit'.[22]

Kerensky was busy during the day. He ordered loyal troops to occupy the
railway stations, established checkpoints at major road intersections, and
raised the bridges across the Neva. The MRC responded by asking the crew
of the battleship *Aurora* to restore movement on the Nikolaevskii Bridge,
thus re-establishing traffic between the city centre and the large working-
class district on Vasilevskii Island. The captain of the battleship refused to
implement the order, but agreed that he could be 'arrested', then dutifully
brought the ship towards the bridge, prompting Kerensky's guards to flee.
The sailors then lowered the bridge. At about the same time MRC commissars
gained access to the telephone exchange and restored the phone connections
to Smolny. Government authority was being challenged, but power was not
yet being seized. In Trotsky's words, 'right up to the evening of the 24th, the
umbilical cord of "legality" was not conclusively severed'.[23]

Around six in the evening of the 24th Lenin wrote a letter to the Central
Committee urging the Party to end the ambiguity and seize power before
what he called the 'wavering vote' of the Second Congress of Soviets. Asking
rhetorically, 'Who must take power?', Lenin answered that it no longer
mattered whether it was the MRC or the Party; action was the essential thing.
So the Bolshevik Military Organisation followed the MRC's lead and dusted
off its plans for the seizure of key installations. The operation began around
two in the morning of the 25th. According to Trotsky's account, small
groups 'usually with a nucleus of armed workers or sailors under the leadership of a commissar' occupied strategic sites such as railway stations, the
electricity network, bridges, the State Bank, big printing plants and the telegraph office. All of this was the work of just 'a few thousand Red Guards and
two or three thousand sailors'.[24]

While these forces were being deployed, Trotsky was called on to address
a preliminary meeting of delegates to the Second Congress of Soviets. At
about three in the morning of the 25th, he finally ended the ambiguity and
made clear that an insurrection was under way in which the Bolshevik Party
was leading the masses.[25] Yet, when dawn broke on the 25th, the insurrection
seemed to stall. By seven in the morning, the Supreme Army Headquarters,
the Petrograd Military Headquarters and Kerensky's government in the Winter

Palace had no telephone service; but there was no sign that they were on the point of surrender. Three hours later, Smolny broadcast that the Provisional Government had been overthrown, but this was not the case. By midday troops had persuaded the Preparliament to disperse; but the government still remained inside the Winter Palace. In the early afternoon, both Lenin and Trotsky addressed an emergency session of the Petrograd Soviet; but the latter's declaration that the Provisional Government had been overthrown was quickly followed by a clarification that the Winter Palace had not yet been taken.

The Bolsheviks were desperate that the overthrow of Kerensky's government should be complete by the time the Second Congress of Soviets was due to open at eight in the evening; but the Winter Palace was still not in their hands even then. A wrangle with the Mensheviks delayed the opening of the congress until well after ten, but as Trotsky paced backwards and forwards between the congress hall and the room where Lenin was based, the continuing sound of artillery fire confirmed that the Winter Palace remained in government hands. It finally surrendered after 2 a.m. on the 26th.[26]

Trotsky claimed in his memoirs that it was while he and Lenin awaited the opening of the Second Congress of Soviets that Lenin became reconciled to the strategy of the insurrection adopted by Trotsky. Lenin was clearly glad that the insurrection had taken place before the congress commenced, but that had not been Trotsky's intention. In his *History of the Russian Revolution* he wrote that 'the insurrection began earlier and ended later than had been indicated'. He had assumed, as he stated repeatedly in public, that the insurrection would be a product of the Congress of Soviets and take place when it was in session, but Kerensky's action had prompted the MRC to act earlier, unexpectedly bringing the timing closer to Lenin's preference. However, by acting before the Congress of Soviets had assembled, the veil of constitutionality had to be dropped – resistance by Kerensky's government was more stubborn and the Winter Palace, unlike some of the earlier targets, held out much longer than expected.[27]

# *RESULTS AND PROSPECTS* IN ACTION

In *Results and Prospects* Trotsky had argued that in the first stage of rule by a workers' government virtually the whole nation would support it. However, as its socialist agenda began to be implemented, the individualist aspirations of the peasantry would be offended and soon the workers' government would come under peasant attack.

The Bolsheviks' relationship with the political voice of the peasantry proved problematic from the start, largely because of the Bolsheviks' initial decision to rule alone. Just as they had failed to agree about whether to stage an insurrection, they could not reach agreement on which sort of government to form. During the day of 26 October Lenin and Trotsky called an informal meeting of those Central Committee members who happened to be around and resolved to form a government comprising only Bolsheviks. Trotsky described this as 'the only thinkable' proposal. However, later in the day the Central Committee invited three representatives of the Left SRs, the radical peasant party, to a more formal meeting and proposed the formation of a coalition government. The Left SRs rejected this proposal and so a purely Bolshevik government was formed, prompting immediate protests from the Left SRs.

The Left SRs then used their control of the Railway Workers' Union to try to force the Bolsheviks to compromise.[28] Those Bolsheviks like Kamenev and Zinoviev who had opposed an insurrection were keen to reach a compromise; Trotsky and Lenin were not. They issued the dissenters with an ultimatum, prompting several Bolshevik commissars to resign. The precise shape of the post-insurrection government began to be clarified only when the Extraordinary Congress of Peasant Soviets was held on 10 November and endorsed the policies of the Left SRs, rather than the mainstream of the SR Party; the Lefts SRs endorsed Kerensky's overthrow, the SRs did not. The Left SRs' triumph was repeated at the Second Congress of Peasant Soviets on 27 November. Confident in their popular mandate, the Left SRs decided to join the Bolsheviks in a coalition government, and this was finally formalised on 8 December. It started work at once on a Land Reform Bill that would give land to the peasantry. It had taken a while, but, as Trotsky predicted, 'proletariat in power' had recognised the importance of revolutionary land expropriation and won peasant support 'in the first most difficult period of the revolution'.

In *Results and Prospects* Trotsky had argued that peasant support for the proletarian revolution would soon evaporate and that the only way out of this dilemma was to spread the revolution to Europe. Two months before the October insurrection he had written, 'a lasting, decisive success is inconceivable for us without a revolution in Europe', and as the newly appointed Commissar for Foreign Affairs he sought to achieve just such a revolution by bringing the First World War to an end. The new Council of People's Commissars instructed the Commander-in-Chief of the Russian Army to begin armistice discussions, but he informed Lenin that he did not recognise the Bolshevik Government. An impasse followed, which ended only with the murder of the Commander-in-Chief on 21 November. The Russian and German armistice delegations had, in fact, first met two days earlier, and during a total of four days of talks Trotsky tried to persuade the Germans to accept a general peace and to agree not to transfer troops to the Western

Front. This proved impossible, but a truce was agreed on 22 November. Still hoping for a general rather than a separate peace, a further appeal was made to the Allies, but when no response was forthcoming the Bolsheviks had no choice but to consider a separate peace. Trotsky appeared before the Soviet Executive on 8 December to justify this stance and in his speech outlined his personal agenda for the next six months [**Document 8**].

> The armistice has made a breach in the war. The gunfire has ceased and everyone is nervously waiting to see how the Soviet Government will deal with the Hohenzollern and Habsburg imperialists. You must support us in treating them as foes of freedom, in ensuring that not one iota of this freedom is sacrificed to imperialism . . . We are becoming more and more convinced that peace talks will be a powerful weapon in the hands of other peoples in their struggle for peace. If we are mistaken, if Europe continues to be silent as the grave, and if this silence gives Wilhelm the chance to attack us and to dictate his terms to us, terms which would insult the revolutionary dignity of our country, then I am not sure whether, given our shattered economy and the general chaos (the result of the war and internal strife), we could fight. I think, however, that we could do so. For our lives, for our revolutionary honour, we would fight to the last drop of our blood . . . [raising] an army of soldiers and Red Guardsmen, strong in its revolutionary enthusiasm.[29]

The talks at Brest-Litovsk got under way on 9 December but progress was slow. After the formal opening there was an adjournment, followed by postponements, and it was only on 25 December that the German demands became clear. On 29 December the Soviet delegation returned to Petrograd, bringing with them what Trotsky called the 'monstrous demands of the Central Powers'. After a brief discussion among the Bolshevik leadership it was agreed that the only thing to do was to play for time in the hope that a European revolution would materialise. The negotiations had to be spun out for as long as possible, and Lenin insisted that 'to delay the negotiations, there must be someone to do the delaying': Trotsky was ordered to head the delegation himself and set off 'as if being led to a torture chamber'.[30] No sooner had he arrived than he asked for another adjournment, arriving back in Petrograd on 7 January 1918.

While he was en route, there had been dramatic developments in the capital. The Constituent Assembly had met and been dissolved on 6 January, and its place had been taken by the Third Congress of Soviets. On 8 January the Bolshevik Central Committee and leaders of the Bolshevik delegation to the Third Congress of Soviets met to consider what to do, and Trotsky proposed a tactic of neither peace nor war; the Bolsheviks would simply not sign the treaty proposed by the Germans, but nor would they resume hostilities. This tactic presupposed that the German proletariat would rise up in fury when it saw how outrageously its imperialist government was behaving.

The meeting accepted Trotsky's suggestion, but this was just an advisory vote; when the Central Committee resumed its discussion on 11 January, without the participation of extraneous delegates, Lenin and Trotsky clashed. Lenin felt they had no choice but to accept the German terms: 'what comrade Trotsky suggests is political showmanship', he argued. If the Germans attacked, the Bolsheviks would be forced to sign an even worse peace. However, the meeting endorsed Trotsky's policy by nine votes to seven.[31] Before returning to the negotiations, Trotsky put an optimistic gloss on the situation when he addressed the Third Congress of Soviets:

> They cannot threaten us with an offensive, as they cannot be sure the German soldiers will take part in one . . . and if German imperialism attempts to crucify us on the wheel of its military machine, then . . . we shall appeal to our elder brothers in the west and say: 'Do you hear?' and the international proletariat will respond – we firmly believe this – 'We hear!'.

Just prior to Trotsky's departure, he and Lenin came to a private understanding, which modified the 'no peace, no war' decision of the Central Committee. Trotsky promised to sign the peace if Lenin's fears were realised and the Germans resumed hostilities.[32]

However, before 'no peace, no war' became an issue, there remained the tactic of spinning out the negotiations, and this was feasible because, initially, both sides were interested in time-wasting. The Germans proposed a democratic peace in line with President Woodrow Wilson's principle of the self-determination of nations. They would effectively break up the Russian Empire, allowing the Bolsheviks to control the Russian heartland but establishing German-sponsored independent regimes in the Baltic and Ukraine. The Germans needed time to persuade Ukrainian politicians to back this scheme, while the Bolsheviks needed time to put an end to the growing Ukrainian autonomy movement and establish Soviet power in Ukraine by force. Just after the Bolshevik army captured Kiev, the Germans had their Ukrainian delegation ready.[33] On 27 January the Central Powers signed a separate treaty with the Ukrainian delegation, and on the 28th Trotsky made his final statement [**Document 9**]:

> In expectation of the approaching hour when the working classes of all countries seize power . . . we are withdrawing our army and our people from the war and issuing an order for full demobilisation . . . At the same

time we declare that the terms proposed to us by the governments of Germany and Austro-Hungary are in fundamental conflict with the interest of all people . . . We cannot put the signature of the Russian revolution under a peace treaty which brings oppression, woe and misfortune to millions of human beings.

Back in the capital, on 16 February (the Gregorian calendar was introduced in Russia at the start of February 1918, so 1 February became 13 February) he told the Petrograd Soviet that the odds against a German attack were nine to one.[34] He was soon proved terribly wrong. The Germans resumed hostilities just two days later. Under the terms of the tacit agreement between Lenin and Trotsky, this was the point at which Trotsky should have agreed to sign the treaty. However, he had changed his mind. Lenin still insisted that the Bolsheviks should offer to sign the treaty at once; Trotsky argued that the offensive should be allowed to begin 'so that the workers of Germany would learn of the offensive as a fact rather than as a threat'. When the Central Committee had met on 17 February he had voted for the principle of peace, but on the 18th he refused to vote for the dispatch of the necessary telegram to the Germans. He reported that the German offensive had indeed begun with an aerial bombardment of the city of Dvinsk, but argued, 'the masses are only just beginning to digest what is happening . . . we have to wait and see what impression all this makes on the German people'. Later that day, Trotsky informed the reconvened Central Committee that Dvinsk had now fallen and it was time to make a direct appeal to the civilian politicians in Berlin and Vienna. Trotsky was behaving recklessly and Lenin once again insisted that the time had come to sign. Trotsky finally backed down and on 19 February the Bolsheviks sued for peace. Trotsky assumed command of a Committee for Revolutionary Defence.[35]

Declaring a willingness to sign the peace treaty was one thing; persuading the Germans to stop their advance was quite another. Fighting had begun and until the Germans agreed to resume talks, they had to be resisted. Allied representatives had responded to the 'no peace, no war' declaration by offering to aid Russia should hostilities resume. On 18 February Trotsky was visited by the British representative in Russia, Bruce Lockhart, who offered British military support. Lockhart found Trotsky surprisingly optimistic: 'even if Russia cannot resist, she will indulge in partisan warfare to the best of her ability'. However, when Trotsky met with his key military advisers on 20 February they persuaded him that partisan operations could not hold back a modern army; the only thing to do was to retreat to a defensible line and hope to build up reserves.

By 21 February a Russian delegation had reached Brest-Litovsk, only to discover that the terms now offered by the Germans were, as Lenin had predicted, far worse than the original ones. At first even Lenin thought there was now no choice but to fight for survival. Given this bleak scenario, it was not surprising that Trotsky maintained contact with the Allies, not only with Lockhart but with French representatives. On 22 February he persuaded a sceptical Central Committee to accept a French offer of military aid, but the military situation was worsening all the time. On 23 February news came of the fall of Pskov and a crisis meeting of military advisers predicted that Petrograd would soon fall, too. When the Central Committee met later that day Lenin insisted that 'this is where the policy of revolutionary phrase-mongering ends'. Trotsky did not agree. He insisted that the Party could 'tackle the task of organising defence'; even if Petrograd and Moscow surrendered, 'we could hold the whole world in tension'. The problem was, he said, that the Party was not united, and 'we cannot fight a revolutionary war when the Party is split'. Reluctantly, he would therefore resign as Commissar of Foreign Affairs and abstain in the forthcoming vote; as a result of this, Lenin's motion to sign the new German proposals was passed.[36]

**Czechoslovak Legion:** In spring 1917 the various units of Czechoslovak prisoners of war which had been operating within the framework of the Russian Imperial Army were transformed into an independent Czechoslovak Legion and greatly expanded. Based in Kiev, the signing of the Treaty of Brest-Litovsk presented them with a dilemma. As the Imperial German Army entered Ukraine, the Czechoslovak Legion helped slow their advance, but once on Russian territory, their future was unclear. Slowly units gradually moved eastwards, heading for Vladivostok and the long journey across America to France, where they hoped to fight on the Western Front. Before the 'English ultimatum' was rejected, Trotsky had plans to keep at least some of the Czechoslovak Legion in Russia as part of an anti-German army, but after the arrival of the German ambassador, this became impossible and so he called for the legion to be disarmed. It was this call which prompted the Czechoslovak Legion to rebel against the Bolsheviks. Since the legion was by then strung out along railway lines from the Volga to Vladivostok, the whole of eastern Russia was suddenly freed from Bolshevik rule.

Even so, Trotsky was convinced that the time to fight Imperial Germany would soon come. The peace was signed on 3 March and the very next day the Bolsheviks established a Supreme Military Council and made Trotsky its chair. He had told the Soviet Executive even before the Brest-Litovsk negotiations had started that if the Germans dictated terms which 'insulted the revolutionary dignitary of our country' then they would raise an army of soldiers 'strong in its revolutionary enthusiasm'. That was precisely what he now set out to do. At the Extraordinary Seventh Party Congress held on 6–8 March to endorse the signing of the treaty, Trotsky followed a justification of his actions with a prediction that would guide his behaviour over the next few weeks: 'the present breathing space can be reckoned to last no more than two or three months at best, and most likely only weeks and days'.[37] War with Germany would resume, and it was imperative to have a capable force ready for that day by disbanding the disintegrating army and building a new one.

During the Fourth Extraordinary Congress of Soviets, 14–16 March, which ratified the Treaty of Brest-Litovsk, Trotsky was appointed Commissar of War and began to draft a plan in the event of renewed German aggression for a fighting retreat beyond the River Volkhov, to be co-ordinated with the construction of defensive 'screens' to protect Petrograd and Moscow. Allied representatives continued to be closely involved in these preparations and, as part of this strategy, Trotsky was also keen to keep in Russia the **Czechoslovak Legion**. Formed by the Provisional Government from Austro-Hungarian PoWs of Czech and Slovak ethnicity, the Legion had been stationed near Kiev when the armistice with the Germans was signed. When, under the terms of the Brest-Litovsk Treaty, the German Army marched into Ukraine, the Legion helped pro-Soviet forces slow its advance. Once back in the

Russian heartland the Legion announced it planned to leave Russia for the Western Front, but Trotsky could see the advantage of keeping this battle-hardened force at hand to fight alongside his newly constructed Russian Army. To help persuade the Legion to stay, on 20 March he temporarily forbade any of their units proceeding further east towards Vladivostok.

Trotsky was equally clear that his new army had to be professional. In a speech to a session of the Moscow Soviet on 19 March, immediately after his arrival in the city, he stated that a properly and freshly organised army meant using military specialists from the old army and imposing discipline. This message was repeated to a conference of the Moscow City Communist Party on 28 March: 'I have had occasion several times already to say at public meetings that in the sphere of command, of operations, of military actions, we place full responsibility upon military specialists and consequently give them the necessary powers.' He therefore dismissed the principle of elected officers and soldiers' committees. To the surprise of many, on 30 March Trotsky appointed to the Supreme Military Council Admiral D. V. Verderevskii, the Navy Minister in Kerensky's last government.[38]

By April 1918, Trotsky's discussions with the Allies had reached the point where both sides envisaged a major British intervention at the moment when the 'breathing space' with Germany ended. The British would persuade the Czechoslovak Legion to stay in Russia, where they would be reinforced by an Allied expeditionary force which would land in Archangel. Trotsky backed the scheme, but pointed out that the German Ambassador was due to arrive in Moscow on 26 April, making close relations between himself and the Allies more problematic thereafter. Yet, even after the arrival of the German Ambassador, such contacts continued. They did so because on 29 April the Germans changed tack in Ukraine. Until then, they had worked with the local democratically elected government, but because of the commitment of that government to land reform, the Germans now decided to overthrow it and establish a dictatorship. For many Bolsheviks, this revealed the true face of German imperialism, and on 4 May Russian troops were instructed to resist any German violations of their new border. The Central Committee then went into a crisis session which lasted the best part of the week of 6–13 May.

A rupture with Germany seemed possible at any minute, but when Trotsky outlined to the Central Committee what he and the Allies were proposing Lenin spoke out against 'the **English ultimatum**' and Trotsky's scheme was dropped. Yet German encroachments on the agreed demarcation line between Russia and Ukraine continued – at Cherkovo station on 9 May and at Bataisk railway junction on 2 June.[39] Obsessed with the possibility of internationalising the revolution through a new war with Imperial Germany, Trotsky took his eyes off the danger of what was, for him, the inevitable and growing peasant dissatisfaction with the proletarian regime.

**English ultimatum:** The term used by Lenin to condemn Trotsky's proposals made during the Central Committee's repeated discussions in early May 1918 over whether to annul the Treaty of Brest-Litovsk. The German imposition of a reactionary puppet regime in Ukraine, coupled with repeated violations of the new border with Russia, convinced many Bolsheviks that the treaty was intolerable. Trotsky had been encouraging the British to send an expeditionary force to north Russia, and hoped that these troops, in combination with the Czechoslovak Legion, could give some backbone to the new Russian army he was hastily constructing. Lenin convinced the Central Committee not only that the Treaty of Brest-Litovsk should be honoured, but also that it should be reinforced by a trade treaty.

# FURTHER READING

As well as Trotsky's *My Life*, his *History of the Russian Revolution* is an essential source, as is another account written by a participant, N. Sukhanov's *The Russian Revolution: A Personal Record*. For the July Days, see A. Rabinowitch's *Prelude to Revolution*; and for Lenin and Trotsky's differing views on how to seize power, see J. D. White's 'Lenin, Trotsky and the Arts of Insurrection: The Congress of Soviets of the Northern Region, 11–13 October 1917'. For events surrounding the Treaty of Brest-Litovsk, see G. R. Swain's *The Origins of the Russian Civil War*. Two important documentary collections are of relevance here: J. L. H. Keep's *The Debate on Soviet Power*; and *The Bolsheviks and the October Revolution: Central Committee Minutes*.

# NOTES

1  A. Rabinowitch, *Prelude to Revolution* (Bloomington: Indiana University Press, 1968), pp. 42–47.

2  L. Trotsky, *History of the Russian Revolution* (London: Sphere, 1965), vol. I, p. 340; N. Sukhanov, *The Russian Revolution: A Personal Record* (Princeton: Princeton University Press, 1984), p. 359; Trotsky, *My Life*, p. 329.

3  Deutscher, *Armed*, pp. 266–67.

4  Sukhanov, *Russian Revolution*, pp. 383–84; Trotsky, *History*, vol. II, p. 296.

5  Sukhanov, *Russian Revolution*, pp. 432–29; Trotsky, *History*, vol. II, pp. 40–42; Trotsky, *My Life*, p. 311.

6  Sukhanov, *Russian Revolution*, pp. 444–47; Trotsky, *My Life*, p. 312.

7  Trotsky, *My Life*, p. 316; for the July Days generally, see Rabinowitch, *Prelude*.

8  Trotsky, *My Life*, p. 317.

9  Trotsky, *History*, vol. II, pp. 289–90; Deutscher, *Armed*, p. 288.

10  Sukhanov, *Russian Revolution*, p. 544; Trotsky, *History*, vol. II, p. 325; for the Preparliament more generally, see G. R. Swain, 'Before the Fighting Started: A Discussion on the Theme of the "Third Way"', *Revolutionary Russia* no. 2, 1991.

11  Trotsky, *My Life*, p. 339.

12  Trotsky, *History*, vol. II, p. 329.

13  R. P. Browder and A. F. Kerensky, *The Russian Provisional Government 1917: Documents* (Stanford: Stanford University Press, 1961), vol. III, p. 1729.

14  Trotsky, *History*, vol. III, p. 90.

15  Trotsky, *History*, vol. III, pp. 140–43.

16  Trotsky, *History*, vol. III, pp. 81, 483.

17  *The Bolsheviks and the October Revolution: Central Committee Minutes* (London: Pluto Press, 1974), pp. 101–02. For the differing tactics of Lenin and Trotsky at this time, see J. D. White, 'Lenin, Trotsky and the Arts of Insurrection: The Congress of Soviets of the Northern Region, 11–13 October 1917', *Slavonic and East European Review* no. 1, 1999.

18 Browder and Kerensky, *Documents*, p. 1767; Trotsky, *History*, vol. III, p. 102.

19 *Central Committee*, p. 110.

20 Trotsky, *History*, vol. III, pp. 114, 116–17.

21 Trotsky, *History*, vol. III, p. 195.

22 Trotsky, *History*, vol. III, p. 198

23 Trotsky, *History*, vol. III, p. 208.

24 Trotsky, *History*, vol. III, pp. 209–12; Trotsky, *My Life*, p. 323.

25 Trotsky, *History*, vol. III, pp. 213–14; Sukhanov, *Russian Revolution*, p. 617.

26 Trotsky, *My Life*, p. 324; Trotsky, *History*, vol. III, pp. 284–85.

27 Trotsky, *My Life*, p. 324; Trotsky, *History*, vol. III, p. 205.

28 Trotsky, *History*, vol. III, pp. 299, 314; *Central Committee*, p. 138. The Railway Workers' Union talks are fully explored in Swain, 'Before'.

29 J. L. H. Keep (ed.), *The Debate on Soviet Power* (Oxford: Oxford University Press, 1979), p. 187.

30 Trotsky, *My Life*, p. 363.

31 *Central Committee*, pp. 175–80.

32 D. Volkogonov, *Trotsky: The Eternal Revolutionary* (London: HarperCollins, 1997), p. 109; Deutscher, *Armed*, pp. 375–76.

33 A more detailed account of events in Ukraine at this time can be found in G. R. Swain, *The Origins of the Russian Civil War* (London: Longman, 1996), pp. 92–118.

34 Volkogonov, *Eternal*, pp. 111–12.

35 Trotsky, *My Life*, pp. 387–88; *Central Committee*, p. 204.

36 Swain, *Origins*, p. 133; *Central Committee*, pp. 218–25.

37 Vokogonov, *Eternal*, p. 116.

38 L. Trotsky, *How the Revolution Armed* (London: New Park Publications, 1979), vol. I, pp. 23, 43–47; for Trotsky's contacts with the Allies, see Swain, *Origins*, pp. 132–48.

39 J. M. Meijer (ed.), *The Trotsky Papers* (The Hague: Mouton and Co., 1964), vol. I, p. 55.

# 4

# Defending the revolution

## PEASANT DISTRUST

In *Results and Prospects* Trotsky had argued that peasant support for a workers' government would only be temporary. What he called 'abolishing feudalism' – that is, land reform – would win the support of the 'entire peasantry', but then 'any legislation carried through for the purpose of protecting the agricultural proletariat' would risk opposition from a minority and force the proletariat 'to carry the class struggle into the villages'.

The signing of the Treaty of Brest-Litovsk wrecked the Bolshevik–Left SR coalition. The Left SRs had achieved their main purpose by enacting the land reform of February 1918, and a treaty with Imperial Germany which condemned Ukraine to German occupation was more than they could stomach, so they left the Bolsheviks to govern alone. No longer held back by the Left SRs, the Bolsheviks abandoned the Left SR policy of collecting grain from the countryside by free-market trading and abolished the market in favour of 'planning'. In their view free trade had fallen into the hands of rich peasants – kulaks – and the only way to break their stranglehold on grain prices was to encourage poor peasants to rise up against them. From May onwards, the Bolsheviks began to encourage the formation of Poor Peasants' Committees, which favoured ending the free market in grain and delivering it instead at low fixed prices to their working-class allies in the towns. Dressed up as 'class struggle in the villages', in reality the policy quickly degenerated into the forced requisitioning of grain. In response, low-level peasant unrest would be endemic over the summer.

The Treaty of Brest-Litovsk infuriated not only the Left SRs but the SR Party. It had won the Constituent Assembly elections in November 1917, but had not responded when that assembly was dissolved in January 1918 because the peace talks with Germany were then at such a delicate stage. They had been prepared to back Trotsky's idea of a short breathing space and co-operation with the Allies, followed by a resumption of hostilities with Imperial Germany. Once Lenin had condemned this as an 'English ultimatum' at the May Central Committee meeting, however, the SRs called for an anti-Bolshevik insurrection. In launching this, the SRs found themselves acting alongside the Czechoslovak Legion, units of which were, by May 1918, strung out along Russia's railway network from the Volga to the Far East. While at the start of the month it was still assumed that those Czechoslovak units west of the Urals would become the core of an Allied intervention force based at Archangel which at Trotsky's signal would resume the fight against Imperial Germany, Lenin's decision to reject the 'English ultimatum' had ended all that. By mid-May Trotsky had no choice but to agree with the German Ambassador that the presence of an armed Allied Army on Russian soil violated the provisions of the Treaty of Brest-Litovsk and that the Czechoslovak Legion should be disarmed. The Legion ignored this order, rebelled, and resumed its journey eastwards. Outside Samara, they faced the prospect of fighting their way through the city at the very moment when the local SRs planned to stage an insurrection there. In a joint action, Samara was taken on 8 June and soon the revolt had spread along the whole length of the Trans-Siberian Railway. Once in control of Samara, the SRs established their own 'People's Army' and declared the formation of a new government – the Committee of the Constituent Assembly (Komuch).[1]

The situation on the Volga worsened in the first days of July. The Fifth Congress of Soviets, which opened on 6 July, saw the final break in relations between the Bolsheviks and the Left SRs. Furious at the way the congress allowed delegates from Poor Peasants' Committees to participate, thus depriving the Left SRs of their anticipated majority, the latter resorted to direct action and assassinated the German Ambassador as the first stage in an insurrection. In Moscow they took control of the telegraph building and much of the centre of the city. Even more devastating for the Bolsheviks was the rebellion of their Volga commander, Colonel Mikhail Muraviev, a prominent Left SR. He seized control of the telegraph and radio station in Simbirsk. The Bolsheviks quickly regained control of Moscow, but on the Volga the situation continued to deteriorate, despite Muraviev's murder by loyal Bolsheviks. Simbirsk fell on 22 July, and the People's Army began its assault on Kazan on 5 August. The Red Army's new Volga commander, Jānis Vācietis, sent daily appeals for reinforcements on 1, 2 and 3 August, but to no avail. Trotsky had resolved to visit the Volga in person on 29 July, but it was only on the night of 7–8 August that his train finally pulled out of Moscow, with Trotsky unaware that his destination, Kazan, was no longer in Bolshevik hands.[2]

# BUILDING AN ARMY

In *Results and Prospects* Trotsky wrote that 'the more definite and determined the policy of the proletariat in power becomes, the narrower and more shaky does the ground beneath its feet become'. It seems likely that Trotsky would have reflected on these words as his train arrived at the Volga front. As he recalled in his memoirs, when he reached the front line, the town of Sviyazhsk, on the Moscow side of the Volga from Kazan, no one knew where Vācietis was, there was panic everywhere: 'the situation looked hopeless . . . the fate of the revolution was hanging by a thread'. The situation was indeed desperate. During his first inspection of the Red artillery, Trotsky found himself diving for cover as his position came under bombardment. No sooner had he returned to his carriage than it came under attack from an enemy airplane. In those early days 'planes came and went, dropping their bombs on the station and railway cars'. Trotsky's first report to Moscow was full of self-criticism [**Document 10**]: reinforcements had been promised but had not arrived and this had created 'a state of psychological collapse'; everything was needed – gunners, engineers, agitators; given the shaky state of morale, officers needed revolvers for 'there is no hope of maintaining discipline without having revolvers'.[3] Morale was worst in the 4th Latvian Regiment. The commander and chairman of the Regimental Committee demanded a period of rest and recuperation lest there be 'consequences dangerous to the revolution'. Summoned by Trotsky to his train, the two men repeated their statement, at which point Trotsky had them both arrested.[4]

Supplies were clearly the key to the situation, and soon men, horses, fuel, field telephones and field guns were all being redirected to the Volga. The journalist Larissa Reissner recalled: 'Here all of Trotsky's organisational genius was revealed, he managed to restore the supply lines, got new artillery and a few regiments . . . Newspapers arrived, boots and overcoats came. Trotsky was able to show this handful of defenders a calmness icier than theirs.'[5] It was not just a question of hustling for supplies; Trotsky was ready to improvise to get things done. The ability of the enemy to bomb his head-quarters at will had convinced him of the importance of air power, so an air squadron was formed. The planes were old and the pilots had no proper flying clothes, but it worked. After a week Trotsky could tell Lenin, 'we have concentrated substantial forces of aviation here, which are terrorising bour-geois Kazan by dropping large quantities of dynamite on it; air intelligence has started to yield fruitful results'.[6]

Trotsky was determined to restore morale. Supplies would help, but more was needed. To improve the welfare of his soldiers, his first report called for the dispatch of a good band, while another demanded a dentist.[7] However, morale was also to be restored through discipline. The commander and chairman of the Regimental Committee of the 4th Latvian Regiment were accused of treason and brought before a revolutionary tribunal. They were not sentenced to death because of fears of provoking a mutiny, but the tribunal made clear that no clemency would be shown in future.[8] Trotsky was as good as his word, for the next case of treachery was dealt with determinedly.

The Red Army launched an offensive on 11 August which, while unsuccessful, did forestall more enemy action and restored a degree of stability to the front. Trotsky decided to move his headquarters from his exposed position in the Sviyazhsk railway siding to a steamboat on the Volga. However, the arrival of this steamer on 14 August prompted some of the reinforcements newly sent from Petrograd to see an escape route; they seized control of the boat and tried to sail upriver to safety. Trotsky had the ringleaders, the commander and the commissar brought before a tribunal and executed. He insisted that no compassion could be shown to Commissar Panteleev, since he had made no attempt to prevent the mutiny and had even participated fully in it.[9]

For Trotsky, discipline simply meant that orders must be implemented. He had to put a stop to the routine discussion and debate of everything. At Sviyazhsk he was furious that what he considered 'a well-conceived operation' was wrecked by the wilful refusal of two divisional commanders to obey orders. The officers concerned got together with their commissars and started criticising the tactics Vācietis was using. Trotsky recalled: 'I had both divisional commanders arrested; five commissars, Party members, came to see me to give explanations and to obtain protection; I handed them over to the courts for abandoning their posts without permission.' After this there were no more conclaves of commanders and commissars against higher authority.[10]

Within a week of arriving at the front, Trotsky was trying to reassure Lenin that the situation was not as dire as reported and that victory would come [**Document 11**]. The enemy was stubborn, but the Red Army was fighting: 'the allegation that our men do not want to fight is a lie'. The key was to have 'a tolerably good commander and a good commissar'. The presence of good, committed Party members could also work wonders. Given the precarious situation at the front – on 28 August Trotsky's train was almost captured in a surprise encirclement by the People's Army – the reliability of former Imperial Army officers was something that caused Lenin increasing concern. However, Trotsky did not share this concern. There had been incidents of disloyalty but by and large Trotsky was full of praise for 'the young General Staffers' who helped him construct the army; he said as much in a report to Moscow dated 11 August. So when Lenin raised the question of excluding General Staffers from the high command, Trotsky replied in fury on 23 August [**Document 12**]: 'It is essential to make the entire military hierarchy more compact and get rid of the ballast by means of extracting those General Staff officers that are efficient and loyal to us and not on any account by means of replacing them with Party ignoramuses.'[11]

After the near disaster of 28 August, Red Army reinforcements had started to flood in and preparations for the reconquest of Kazan could begin. The assault was to be carried out by torpedo boats transferred from the Baltic Sea. Trotsky took part in the attack which began on the night of 7–8 September and recalled how his boat was hit and the steering gear shot to pieces. On the eve of the assault Trotsky was supremely confident:

> Propaganda, organisation, revolutionary example and repression produced the necessary change in a few weeks. A vacillating, unreliable and crumbling mass was transformed into a real army. Our artillery had emphatically established its superiority. Our flotilla controlled the river. Our airmen dominated the air. No longer did I doubt that we would take Kazan.[12]

It was not an easy victory – both Trotsky and Larissa Reissner remembered 'great losses' – but Lenin summed up the situation accurately when Trotsky visited him to report his triumph at Kazan in person. Lenin stated laconically that 'the game is won', and although the Bolsheviks would face plenty of difficulties before victory was achieved, they would never again be on the verge of defeat.[13]

The pattern of events at Sviyazhsk was to be repeated many times during the Civil War. Looking back, Trotsky commented 'I almost never had occasion to accompany a victorious army . . . I retreated with troops but never advanced with them.' His great ability was to turn around the retreating soldier.

> Even after defeats and retreats, the flabby, panicky mob would be transformed in two or three weeks into an efficient fighting force. What was needed for this? At once much and little. It needed good commanders, a few dozen experienced fighters, a dozen or so of communists ready to make any sacrifice, boots for the barefooted, a bath-house, an energetic propaganda campaign, food, underwear, tobacco and matches. The train took care of all this. We always had in reserve a few zealous communists to fill the breaches, a hundred or so of good fighting men, a small stock of boots, leather jackets, medicaments, machine guns, field-glasses, maps, watches and all sorts of gifts.

When the rout had stopped, it was just a question of supply, but with nothing left in central depots after spring 1919 constant improvisation was needed to keep supplies coming, and Trotsky proved a master at organising improvisation.[14]

## STALIN AND MILITARY SPECIALISTS

After the capture of Kazan, the Red Army advanced steadily against the People's Army, approaching Samara on 19 September; but bitter fighting meant that the People's Army did not abandon the town until 6 October. As the Red Army advanced towards Ufa, its progress slowed still further, and by the end of the month the People's Army had staged a counter-offensive, forcing the Red Army to begin a rather panicky retreat in early November. Political developments then completely changed the nature of the fighting on the Eastern Front. On 18 November, acting in the spirit of General Kornilov, with whom he had first discussed counter-revolution in April 1917, Admiral Alexander Kolchak staged a coup against the SRs and their Czechoslovak allies, who owed allegiance to the Constituent Assembly, and established a right-wing dictatorship. Henceforth, the Bolsheviks would be fighting not the SRs, whose democratic mandate as victors in the Constituent Assembly elections was impeccable, but counter-revolutionary generals, hell bent on restoring the old order, men the revolutionaries always branded as 'Whites'. Kolchak's coup and his subsequent persecution of the SR Party in Siberia ended serious fighting in the east until the end of December. The Red Army could resume its advance and capture Ufa, leaving Trotsky free to look to other fronts.

Fighting in southern Russia pre-dated the SR insurrection and Czechoslovak rebellion, but until October 1918 it had been desultory and never seriously threatened the survival of the Bolshevik regime. In the first months after the Bolshevik seizure of power General Kornilov and other leading counter-revolutionary generals had headed south to the Don and Kuban regions; but their attempt to break out of this isolated, peripheral region had been frustrated by Red forces and by the end of February 1918 they were confined to the remote Kuban steppe. German occupation of Ukraine meant that these White forces were protected on one flank and from August 1918 they began a series of assaults on Tsaritsyn. The third assault, in early October, nearly succeeded, but reinforcements arrived in the nick of time and Stalin, who had been sent to the town on 7 June, took the credit for the subsequent Red victory.

Stalin was therefore full of confidence about the performance of both himself and his men when he clashed seriously with Trotsky for the first time. The roots of this lay in September, when the overall command of the Red Army was thoroughly reformed. Until the end of August, those Red Army forces sent to deal with internal counter-revolution had not been subject to the control of the Supreme Military Council, which was only responsible for the troops being prepared for a possible war with Germany. The extent of the Volga fighting made this distinction nonsensical, so Trotsky decided to put all of Russia's military formations under the control of a single new Revolutionary Military Council (RVS), abolishing the Supreme Military Council. This meant that Stalin's forces were for the first time to be subjected to a new hierarchy of military regulation. In particular, Stalin had to accept the deployment of 'military specialists', the term used for officers from the old Tsarist army.

Stalin was suspicious of these military specialists. As soon as he arrived in Tsaritsyn he discovered a counter-revolutionary plot involving them, which prompted him to put all his faith in bringing forward young pro-Bolshevik non-commissioned officers to form a new officer corps. At the same time, he had institutionalised a system whereby Bolshevik political commissars were able to influence decisions on purely military matters, a form of collective decision-making which contradicted a promise that Trotsky had made to officers in the army deployed against Germany that they would have absolute authority in military matters. Stalin's distrust of the military specialists meant that he had already written to Trotsky in mid-July criticising their work.[15]

The dispute between Stalin and Trotsky began in earnest on 2 October. Having established an RVS at national level, designated for the sake of clarity the 'Republican RVS', Trotsky envisaged a series of subordinate RVSs on the individual fronts. Similarly, having appointed Vācietis the new Commander-in-Chief, he now designated a series of front commanders. But Stalin seemed to be in no hurry to establish an RVS for the Southern Front or even, when it was established on 17 September, to co-ordinate his actions with the new commander of that front. Trotsky left the Eastern Front, had a hasty meeting in Moscow on 3 October, then travelled south, explaining his standpoint in a message sent from his train on the 4th. He informed Moscow that he would, of course, 'be careful with the Tsaritsyn people', but the essence of the conflict was this: Stalin 'had established a collective command, which we have categorically rejected and which, independently of the personality of the commander, leads to a dissipation of command and anarchy; here is the crux of the matter'.[16]

He was equally blunt in a letter to Lenin sent the same day which attacked not only Stalin but Kliment Voroshilov, one of the non-commissioned officers Stalin was keen to promote [**Document 13**].

> I categorically insist on Stalin's recall. Things are going from bad to worse on the Tsaritsyn Front, despite the superabundance of military forces. Voroshilov is able to command a regiment, but not an army of 50,000 men. Nonetheless, I will retain him as commander of the 10th Tsaritsyn Army on condition that he places himself under the orders of the Commander of the Southern Front . . . [Because autumn is approaching] there is no time for diplomatic negotiations. Tsaritsyn must either obey orders or get out of the way. We have a colossal superiority of forces but total anarchy at the top. This can be put right within 24 hours given firm and resolute support your end.

To reinforce the point, the next day Trotsky forwarded to Lenin a telegram from Vācietis demanding 'Stalin's military order no. 18 must be counter-manded since the actions of Stalin are destroying all my plans'.[17]

Stalin had written to Lenin about Trotsky's behaviour in a similarly forthright manner on 3 October:

The point is that Trotsky, generally speaking, cannot get by without noisy gestures. At Brest he delivered a blow to the cause by his incredibly 'Leftist' gesturing . . . Now he delivers a further blow by his gesture about discipline, and yet all this Trotskyiste discipline amounts to in reality is to the most prominent leaders on the war front peering up the backside of military specialists from the camp of the 'non-party' counter-revolutionaries and not preventing them from wrecking the front. (Trotsky calls this not interfering in operational matters.) . . . Remove Trotsky, since I am afraid that his unhinged commands, if they are repeated, will put the front into the hands of so-called military specialists who merit no trust at all.[18]

On 5 October Stalin insisted in a message to Sverdlov that Trotsky had been insulting and had suddenly broken off the talks aimed at reconciliation.[19] It was not until the end of October that a working relationship between Trotsky and Stalin had been restored, but the tension between the two men would remain an important component of Soviet politics over the next decade.

By the time of the Eighth Party Congress on 18–23 March 1919 opponents of the use of military specialists had formed themselves into a political faction, the Military Opposition, determined to challenge what they saw as Trotsky's undue reliance on 'Tsarist officers'. To many Bolsheviks, Trotsky's support of the military specialists seemed cavalier. Although on 2 October he had learned of the betrayal of a certain Lebedev and had ordered the arrest of his family, it was more usual for Trotsky to intervene to get arrested officers released. On 4 October he asked the Bolshevik secret police (*cheka*) in Tver to release a certain Sulimov, whom he argued was needed at the front. A week later he sent two telegrams on the subject of arrested specialists. In the first, written on 13 October to Zinoviev, he responded to the arrest of 16 communication officers and asked for the release of those 'for whom there were not individual charges'. The second was sent to Felix Dzerzhinsky, the head of the *cheka*, and asked for the release of the Tver Aviation Group commander, who had been arrested 'just because he was a former officer'. On 13 October he also wrote to Lenin [**Document 14**], proposing that 'in those cases where there are no direct, serious charges against arrested officers' they should be asked to serve in the Red Army; if they agreed, they would have to understand that in the event of betrayal, their families would be arrested. On 16 October he complained about the activities of the Nizhnyi Novgorod *cheka*, which was persecuting army officers in the town who were going about their legitimate business of touring barracks and bases. The *cheka*'s duty, he reminded them, was not to interfere with the work of military officers, but to keep tabs on the families of those suspected of being unreliable and arresting those families should the need arise. Early in November he took up the case of an officer arrested by the Tsaritsyn *cheka* while Stalin was in charge.[20]

Those opposed to Trotsky began to argue that he was not only soft on officers, but persecuted Bolshevik commissars. His decision to execute Panteleev while in Sviyazhsk in August suddenly assumed greater significance. Documents which his critics had studied revealed that no individual charges had been brought against Panteleev. Trotsky was forced to explain to Lenin that Panteleev had not been executed because his regiment had deserted, but because he too had deserted and tried to seize a steamer and escape to Nizhny; there were no individual charges because there was nothing individual about his conduct – he was just another deserter. It was not only those close to Voroshilov and Stalin who made such charges. Zinoviev had concerns, too, and a commissar close to him protested at the end of October when Trotsky put the blame for the way the Red Army had faltered and then retreated on the Eastern Front on poor work by the commissars; not surprisingly, in turn, the commissars blamed disloyal officers.[21] By late December 1918 the Panteleev case was being aired publicly on the pages of *Pravda*, and Trotsky wrote to the Central Committee in protest [**Document 15**]. Despite the various rumours that were circulating, he insisted that Panteleev was the only commissar to have been shot, that he was justly executed, and that the Central Committee needed to give a clear endorsement of the policies of the Commissariat of War.

Under the insistent criticism of the Military Opposition, Lenin began to doubt whether Trotsky was right. He finally decided to back him only towards the end of February 1919. Trotsky returned to Moscow for the opening of the Eighth Party Congress and during a government meeting Lenin passed him a note which suggested firing all the military specialists and appointing a Bolshevik as Commander-in-Chief. Trotsky passed back a note of his own which read, 'infantile nonsense'. When Lenin later asked Trotsky why he had been so dismissive, Trotsky asked Lenin how many former officers were serving in the Red Army. Lenin confessed he had no idea, and he was astonished when Trotsky explained that 76 per cent of their officers had served in the Tsar's army and only 12.8 per cent were 'fledgling red commanders'. From that point on, Lenin backed Trotsky on the issue of military specialists.[22] However, he offered no support to Trotsky when it came to the commissars. In an order issued on 2 March Trotsky noted that the internal service regulations of the Red Army made no mention of the rights and duties of commissars. He explained that this was completely logical since it was clear that 'the institution of commissar is not a permanent institution'; sooner or later, he believed, 'one-man management in the sphere of administration and command' would be established.[23] Although the Eighth Party Congress defeated the Military Opposition to the extent that it put an end to the baiting of military specialists, it reinforced the position of the military commissars rather than bringing their role to an end. Moves by both Stalin and Zinoviev ensured that Trotsky should be instructed to pay more attention to communist opinion in the army.

Trotsky responded with one of the long, slightly supercilious memorandums for which he became infamous [**Document 16**]. The ambition of the Party to have more control over Field Headquarters and the Republican RVS had resulted in vaguely drafted guidelines which misunderstood the correct relationship between the Party and the Red Army. In fact, many of the proposed changes simply codified existing practice. Trotsky's real concern was that Zinoviev's attitude was not so different from that of Stalin. He had misunderstood the nature of the Military Opposition and his 'solution' of close Party oversight of the army was 'extremely dangerous'. Trotsky's clash with Zinoviev would be as fateful for the Russian Revolution as was his clash with Stalin.

# PEASANTS DURING WARTIME

Towards the end of November 1918, Lenin began to have doubts about his peasant policy. If in the first week of that month he had been talking about advancing towards large-scale socialised farming with the support of the poor peasants, by the end he was identifying middle peasants as the Party's main allies and even hinting that kulaks could be managed:

> for the middle peasant we say – no force under any circumstances; for the big peasant we say – our aim is to bring him under the control of the grain monopoly and fight him when he violates the monopoly and conceals grain.[24]

By December 1918 he had gone further and taken it on himself to resolve a number of incidents in Yaroslavl, Tver and Vologda where local soviets had gratuitously antagonised the middle peasants. On 4 December 1918 he quietly signed a decree that abolished the Poor Peasants' Committees. When Stalin was sent to investigate why the strategically sensitive town of Perm had fallen with such ease to Admiral Kolchak on 24 December, he focused on the failings of the Poor Peasants' Committees; the key lesson of Stalin's report was that peasants opposed the agrarian policies of the Bolsheviks.

Trotsky had found the same. In late November 1918 he had faced a widespread peasant rebellion in the rear near Voronezh; this was followed in late

December by a rebellion of peasant troops further to the south and west in Valuiki, Urazovo and Kupyansk. Trotsky had not yet taken on board Lenin's views about the middle peasants, though, and condemned the rebellion as the work of 'Left SRs, Anarchists and Counter-revolutionaries'. He brought in loyal troops, surrounded the insurgents and on 27 January issued the following proclamation:

> I have come to the front in order to put an end to your shameful and dishonourable mutiny . . . I have instructed the Soviet authorities to place your families under temporary arrest and to seal all your property in villages and towns. On behalf of the Council of People's Commissars I order that all instigators, traitors, self-seekers are to be crushed, shot, wiped off the face of the earth.

Given this, it was perhaps not surprising that, in the popular view, Lenin gained a reputation for being pro-peasant, whereas Trotsky was branded anti-peasant. On 6 February 1919 Trotsky wrote *A Letter to the Middle Peasants* [**Document 17**] to counter the rumours that Lenin favoured this group, whereas Trotsky was their irreconcilable enemy. He expressed regret for a number of cases where peasants had been mistreated by soldiers with a low level of political consciousness and stressed that 'the middle peasant, provided he has not been duped by kulak lies, ought to be our friend', because the Bolsheviks had fulfilled their promise and given land to the peasantry. However, while Lenin talked of the kulaks as 'the enemy', Trotsky articulated this still in terms of class war: 'only soviet power is conducting and will continue to conduct a war of extermination against the kulaks'. He then denounced most stories about the Red Army's misbehaviour as Left SR slander, and argued that 'the White Guard . . . have repainted themselves as Left SRs'.[25] As the Civil War ebbed and flowed, Trotsky's fear of the kulak danger constantly resurfaced.

Early in March 1919 Kolchak renewed his offensive, and the speed of his advance was linked to the continued hostility of the middle peasants to Bolshevik agrarian policy. As Kolchak advanced, so peasant disturbances broke out on the Volga, in Syzran, Simbirsk and Samara. As a consequence Trotsky rushed to the front in mid-March and took up the cause of the middle peasants with renewed enthusiasm. On 15 March he wrote of justified complaints at the behaviour of the Red Army and reminded soldiers that 'the kulak is our enemy; but the middle peasant, the labouring harvester, should be our friend and brother worker'. The impact of his message was limited; as Trotsky travelled east, his train was delayed when peasant insurgents blew up the track. On 21 March he called on Lenin and Stalin to establish 'an inspection team of the highest authority for work in the rear of the Eastern Front . . . the middle peasants are exasperated by the manifest malpractices of official institutions'.[26] Kolchak, of course, had absolutely no intention of giving land to the peasantry, and once this became clear the peasant insurrections ceased. Only a month after Trotsky had left Moscow, he was able to return for a Central Committee meeting on 18 April and report that the situation had improved dramatically. Vācietis reported on 1 May that 'we are holding the enemy's attack and on certain sectors have begun to go over to the offensive'. The Kolchak danger was over.[27]

A fortnight after the start of offensive operations against Kolchak, Trotsky completed work on a report about a different crisis he faced – the Don Rebellion. He had intended to bring this report to a meeting of the Politburo in Moscow in mid-May, but he turned back to Kharkov on the 16th because the situation there had become grave. Lenin's message about wooing the middle peasantry had not been taken on board by the Don Bureau of the Communist Party. It had one aim: to destroy the power base of the Cossacks who had for so long been a symbol of the Tsar's repressive regime. Although military commanders on the Southern Front saw the value of co-operating with those Cossacks who were sympathetic to the new regime, of which there were quite a number, the Don Bureau did not. Calling at the end of January for 'the wholesale destruction of upper elements of Cossack society', the Don Bureau disarmed the Cossacks, seized their grain surpluses and confiscated their land in preparation for the introduction of collective farms. Those who resisted were subjected to terror; in possibly the worst incident 260 Cossacks were killed in one village.

By 10 March resistance to this policy had become open rebellion and by the end of the month much of the Don region had been 'liberated' from Bolshevik control. Initially these Don rebels fought completely independently of the White generals still confined to the Kuban. However, on 9 May, General A. I. Denikin, who had become leader of the White forces after General Kornilov had died in action, decided to contact the rebels and sent an emissary to them in one of his British-supplied biplanes. Soon they were receiving regular air drops. By 8 June the rebels and Denikin had linked up and the Whites had escaped from their confinement in Kuban and gained access to Ukraine.[28] What made this doubly disastrous for the Bolsheviks was that they had effectively also lost control of Ukraine. German forces had been driven from the region by an *ad hoc* alliance of Bolsheviks, Left SRs and anarchists, but when the Bolsheviks formally established the Ukrainian Soviet Government on 6 March 1919 they not only assumed power alone but ignored Lenin's calls to appease the middle peasantry, instead drawing up plans for collective farming.

The peasant response was immediate: revolts broke out on a wide scale, 93 in April with a further 26 in May. Lenin, happy to see a change in land policy, rejected out of hand the view of the commander of the Ukrainian Red Army that the situation had become so severe in Ukraine that the Left SRs needed to be brought into a coalition government. Trotsky was also concerned about the military implications of what the commander of the Ukrainian Red Army was proposing. Conciliating the Left SRs and anarchists meant, in the military sphere, co-operating with their partisan guerrilla forces. In Trotsky's view, these might have been effective in harrying the retreating Germans and their Ukrainian nationalist allies, but they would be no match for Denikin with his Allied supplies. Just as it had been essential to create a centralised professional army in Russia in summer and autumn 1918, so in spring 1919 it was essential to create a centralised Red Army in Ukraine, an army which would recognise its historic duty and concentrate its forces against Denikin. On 1 May Trotsky sent a detailed memorandum to the Central Committee criticising the commander of the Ukrainian Red Army.[29]

However, the commander ignored this and headed a delegation in person to the two main partisan leaders – the Left SR sympathiser Ataman Nikifor Grigoriev and the anarchist Nestor Makhno. The sticking point in their talks was political representation in the Ukrainian Soviet Government, and before any progress could be made, on 7 May, Grigoriev rebelled against the Bolshevik Government. The rebellion was quickly suppressed, but its outbreak reinforced Trotsky's belief that the partisan movement had to be crushed. On 22 May he ordered the formation of a special *cheka* battalion 'to discipline Makhno's anarchist bands'.[30] The strategic problem for Trotsky was that Makhno, based in the town of Gulyai Polye in southern Ukraine, was the first to confront Denikin's forces as they emerged from Kuban. By the end of May, his forces were in steady retreat and as Denikin continued to advance Trotsky railed against Makhno. It was time, he said, on 2 June, 'to finish with this anarcho-kulak debauchery'.[31]

Lenin had long been worried that the existence of a separate Ukrainian Soviet Government, especially one with its own Commissariat of War and its own Red Army, was producing a dangerous division of authority. The behaviour of the commander of the Ukrainian Red Army seemed to prove this. At first sight, it seemed even more worrying that Trotsky, despite his clash with the commander, had not dismissed him, as Lenin had instructed. Lenin wrote angrily to Trotsky on 2 June demanding an explanation. Trotsky replied the next day and stated that the 'reproaches are unfounded': he had started to carry out the decisions of the Central Committee, but before this work could be finalised he had been forced to move to the Don, from where communication with both Moscow and Kiev had been difficult. As soon as a replacement could be found, the commander would indeed be sacked; nothing else was delaying his enactment of the Central Committee's decision.[32]

# FROM COMMAND CRISIS TO VICTORY

In May 1919 a new front suddenly opened up in Russia's Civil War. From newly independent Estonia, formed after the withdrawal of German troops from the Baltic, General Nikolai Yudenich sent a force against Petrograd. This surprise attack very nearly succeeded. Stalin was ordered to Petrograd on 17 May and from the moment of his arrival on the 19th he instigated a number of desperate measures to save the former capital. At once he sensed that counter-revolutionary intrigue was part of the problem, something he had long suspected and had raised with Lenin previously. Stalin sent Lenin a long report on 4 June which detailed his suspicions, and confirmation came nine days later when two forts which protected the approaches to Petrograd rebelled. Their action was supported by British motor launches operating from Finland called in by the British spy Paul Dukes, who had access to all the decisions made by the Northern Front RVS. It was a close shave for the Bolsheviks, but the loss of the forts proved to be the worst of the crisis; two days later they were recaptured and Stalin could return to Moscow. He had claimed in his report of 4 June that 'it is evident that not only the Chief of Staff of 7th Army [based near Petrograd] works for the Whites', but 'also the entire Staff of the Republican RVS'. It was, he insisted, 'now up to the Central Committee to draw the necessary inferences' and among several suggestions he made was that 'Party workers who urge the military specialists on against the commissars' should be assigned to other duties. Thus, by June 1919, not only had a combination of the Don Rebellion and the collapse of Ukraine enabled Denikin to enter southern Russia, but a combination of genuine misunderstandings on Lenin's part and deliberate stirring on Stalin's part had reopened the issue of Trotsky's conduct of the war and the absence of close Party control.[33]

Although Vācietis had first suggested as early as 7 May that it was time to concentrate on the danger posed by Denikin, at the start of June it was still the common currency of all Bolsheviks that Kolchak and the Eastern Front remained more important. There were, however, differences of emphasis even before the crisis on the Southern Front forced a reassessment of this conviction. In a telegram of 1 June Trotsky emphasised that, since it was 'clear we cannot at present advance to Vladivostok', the offensive should continue only until an agreed defensive line was reached. This was not the view of the Eastern Front commander, S. S. Kamenev, who on 6 June submitted plans for an immediate advance on Krasnoufimsk en route for Ekaterinburg. Vācietis shared Trotsky's assessment and considered an advance on Krasnoufimsk quite unrealistic, given the pressure on the Southern and Petrograd fronts. On 12 June he ordered Kamenev to establish a defensive line on the Kama and Belaya rivers. Kamenev, however, was supported by his military commissar, who believed that, since plans for an insurrection in Kolchak's rear were already well advanced, the admiral's forces could be annihilated within a few weeks. So he decided to take up Kamenev's case when the Central Committee held a plenary session, in Trotsky's absence, on 15 June. This lobbying worked and Vācietis was instructed 'to continue the offensive against Kolchak'. Vācietis appeared to accept this, but on 22 June he ordered Kamenev to shift the direction of his advance from due east to south-east, towards Zlatoust, away from Ekaterinburg, and towards the railway network leading back to the Volga and the south. The fall of Kharkov on 25 June and both Ekaterinoslav and Tsaritsyn on the 30th seemed to justify Vācietis' caution, but, to Trotsky's fury, on 3 July Vācietis was dismissed by the Central Committee for failing to support its policy in the east; he was replaced by Kamenev.

The removal of Vācietis was not the only decision taken by the Central Committee at this fateful meeting. An issue left unresolved after the Eighth Party Congress was the location of the Field Headquarters of the Republican RVS; this was now moved from its base at Serpukhov, 60 miles south of Moscow, to Moscow itself. At the same time the composition of the RVS itself was changed: its overall size was reduced, some of Trotsky's allies were removed, and supporters of the campaign for an eastern offensive were added. Opposed to all these moves, and supported by none of his Politburo colleagues, Trotsky resigned, left the Central Committee meeting, slammed the door and took to his bed complaining of ill health. However, the Central Committee did not accept his resignation when it met again on 5 July, and in a series of conciliatory gestures made clear that it would continue to supply the Southern Front, where Trotsky was urged to concentrate his efforts. Back there on 8 July, Trotsky learned that Stalin's vendetta against Vācietis had succeeded and that the former Commander-in-Chief had been arrested on charges of counter-revolutionary activity. The only 'evidence' against him was that he had shared lodgings with a General Staff officer who had allegedly been linked to a conspiracy of other General Staff officers within Field Headquarters.[34]

Trotsky immediately went on the offensive to prevent a new assault on the military specialists. When a Kharkov paper put the collapse of the Southern Front down to the treachery of officers who had gone over in droves to Denikin, Trotsky set the record straight [**Document 18**]:

We must and will keep a sharp look-out for the activity of counter-revolutionary scoundrels who have penetrated our ranks. But at the same time we shall not allow unbalanced windbags and demagogues to hinder serious Party workers in their task of building a properly organised army, especially by employing qualified commanders on a wide scale.

At a series of rallies on 11 and 14 July Trotsky pushed through resolutions stressing that the policy towards military specialists should not and would not change.[35]

The tension between Trotsky and the rest of the Bolshevik Party leadership increased as Kamenev turned his attention to the Southern Front. Kamenev wanted a two-pronged assault, one on the right flank to the east of Kharkov, and the other – larger – attack on the left flank down the lower Volga and then, to Denikin's rear, into Kuban. Trotsky, supported by the discredited Vācietis, argued that Denikin had to be tackled head on in the Donets Basin, where there were large industrial towns that could be expected to rally to the Bolshevik side. Nevertheless, the Central Committee backed Kamenev on 23 July and called for the offensive to begin three weeks later.

From Lenin's perspective, Trotsky's subsequent behaviour was unhelpful. The more he called for extra supplies in the south, the more he seemed to imply criticism of Kamenev. When the Kamenev offensive opened on 14 August the right flank to the east of Kharkov soon faltered. Although Kupyansk was briefly captured, the Red Army had been driven back to its starting point by early September. The outflanking assault down the Volga was more successful, and by 5 September the Red Army was approaching Tsaritsyn; but it was unable to consolidate its position. This was largely because of stiff opposition from Denikin's British tanks and aircraft, and partly because the Bolsheviks had to divert troops to combat a daring White cavalry raid behind Red lines which briefly resulted in the loss of Tambov.

By mid-September the Red offensive had petered out and Denikin had resumed his advance, even though the Red Army was beginning to outnumber Denikin's forces. On 6 September the Politburo expressed its astonishment at Trotsky's 'attempts to revise the basic strategy plan decided upon' (he had written to Kamenev urging him to reconsider his priorities). Trotsky refused to be put down, though, replying the same day to the whole Central Committee that the plan was disintegrating; the centre of gravity of the fighting had moved towards a line between Kursk and Voronezh, where there were no reserves and the poor state of the roads meant that, while some cavalry groups could be brought back from the Tsaritsyn line of attack, the vast majority were trapped on the left flank, unable to help. The Politburo's response was to question the loyalty of the commander of the left flank attack and accuse Trotsky on 18 September of failing to subject him to sufficient political surveillance as instructed.[36]

Yet, towards the end of September, the situation on the ground forced the Politburo to adopt a stance closer to that of Trotsky. The Central Committee plenum of 21–26 September accepted that the two flanks of the earlier attack were now entirely separate, necessitating the creation of both a Southern Front and a South-Eastern Front. Because Denikin's advance in what was now the Southern Front was so alarming, this had to become the major front, something agreed by the Republican RVS on 27 September and implemented by Kamenev on the 30th. Trotsky could therefore 'consign to the archives' the long memorandum he had planned to submit to the Politburo which once again went over the rationale behind his plan for the Donets Basin. The fall of Orel on 13 October finally convinced the Politburo to throw itself fully behind Trotsky once more. On 15 October he attended a Politburo meeting in person and insisted that, unless troops were moved from the South-East Front to the Southern Front, he would be forced to evacuate Tula; the Politburo agreed. Ten days later, while relations between Trotsky and Kamenev remained tense, Lenin was successfully mediating between them.[37]

In mid-October Petrograd again came under attack from Yudenich. Lenin suggested surrendering the city, given the desperate fighting at Orel, but Trotsky opposed him and on this, for the first time in many weeks, he had the full backing of the Politburo. He set off for Petrograd on 16 October and found when he arrived a scene of demoralisation and panic, for which he was quick to blame Zinoviev. Trotsky assessed the situation quickly and accurately in an order issued on 18 October. The Red Army outnumbered Yudenich's forces, but the enemy's British tanks made them highly mobile; the answer was to keep calm, avoid encirclement, then, at the right moment, advance and overwhelm the enemy. Trotsky gained first-hand experience of the danger the city faced as soon as he issued this order. A rifle regiment based near his headquarters began to retreat in panic when a rumour spread that it was being outflanked. Trotsky mounted the first horse he could find and helped turn the lines back.[38] Although Yudenich's men continued to advance, and reached as far as Pulkovo Hill – the site of the city's airport today – the mood in the Red Army command had changed. On the 21st the line was held at Pulkovo and then the Red Army went on the offensive. On the 23rd nearby Tsarskoe Selo and Pavlovsk were retaken after bitter fighting and the danger was over.

By then, the situation had also been transformed at Orel. On 20 October the town was recaptured by the Red Army and four days later Voronezh fell to the Red cavalry. After a further three weeks of fierce fighting, the Red cavalry led the assault on the strategic railway junction at Kastornoe, capturing it on 15 November and opening up the line to Kharkov, thus threatening Denikin's advance troops with encirclement. Denikin's retreat suddenly degenerated into a rout as he struggled to hold a defensive line on the River Don. The Civil War was over.

Ironically, Trotsky played little part in this triumph. On 14 November the Politburo resolved that he should resume diplomatic duties, leaving Stalin to finish off Denikin. Trotsky was sent to Dvinsk (today Daugavpils in Latvia), where it was hoped secret talks could begin with the Poles about agreeing a common border. He arrived on 28 November, only to be told that the Poles had changed their minds.[39]

The past few months had been a bruising time for Trotsky. He had been proved right, but in the process he had clashed bitterly with the Party conclaves in Moscow, especially with Stalin and Zinoviev over their obsessive desire for Bolshevik organisational control of the army. Trotsky had evolved his own, rather different way of operating. As he recalled in his memoirs:

> After making the round of a division and ascertaining its needs on the spot, I would hold a conference in the staff-car or dining car, inviting as many representatives as possible, including those from the lower commanding forces and from the ranks, as well as from the local party organisations, the soviet administration and the trade unions. In this way I got a picture of the situation that was neither false nor highly coloured. These conferences always had immediate practical results.

Observers noted that 'he spent at least six hours every day presiding over conferences of commissars, railway officials, factory men and even doctors'. This was not democracy, but nor was it the closet politics of administration.[40]

## FURTHER READING

Not much has been written about Trotsky's role during the Civil War, apart from the current author's 'Trotsky and the Russian Civil War', in I. D. Thatcher's *Reinterpreting Revolutionary Russia*. Trotsky recalls some incidents in *My Life*, and the revolutionary journalist Larissa Reissner gives a pen portrait of life in Sviyazhsk in 'Sviyazhsk', in J. Hansen *et al.* (eds), *Leon Trotsky: The Man and his Work*. Another pen portrait describes Trotsky's working methods during the Civil War: see F. McCullagh's 'Trotsky in Ekaterinburg'. Otherwise, it is a question of interpreting two substantial document collections: Trotsky's *How the Revolution Armed* and J. M. Meijer (ed.), *The Trotsky Papers*.

## NOTES

1 The events from the Brest-Litovsk Treaty to the formation of Komuch are explored in depth in Swain, *Origins*.

2 Trotsky, *My Life*, pp. 414, 419. For more on Muraviev and the appointment of Vācietis, see G. R. Swain, 'Russia's Garibaldi: The Revolutionary Life of Mikhail Artemovich Muraviev', *Revolutionary Russia* no. 2, 1998; and G. R. Swain, 'Vācietis: The Enigma of the Red Army's First Commander', *Revolutionary Russia* no. 1, 2003.

3 Trotsky, *My Life*, pp. 396–400. The drama of Sviyazhsk at this time is captured in L. Reissner, 'Sviyazhsk', in J. Hansen *et al.* (eds), *Leon Trotsky: The Man and his Work* (New York: Merit, 1969).

4 Trotsky, *My Life*, p. 401.

5 Reissner, 'Sviyazhsk', pp. 114–15.

6 Trotsky, *My Life*, p. 402; *Trotsky Papers*, vol. I, p. 81.

7 *Trotsky Papers*, vol. I, pp. 69–71.

8 *The Military Papers of Leon Trotsky, 1918–24* (microfilms from the Russian State Military Archive filmed by Research Publications, an imprint of Primary Source Media, hereafter RGVA), fond 33987, opis' 2, ed. Khr 18, p. 53.

9 Trotsky, *My Life*, p. 402; Trotsky also discusses the incident in his *Stalin: An Appraisal of the Man and his Influence* (London: Panther, 1969), vol. II, p. 89.

10 *Trotsky Papers*, vol. I, p. 333.

11 *Trotsky Papers*, vol. I, p. 107.

12 Trotsky, *My Life*, pp. 405–08.

13 Reissner, 'Sviyazhsk', p. 117; Trotsky, *Stalin*, vol. II, p. 103; *Trotsky's Diary in Exile* (London: Faber, 1959), p. 83.

14 Trotsky, *Stalin*, vol. II, p. 119; Trotsky, *My Life*, pp. 415–17.

15 *Bolshevitskoe rukovosdstvo: perepiska, 1912–27* (Moscow: ROSSPEN, 1996), p. 42; Stalin's activities in Tsaritsyn are dealt with by R. Argenbright, 'Red Tsaritsyn: Precursor of Stalinist Terror', *Revolutionary Russia* no. 2, 1991.

16 RGVA, 1.1.142, p. 92.

17 *Trotsky Papers*, vol. I, pp. 135–37; the cancellation of Stalin's order is in Trotsky, *Stalin*, vol. II, p. 75 and RGVA, 33987.2.40, p. 30.

18 R. Service, *Stalin* (Basingstoke: Macmillan, 2004), p. 168.

19 *Rukovosdstvo*, p. 54.

20 RGVA, 1.1.42, pp. 87, 90; 33987.2.40, pp. 117, 147, 179, 182, 281, 283, 290, 291.

21 *Trotsky Papers*, vol. I, p. 155; RGVA, 33987.2.40, p. 190.

22 Trotsky, *My Life*, p. 447; Trotsky, *Stalin*, vol. II, pp. 60–61.

23 L. Trotsky, *How the Revolution Armed* (London: New Park Publications, 1979–81), vol. II, pp. 125–26.

24 G. R. Swain, *Russia's Civil War* (Stroud: Tempus, 2000), p. 57.

25 Trotsky, *How*, vol. III, pp. 314–17.

26 RGVA, 4.3.202, p. 14; *Trotsky Papers*, vol. I, pp. 307, 309, 311.

27 *Trotsky Papers*, vol. I, pp. 323, 361, 367; Trotsky, *How*, vol. II, p. 522.

28 V. P. Butt *et al.* (eds), *The Russian Civil War: Documents from the Soviet Archives* (Basingstoke: Macmillan, 1996), p. 81; the above summary is from Swain, *Russia's Civil War*.

29 *Trotsky Papers*, vol. I, p. 391.

30 *Trotsky Papers*, vol. I, pp. 431, 459–61.

31 Trotsky, *How*, vol. II, pp. 278–81, 294.

32 *Trotsky Papers*, vol. I, pp. 515–17.

33 Trotsky, *Stalin*, vol. II, p. 101; Trotsky, *My Life*, p. 423; for the Petrograd campaign, see Swain, *Russia's Civil War*.

34 *Trotsky Papers*, vol. I, p. 595; Trotsky, *My Life*, p. 398; for the dismissal of Vācietis, see Swain, 'Vācietis'.

35 Trotsky, *How*, vol. II, pp. 135, 337; *Trotsky Papers*, vol. I, p. 597.

36 *Trotsky Papers*, vol. I, pp. 667, 671.

37 *Trotsky Papers*, vol. I, pp. 682 (editorial note), 687; Trotsky, *How*, vol. II, pp. 430–32; the memo, which Trotsky consigned to the archives and then had published in *How*, is also reproduced in R. Pipes, *The Unknown Lenin* (New Haven: Yale University Press, 1998), p. 70.

38 Trotsky, *My Life*, p. 429.

39 *Trotsky Papers*, vol. I, pp. 759, 765; for the rout of Denikin, see Swain, *Russia's Civil War*.

40 Trotsky, *My Life*, p. 416; F. McCullough, 'Trotsky in Ekaterinburg', *Fortnightly Review* vol. 108, 1920, p. 541.

# 5

# Building a workers' economy

## LABOUR ARMIES

Although Trotsky would remain Commissar of War until 1925, his main concern from the end of 1919 onwards was the economy. Even during the Civil War Trotsky argued that the key to post-war recovery would be universal labour service. This was his theme at the Seventh Congress of Soviets in early December 1919, and the Central Committee meeting on the 16th of that month adopted his proposals.[1] When these were published in *Pravda* there were widespread protests from the trade unions, which, not surprisingly, had hoped that peace might bring an end to the restrictions on their activity. On 12 January 1920 both Lenin and Trotsky appeared before the trade union leaders, but they were unable to win them around. However, support for the idea came from the commander of the Third Army operating in Siberia. On 10 January 1920 he proposed adopting a new name; since Kolchak had been defeated, his army would transform itself into the First Labour Army. Economic recovery was clearly the order of the day, so the Siberian Red Army would become a Labour Army and restore the economy. Trotsky became the most enthusiastic advocate of the Labour Army idea.[2]

Keen to see a Labour Army in practice, he returned to his train and on 8 February set off for Ekaterinburg, the base of the First Labour Army, for a month-long visit. His journey showed how much still needed to be done. The train got stuck in a snow drift and had to be dug out. This prompted a flurry of invective against sabotage by railway workers and the 'kulak executive committees' of soviets which 'loafed around' rather than keeping the tracks clear; the whole of the local soviet concerned was duly placed under arrest. On arrival, he informed Lenin straight away that the militarisation of the railways should continue into the post-war era, since the centre had no control over railways in the provinces. He added that the coal mines of the Urals also had to be put under martial law [**Document 19**]: 'On this question the opposition of local "trade unionists", indeed those of the centre too, must be overcome'. It was also essential to clarify the powers of the Labour Army when these came into conflict with those of the Commissariat of Supply; Trotsky urged Lenin to confirm that only the Labour Army had the power to reroute supplies.[3]

Trotsky's robust attitude towards labour meant that exemplary treatment was handed out 'to all scoundrels and traitors who take advantage of calamities and intensify these calamities through counter-revolutionary strikes and demonstrations'. Desertion from the Labour Army would be treated in exactly the same way as desertion from the Red Army.[4] Trotsky never saw discipline alone as the solution, however. Just as he had favoured the use of military specialists from the Tsar's army to win the Civil War, he favoured the recruitment of industrial specialists to bring about socialist reconstruction. As he told the Ekaterinburg Party organisations on 25 February 1919, 'extensive recruitment of specialists (engineers and technicians) is needed for the reorganisation of disordered industry; it must be explained to less conscious workers that, whereas in the past the specialists may have served capital, today they will serve the working class'. For Trotsky it was less conscious workers who opposed his economic plans, just as it had been less conscious commissars who supported the Military Opposition.[5]

Trotsky returned to Moscow to attend the Ninth Party Congress, which took place from 29 March–4 April 1920, and was quickly followed by the Third Congress of Trade Unions on 9 April. He was determined to push ahead with labour conscription, arguing in *Pravda* on 23 March that 'since the Soviet state organises work in the interests of the workers themselves, compulsion is in no way opposed to the personal interests of the workers'; in his keynote speech to the Party Congress on the economy he made very clear that the new communist society would remain highly regimented for many years to come. The organisation of labour, he believed, was the essence of organising a new society. 'We are making the first attempt in world history to organise the labour of working people in the interests of the working majority; but that, of course, does not mean the destruction of the element of compulsion.' Compulsion, he added, 'is playing and will continue to play a great role for a considerable historical period'. Trade unions had played a valuable role in a free market economy but now 'the work force should be distributed according to an economic plan for the current state of our development; the working masses cannot be wandering around the Russian land, but must be collected together, ordered and commanded just like soldiers'.

This required a change in the role of the trade unions. In his view trade unions would not be abolished as labour was militarised but would themselves become the agents of militarisation. The militarisation of society was 'unthinkable without the militarisation of the trade unions'. Trotsky was equally firm about the use of specialists. Echoing his experience of the Civil War, he called on the congress to recognise that a single authority was needed to head industry, and if that meant 'bourgeois specialists' then so be it. In his address to the Third Congress of Trade Unions on 9 April [Document 20] he repeated these arguments and explained how the War Commissariat was in a unique position to turn the constitution's vague reference to 'labour service' into a practical proposition through the 'militarisation of labour':

> We . . . counterpoise to capitalist slavery socially regulated labour on the basis of an economic plan, obligatory for the whole people and, therefore, compulsory for every worker in the country. Without this we cannot even think of the transition to socialism . . . Without labour service, without the power to give orders and demand that they be carried out, the trade unions will be transformed into a mere form without content, for the socialist state which is being built needs trade unions not for a struggle for better conditions of labour . . . but in order to organise the working class for production.

Trotsky saw few limitations to Russia's socialist development if his policies were followed, even if Germany did not have the revolution that he, and all Bolsheviks, still hoped was coming. He told the Party Congress:

> It is quite possible that we can go over to a more or less developed socialist economy in the course of the next three, four or five years . . . in the course of three or four years we can make gigantic steps forward and the remnants of class struggle here will be broken up and eliminated once and for all.[6]

Trotsky was not denying the possibility of building a workers' state in the medium term, even without a European revolution; but he was insisting that, for this to happen, very particular policies needed to be implemented.

# WAR WITH POLAND

When Poland attacked Soviet Russia on 25 April 1920, Trotsky immediately returned to military concerns and his tactics were identical to those employed during the Civil War. He left Moscow on 7 May and by the 9th was in Bryansk, from where he reissued the blood-curdling decree on desertion first issued during the Civil War. However, by the time he got to Gomel on the 10th he had decided to introduce a radical change in the command structure. Because 'we have operating against us for the first time a regular army led by good technicians', he needed to have many more skilled officers operating at even the most junior level. So in future those with the rank of army commander would be put in charge of divisions as divisional commanders, with similar changes cascading down the hierarchy of command; all affected officers would retain their original rank and salary. By mid-June the situation on the Western Front had stabilised and the Red Army had recaptured Kiev, which had been lost in the first weeks of fighting.[7] However, an early victory was prevented by the resumption of Russia's Civil War. After his forces had been beaten back to the Black Sea, Denikin had fled to the Crimea, which remained an isolated pocket of territory beyond Bolshevik control. There Denikin had been replaced as White commander by General Peter Wrangel, who prepared to take advantage of the Polish War by breaking out of Crimea and advancing towards Moscow. He began this advance on 6 June.

The Polish War prompted more tension between Trotsky and Lenin. In July the British Foreign Minister, Lord George Curzon, proposed a negotiated end to the war, which would establish a border for Poland that was roughly in accordance with the ethnic dividing line between Poles, on the one hand, and Ukrainians and Belorussians, on the other. When this 'Curzon Line' was put to the Politburo on 13 July, Trotsky called for its acceptance while Lenin called for a continued advance towards Warsaw. Trotsky argued that, if the Red Army were not to appear in Poland as conquerors, the Bolsheviks had to exhaust all peace efforts before entering the country; otherwise they would simply play into Poland's hands. Lenin, rather than Trotsky, was trying to export revolution, but as Trotsky told the Moscow Soviet on 12 August, Wrangel was now the main danger, and the Party should abandon the chimera of spreading revolution to Poland. When asked to tour the Warsaw Front as the Battle of the Vistula raged on 14–17 August, Trotsky refused; it was Lenin who insisted that Warsaw be taken and that the Red Army plan an advance on Danzig. Reality dawned on 19 August when the Politburo endorsed a paper citing Wrangel as the priority and instructing Trotsky to make suitable preparations on that basis. On 23 August, having refused to travel to Warsaw, Trotsky boarded his train and headed south.[8]

He recalled on his return from the Wrangel Front that he found Moscow favouring a second Polish war. 'I declared that a repetition of the error already committed would cost us ten times as much, and that I would not submit to the decision that was being proposed, but would carry an appeal to the Party.' Lenin still defended the continuation of the war, but without his former conviction. Trotsky then toured the Polish Front in September: 'the two or three days that I spent at the front were enough to confirm the conclusion I had brought with me from Moscow'. On his return the Politburo almost unanimously resolved in favour of an immediate peace. When the armistice was signed on 12 October, its terms were such that the majority of the Politburo at first suggested a resumption of hostilities. They were brought to their senses only by Trotsky's threat of resignation. At the end of the month he set off for his final tour of the front to oversee Wrangel's defeat, which was secured at a battle on the frozen Sivash salt marshes on the third anniversary of the October Revolution.[9]

## THE TRADE UNION CONTROVERSY

Before the outbreak of the Polish War, Trotsky had been able to rely on Lenin's support when it came to economic matters; after the war, this was no longer the case. The key to success for Trotsky remained what he called 'the organisation of labour', and on 3 September he established a new trade union for all transport workers, Tsektran, which was under central Party control and chaired by Trotsky himself.[10] Lenin was not happy with this decision and turned to Zinoviev, who was asked 'to re-establish proletarian democracy in the trade unions'. Zinoviev told the Ninth Party Conference on 22–25 September that Tsektran was a temporary body which would disappear as soon as normal trade union life resumed; in the interim 'petty interference' in trade union affairs would be kept to a minimum. By the time of the Fifth Trade Union Conference (2–9 November), the Trotsky–Zinoviev clash was in the open. Trotsky made clear in his speech that labour conscription would continue and that in future other trade union leaders would be appointed rather than elected, as was the case with Tsektran. When, on 8 November, the Central Committee discussed the future of the trade unions, Lenin showed his hand. Trotsky proposed that in a future socialist society trade unions would cease to play the role they had traditionally played under capitalism and would become administrative organs of the state. This meant, he stressed, that the administrative controls over trade union activity seen in Tsektran should be extended to other trade unions. The Bolshevik trade union leader protested that the existing powers of Tsektran were bad enough, and to extend such powers was out of the question. Lenin then submitted his own paper, distancing himself from Trotsky and suggesting that the trade unions should survive as independent, non-state organisations, but with a remit that was educational rather than managerial. In a clear warning to Trotsky, he stated that the era of the Labour Army was over.

The Central Committee backed Lenin, but since it had done so by just one vote it resolved to establish a commission chaired by Zinoviev to work towards consensus and report back on 8 December. Until then, only Zinoviev should speak for the Party on trade union matters, so it was he who told the Fifth Trade Union Conference on 9 November that militarisation could lead to 'petty officialdom and interference in trade union work'.

Trotsky felt that he was being gagged as a result of the powers given to Zinoviev by the Central Committee, and, although he was appointed to Zinoviev's Commission on the Trade Unions, he did not remain on it for long. He resigned in early December because the commission refused to give him the same access to the press that it gave Zinoviev. In Trotsky's view 'a reasonable' accommodation on the trade union question was impossible. When Zinoviev presented his report to the Central Committee on 8 December he called for the abolition of Tsektran. Trotsky fought a rearguard action but the best he could achieve was a compromise whereby Tsektran would continue operating until February 1921.[11]

Lenin's solution to this crisis was to continue to press for consensus and compromise. He asked Zinoviev's commission to resume its work. However, Trotsky continued his boycott and when it finally adopted trade union proposals known as the 'Platform of the Ten', he would not sign them. Trotsky did not want this issue resolved in the privacy of an internal Party commission but through broad Party debate. It was due to his persistence that the Central Committee agreed on 24 December that 'a wide pre-congress discussion' should be held within the Party as preparations began for the Tenth Party Congress in March 1921. Trotsky launched his campaign with a speech to the Eighth Congress of Soviets on 30 December. Here he called for the sort of fusion between trade union activists and factory administrators that he had previously suggested for commissars and commanders in the army. Just as he had thought the military leaders were increasingly doing the same job and would not remain separate entities for ever, he now believed 'it is essential to step firmly forward to the point that the separation into trade unionists and industrialists decreases . . . these two categories of work, these two streams need to get closer and become one; these two apparatuses should merge'. As always, he was keen to stress that the trade union question, the organisation of labour, was just one element, albeit a key element, in the question of how the economy would operate in a socialist society.[12]

Zinoviev countered with organisational measures. On 3 January 1921 his Petrograd Party organisation called for elections to the Tenth Party Congress to take place on the basis of platforms and proposed as its platform Lenin's Platform of the Ten, which was published in *Petrograd Pravda* on 6 January. Trotsky objected and on 11 January persuaded the Moscow Party organisation to pass a resolution supporting his stance. On 12 January the Central Committee endorsed the idea of elections by platform and *Pravda* published both Lenin's Platform of the Ten and Trotsky's resolution.[13]

Trotsky returned to Ekaterinburg in February 1921 and it was while he was there that the disturbances which were to culminate in the Kronstadt Mutiny began. For Trotsky the whole Kronstadt affair was a side-issue in his clash with Zinoviev. The latter was in charge of Petrograd, and on 15 February, in a controversial vote, the Party organisations within the Baltic Fleet decided to put themselves under the authority of Zinoviev's Petrograd Committee, rather than Trotsky's Red Army Party structure. When the Kronstadt Mutiny began in the first days of March, Trotsky saw it as Zinoviev's problem, since he had won the confidence of the sailors in the February vote. However, when it was clear negotiation was impossible, Trotsky, as Commissar of War, was called on to issue a warning to 'the garrison and population of Kronstadt and the rebellious forts', which he did at 2 p.m. on 5 March. All the rebels were ordered to hand over their arms immediately and release the Bolshevik representatives they had captured; 'only those who surrender unconditionally can count on the clemency of Soviet power'. The statement concluded that measures to retake the base were being prepared and there would be no further warnings. The military assault began on 7 March and was over ten days later, but Trotsky took no part in it.

The Tenth Party Congress met as scheduled, which meant it took place during this assault, from 8–16 March. It brought the trade union debate to an end on 14 March. Zinoviev introduced the discussion and was greeted by applause; Trotsky seemed petulant, since he took every opportunity to accuse Zinoviev of abusing Party rules to achieve his victory, and even condemned Lenin for giving the impression of standing above the fray while actually backing Zinoviev. Lenin was furious with Trotsky's behaviour and was convinced he had tried to wreck the work of the Zinoviev Commission by boycotting it. He confided to some of his closest supporters during the congress: 'I have been accused: "You are a son of a bitch for letting the discussion get out of hand." Well, try to stop Trotsky! How many divisions does one have to send against him?' He went on to stress that he would come to terms with Trotsky, even though Trotsky, 'a temperamental man', wanted to resign. Lenin's political solution to the crisis was to make the Tenth Party Congress pass a resolution on Party unity that would henceforth ban the sort of factional struggle that had played out between December 1920 and March 1921.[14]

# PLANNING PROPOSALS

The Kronstadt Mutiny was only one of many crises facing the Bolshevik Party during the Tenth Party Congress. Since autumn 1920 the peasants of Tambov Province had been in open revolt and the situation was no better in Western Siberia. Lenin decided that a change of policy was essential. On 8 February he presented the Politburo with 'Preliminary Rough Draft Theses Concerning the Peasants'. These proposed that in the place of grain requisitioning, a tax in kind should be set at a level lower than the previous year's procurement target, to be linked to a free trade in grain above that tax threshold.

Lenin then organised a series of high-profile meetings with peasants from Tambov, while the Politburo reflected on the issues concerned. By 24 February an agreed paper had been endorsed by the Central Committee to be presented to the Tenth Party Congress. With the Kronstadt crisis concentrating the minds of delegates, Lenin's 'New Economic Policy' (NEP) was endorsed by the congress on 15 March.

After the congress Trotsky took two months' leave, his first since returning to Russia. The militarisation of the trade unions had always been for him just part of the greater project of organising labour, which was, in turn, just part of the need to introduce a proper economic plan. The introduction of NEP complicated the issue of planning. Agriculture now operated according to a free market, and in a series of moves introduced quickly after the Tenth Party Congress large sectors of light industry geared to satisfying peasant demand were privatised as well. Meanwhile, the state retained control of the banks, heavy industry and foreign trade, what the Bolsheviks called the 'commanding heights'. However, Trotsky felt that introducing a market link between privately owned agriculture, with its associated enterprises, and state-controlled heavy industry might complicate the planning process; but it did not make it any less necessary.

On 7 August 1921 Trotsky presented a paper to a Central Committee plenum in which he suggested that many of the economic changes agreed at the Tenth Party Congress were being implemented erratically [**Document 21**]. He encapsulated the problem thus:

> The lack of a real economic centre to watch over economic activity, conduct experiments in that field, record and disseminate results and co-ordinate in practice all sides of economic activity and thus actually work at a co-ordinated economic plan – the absence of a real economic centre of this sort not only inflicts the severest of shocks on the economy, such as fuel and food crises, but also excludes the possibility of the planned and co-ordinated elaboration of new premises for economic policy.

The solution, he suggested, was to reorganise the state planning body, Gosplan. It had been agreed to set up Gosplan in February 1921, and, despite the onset of NEP, this had been done on 1 April, although the tasks of the new body were only vaguely defined. Not even Trotsky was clear how economic planning would work at this stage, but he stressed two things: first, 'an economic plan cannot be worked out theoretically', it had to be worked out through monitoring practice; and, second, the plan had to be 'put together around large-scale nationalised industry as a pivot'. Trotsky was determined to refine his views on planning and present them to the Eleventh Party Congress when it met between 27 March and 2 April 1922.[15]

By then, two concerns had come to the fore. First, Trotsky was keen to establish that, despite the privatisation of agriculture and large sectors of light industry, the economy remained socialist and therefore amenable to planning. For him, resorting to the market was just a way of introducing a more sophisticated mechanism for distribution than that offered by central direction; it did not fundamentally change the socialist nature of the Soviet economy.[16] His second point was that planning was not the same as Party interference in the management of the economy.

The apparatus of the Party had grown enormously by the start of 1922: on 4 February Trotsky informed an astonished Lenin just how much of the state's budget was allocated to running the Communist Party. Then, two weeks before the opening of the Eleventh Party Congress, he sent the Politburo a detailed memorandum insisting that excessive Party interference in economic affairs was wasteful; the economy needed the economic guidance of experts, not Party interference [**Document 22**]. 'If the New Economic Policy requires that the trade unions be trade unions,' he wrote, 'then this same policy requires that the Party be a party.' In his view it was the duty of the Party 'to govern only through the properly functioning state apparatus', not to interfere at every level; the Party should 'send back 99 per cent of the matters submitted to it for decision, on the grounds that they contain nothing of concern to the Party'. Distancing the Party from the management of the economy was not a policy Lenin shared. On his copy of Trotsky's memorandum he wrote, 'to the archives'.[17]

Trotsky repeated his key themes in his speech to the Eleventh Party Congress, stressing in particular the need for specialists if the market were to be used to build socialism. The only way forward was to understand each economic sector in detail and devise a plan, and this had to be the task of specialists.

> It is clear that the Party, even in the role of Party organisations, cannot decide all questions. Every economic question is complicated, yet round and about there are people who think that if this complicated question is put to the provincial Party committee or the **Orgburo** or the Politburo it will suddenly become a simple question.

**Orgburo:** The Organisational Bureau of the Central Committee, or Orgburo, was, after the Politburo, the most important executive body of the Central Committee.

As a result, the provincial Party committee, this 'unspecialised apparatus, always in a hurry' contained the worst elements of bureaucratism – 'that is addressing a problem without ever understanding the essence of that problem'. For Trotsky 'the ruling party does not at all mean the Party directly administering every detail of every affair'. Zinoviev took the lead in challenging Trotsky, arguing that it was quite impossible to say 'the Party will be a party and will only concern itself with agitation and propaganda'. The Bolshevik Party 'must direct economic life'.[18]

After the congress, on 11 April 1922, Lenin tried to win over Trotsky by appointing him one of his three deputies. Trotsky explained at extraordinary length why he could not accept this offer [**Document 23**]. Going paragraph by paragraph through the job specification, Trotsky stressed that the role of deputy was ill-conceived and therefore impossible to fulfil. In Trotsky's summary, the deputy had 'to ensure all is well in every field and in every connection'. However, the Bolshevik Party had already established the Workers' and Peasants' Inspectorate (Rabkrin) to do just that. It was beside the point that Rabkrin was staffed by 'useless has-beens intriguing against their former managers'; the deputy was bound to find himself duplicating its work and clashing with its leaders. A deputy could not be appointed as a Jack of all trades; a deputy needed a specific brief, such as chairing Gosplan. Thus, Trotsky got to the essence of the matter:

> At the beginning of last year it was already plain that there was no organ for co-ordinating and actually controlling economic matters. The present organisation of the State Planning Commission approximates outwardly to what I proposed last year, but only outwardly. In essence the parcelling out of responsibilities remains a fact, and it is absolutely unknown who in practice controls the indents for fuel, transport, raw materials or money . . . these questions are put before the Council of Labour and Defence or the Politburo and are solved by rule of thumb.[19]

Lenin may well have intended to make an immediate effort to persuade Trotsky to change his mind, but on 25 May he suffered a severe stroke from which he would never fully recover. This coincided with an injury Trotsky suffered while on a fishing trip on the Moscow River, which kept him out of action for much of the summer. In mid-July, by which time Lenin was well enough to return to the question of Trotsky's future, he was horrified to learn that Zinoviev, Kamenev and Stalin, rapidly emerging as the dominant triumvirate, had concluded that it was time to remove Trotsky from the leadership in view of his refusal to accept the post of deputy. Lenin responded: 'throwing Trotsky overboard is the height of stupidity. If you do not consider me already hopelessly foolish, how can you think of that?' Consequently, Trotsky was not sacked; but now he operated from the sidelines.

On 23 August he again sent a memorandum to the Politburo [**Document 24**]: 'It may be that the moment for serious discussion and settlement of the question of a planning organ is not yet', but with the change over to NEP state funds had become a vital lever in the economic plan; their allocation should be pre-determined by the economic plan, yet Gosplan had no responsibility for these fundamental questions. 'How can it have happened that when discussing the question of the allocation of funds and the volume of

money in circulation, no one in the Politburo called Gosplan to mind?'
Lenin's response was to try once again to persuade Trotsky to become a
deputy. On 11 September he asked Stalin to organise a telephone vote of
Politburo members. Trotsky replied, 'categorically refuse'.[20]

## PLANNING PROGRESS

In November 1922, with Lenin still ill and Trotsky out of the capital, the Central
Committee decided to weaken the state's monopoly over foreign trade.
However, it rapidly backtracked when it learned that both Lenin and Trotsky
were opposed to the proposal, and this brought Trotsky's views – including his
ideas on the future of Gosplan – back to the forefront of Lenin's attention. Lenin
could accept that Gosplan needed to have a role in regulating the export trade,
but Trotsky had used this incident to propose that it needed to have additional
administrative rights, too. On 23 December Lenin let it be known that he
backed Trotsky's idea that Gosplan's resolutions should have legislative power
'up to a certain point and under certain conditions'. A few days later he clarified
that Trotsky 'could be met halfway'. Gosplan would have legislative powers,
although these could be overruled on occasion. Lenin also insisted on selecting
the person to head Gosplan. He wanted a man with an academic background,
not an administrator, but that person also had to be politically reliable: 'the
overwhelming majority of academics, of which Gosplan is naturally made up,
is heavily burdened with bourgeois views and prejudices', he felt. The caution
he had once shown towards military specialists had not left him.[21]

   With Lenin displaying open support for Trotsky, the question of Trotsky's
position inevitably came back on to the agenda. On 6 January 1923 Stalin
again proposed to the Politburo that Trotsky should be appointed a deputy,
but this time with a specific brief to preside over the Council of Labour and
Defence. On 15 January the Politburo received another of Trotsky's lengthy
and closely argued memoranda, highlighting what he saw as the weakness of
Stalin's proposal [**Document 25**]. Trotsky was concerned that short-term financial considerations were hampering long-term planning, yet Stalin's planned
reorganisation would mean that the only commissariat fully represented in
economic discussions would be the Commissariat of Finance, while Gosplan
would not be included. He ended his memorandum with this telling analogy
for Gosplan's role in the economy: 'I would say that Gosplan would discharge
the role of staff headquarters and the Council of Labour and Defence that of
the Military Revolutionary Council.' Although Stalin responded by suggesting
that Trotsky combine the role of deputy with that of heading Gosplan, Trotsky
was convinced that none of these proposals addressed the real issue: 'the
Politburo sought to settle ten or twelve practical economic questions of vast

importance in a single session, without the slightest preparation, after ten minutes' discussion beforehand', he argued, and that was not planning.[22]

Yet, for all this dissension, Trotsky's campaign that the issue of planning should be taken seriously was making progress. On 13 February the Politburo backed Trotsky rather than the Commissariat of Finance on the issue of enterprises having the right to use their turnover capital to provide credit; and on 20 February it was agreed that Trotsky's theses on organising industry would be the basis for discussion at the Central Committee plenum on 22–23 February. In turn, that plenum resolved to accept Trotsky's theses as a basis for debate at the Twelfth Party Congress.[23] It was because Trotsky felt he was making progress on his campaign to introduce a genuine system of economic planning through Gosplan that he behaved so cautiously when Lenin suggested he should confront Stalin over what had become known as the Georgian Affair. One of the main political events of 1922 had been to transform Soviet Russia, Soviet Ukraine and other Soviet republics formed within the former Russian Empire into a newly constituted Soviet Union. In this process Lenin and Stalin had disagreed about the degree of autonomy the constituent republics of the Soviet Union should have.

However, it was not so much Stalin's disagreement on points of principle which infuriated Lenin, for Stalin was always ready to compromise on these, but the brutal way Stalin had forced his opponents into submission, in the case of Georgia by condoning physical assaults on any communists who disagreed with him. Behind the Georgian Affair stood a purely personal matter. Stalin, as Party General Secretary, was responsible for ensuring Lenin followed the health routine imposed by the Politburo. But Lenin was not just a Party symbol, he was a person with human relationships, and his wife Nadezhda Krupskaya understandably felt she had a part to play in Lenin's welfare. This tension caused a number of minor incidents, and finally exploded when Stalin lost his temper with Krupskaya and swore at her. This prompted Lenin to draft a testament to be read out at the Party Congress following his death. The testament was critical of Stalin, the power he had accumulated, and the way he was using that power. It concluded by calling for Stalin to be removed from the post of Party Secretary.

Despite giving Lenin the impression that he would take up cudgels against Stalin, Trotsky told Kamenev, who was deputising for Lenin as the Head of Government, 'I am for preserving the status quo . . . I am against removing Stalin.'[24] And despite a bitter row with Stalin in April, he opposed Kamenev's view that Lenin's critique of Stalin should be published. Instead, he endorsed Stalin's suggestion that only leading provincial delegates to the congress be given a summary of Lenin's views at a special private meeting.[25]

Trotsky used the Twelfth Party Congress (17–25 April 1923) as a platform to give his overview of how economic policy should develop [**Document 26**].

His vision was simple. Under NEP the key task was to increase production and at the same time ensure that the benefits of any increased production flowed to the socialist sector of the economy. The economy was a little richer, but, he asked, had the socialist or the capitalist sector benefited? The picture was not good: trade between the countryside and the towns was still essentially only in consumer goods, yet economic recovery demanded that industrial goods find a market, too. Trotsky's message was Thatcherite. It would not be enough for industrial trusts as a whole to be profitable; within trusts, *every factory* had to be profitable, even if that meant redundancies. Profits accumulated by the state as a result of this rigour would be diverted into state investments, and for this to happen it was essential to plan; organising a proper system of centralised planning was the key task the Twelfth Party Congress had to address. Trotsky then went on to sing the praises of Gosplan and to repeat his view that it should be the Staff HQ of the Council of Labour and Defence. Zinoviev was quick to contradict this Civil War analogy, pointing out, 'it is impossible to say that the time has come when the Party should refuse to lead the economy; the very opposite, the organised and planned interference of the Party, will alone lead to that aim which stands before us'.[26]

## BUREAUCRATIC OBSTRUCTION OF PLANNING

Almost immediately this new disagreement between Trotsky and Zinoviev was diverted into other channels. By summer 1923 the political crisis that had arisen in Germany aroused hopes among the entire Bolshevik leadership that the Soviet Union's isolation as the only socialist state in the world would end. When the German Government declared early in 1923 that it was incapable of paying the reparations owed to the wartime Allies, French troops occupied the Ruhr. The resulting economic chaos caused hyperinflation and widespread labour unrest which culminated in a general strike early in August, forcing the resignation of the government. In this atmosphere the German Communist Party made rapid progress, especially in its campaign to wrest control of the trade union movement by building up communist-dominated factory committees. In July more than half the votes in the Metal Workers' Union had gone to communists, and between July and October the number of Communist Party cells in the trade unions rose from 4,000 to 6,000. By late summer, half of Germany's labour force supported the communists, and on 23 August the Politburo held a special session to discuss the situation there.[27]

Trotsky was worried by what he called 'the temporising policy with regard to the armed insurrection' on the part of the German Communist Party leadership, and wrote in *Pravda* on 23 September about the need for a clear timetable for revolution. In October 1917, although there had been 'a deliberate postponement of ten days', the Bolsheviks had set themselves a clear timetable.[28] In this article Trotsky assumed that in setting a date for insurrection 'the toiling masses were in constant ferment and the Party obviously supported by an unquestionable majority of toilers'; it was precisely because this was not the case in Germany in autumn 1923 that the German Communist Party leadership was so 'temporising'. It recognised that, at best, the communists were supported by half the organised working class, a long way short of 'an unquestionable majority of toilers'.

Nevertheless, when the Politburo again debated Germany at the end of September all doubts were put aside. As in October 1917, it was a question of making an essentially offensive action seem defensive: the Politburo's plan was that the communists would organise mass demonstrations on 7 November, the anniversary of the October Revolution; this would provoke counter-measures by the authorities; then the communists could respond with renewed and 'justified' demonstrations, culminating in a seizure of power on 9 November, the fifth anniversary of the overthrow of the Kaiser. The German Communist Party leadership refused point-blank to accept this timetable.

The German October went off at half-cock. The communists joined the regional governments in Saxony and Thuringia and started to arm a proletarian militia. When Berlin ordered this to stop, the communists refused, then organised a conference of factory councils and proposed that it organise a general strike in defence of the workers' right to bear arms. Thus they tried to present the 'offensive' action of forming the proletarian militia as a 'defensive' one. The factory councils were not fooled, and voted to reject the strike call. With this, the German October fizzled out.

This would not have been so dispiriting for the Politburo had it not coincided with a new domestic crisis in Russia. Provoked largely by lay-offs in the state industrial sector and delays of several months in the payment of wages – policies which followed on logically from Trotsky's insistence that state enterprises must run at a profit – there was a rash of strikes in September and October. Some of these involved dissident communists who branded NEP 'New Exploitation of the Proletariat' and called for the return of soviet democracy. The Politburo responded by deciding on 23 September that it was the duty of all Party members to inform not only the Central Committee and the Central Control Commission (CCC) but the *cheka* about factional activity.[29]

Trotsky had long campaigned against Party 'interference' in economic matters it did not understand. The German October prompted Party 'interference' in military matters, too, which until then had been Trotsky's prerogative. He himself had talked about the danger of war if the revolution in Germany succeeded and the Red Army was forced to mobilise in support of it.

However, since the Civil War had ended the Red Army and the RVS had been left to run themselves, and the latter was still dominated by non-Party military specialists, perhaps not the best people to command when a revolutionary war in Europe was in prospect. So, at the Politburo meeting of 23 September, a radical revision of the composition of the RVS was proposed. Trotsky, who had not been consulted about this, was incandescent with rage. He stormed out of the meeting and argued that what the Party leadership had dressed up as a routine reorganisation was in fact part of a political struggle directed against him.[30]

Faced with a real or imagined assault on his position, he decided to counter-attack. The crux of his discontent had nothing to do with the army but was something quite different. At the Twelfth Party Congress Trotsky had insisted that his resolution on the economy should be adopted in practice, not just used as a piece of propaganda rhetoric. He had warned what would happen if the planned economy and strict reduction of overheads in industry were not addressed, but despite what the congress decided about strengthening Gosplan, in practice it had been relegated in importance, doing useful work but not introducing the planned regulation of the economy.

Looking for the reason why the resolution had not been implemented, Trotsky turned to Stalin and his work in the Party's Secretariat and Organisation Bureau. Conceding that the Twelfth Party Congress had, as Zinoviev insisted it should, resolved to increase Party control over economic management, the Party, under Stalin's guidance, had gone about this in the most inappropriate way, Trotsky argued. Instead of 'a thorough selection of managerial personnel', the Organisation Bureau had developed its own criteria: 'in the last eighteen months a specific secretary's psychology has been formed', secretaries were chosen for their political loyalty, and the net result was 'an unprecedented bureaucratisation of the Party apparatus'. Given the takeover of the Party's official channels by those sharing the 'secretary's psychology', it was scarcely surprising that 'the most acute and pressing problems were being discussed outside the official Party apparatus, thus creating the conditions for illegal factions inside the Party'. And yet, instead of addressing the interests of industry, the September plenum decided to extend the tentacles of that 'secretary's psychology' into the RVS.[31]

Trotsky's views quickly began to circulate more widely than merely within the Central Committee. On 15 October 46 prominent Party leaders, some of them long associates of Trotsky and others the sort of economic leaders instinctively hostile to the hierarchy of secretaries, signed a common platform which echoed Trotsky's demands. Trotsky was accused of trying to incite factionalism.[32] His response was that it was not 'factional' to point out irregularities in the way the Central Committee worked and reminded the Politburo of his main concern – that the poor regulation of the economy was the root cause of the economic crisis, and that Lenin had agreed that Gosplan should have legislative powers. Provocatively, he ended this letter with a pointed aside for the future: 'in October 1917 some important executives deserted their posts'.

Throughout October and November the Party worked to resolve this dispute and on 5 December a sub-committee met at Trotsky's flat and hammered out an agreement. Trotsky accepted Kamenev's and Stalin's repeated assurances that the Politburo would implement a new course. Indeed, it seems clear that Stalin once again proposed that Trotsky should 'take charge of industry', for at this and other meetings the two men were overheard as they 'talked about Gosplan'.[33]

# FURTHER READING

To the documentary collections *How the Revolution Armed* and *The Trotsky Papers* can be added V. Vilkova's *The Struggle for Power in Russia in 1923* and, for readers of Russian, *Arkhiv Trotskogo*. Otherwise, on the trade union debate, it is worth considering W. G. Rosenberg's 'The Social Background to Tsektran' and sections of A. J. Heywood's *Modernising Lenin's Russia*. On Lenin and Trotsky in 1922, see Erik van Ree 'Lenin's Last Struggle Revisited'. B. Bazhanov's *Bazhanov and the Damnation of Stalin* gives useful insights into Stalin's handling of the Politburo at this time. On the situation in Germany, see G. R. Swain, 'Was the Profintern Really Necessary?'

# NOTES

1  L. Trotsky, *Terrorism and Communism* (Ann Arbor: University of Michigan Press, 1961) p. 47; Trotsky, *How*, vol. III, p. 23.
2  Deutscher, *Armed*, pp. 493–96.
3  Trotsky, *How*, vol. III, pp. 75–76.
4  Trotsky, *How*, vol. III, pp. 83, 89.
5  Trotsky, *How*, vol. III, p. 83.
6  For Trotsky's contributions to the debates at the Ninth Party Congress, see *Devyatyi s'ezd RKP: stenograficheskii otchet* (Moscow, 1920), pp. 79–97, 163, 171, 360.
7  *Trotsky Papers*, vol. II, p. 175.
8  *Trotsky Papers*, vol. II, pp. 209, 215, 229, 241, 257; Trotsky, *How*, vol. III, pp. 224, 253.
9  Trotsky, *My Life*, pp. 457–59.
10  Trotsky, *My Life*, p. 465; A. J. Heywood, 'A Tale of Two Policies: Trotsky, Foreign Trade and the Plight of the Soviet Railway System, December 1919–March 1921', unpublished paper, kindly made available to the author.

11 L. Schapiro, *The Origin of the Communist Autocracy* (London: Macmillan, 1977), pp. 273–84.

12 RGVA, 4.14.4, pp. 190, 208. (The drafts of all Trotsky's writings while he was Commissar of War are kept in the Military Archives and are therefore reproduced in the microfilm of this collection. It proved easier to consult these drafts rather than the incomplete edition of Trotsky's *Collected Works* available in Great Britain.)

13 Schapiro, *Origin*, p. 289.

14 *Stenograficheskii otchet X s'ezda RKP* (Petrograd, 1921), p. 147; Deutscher, *Armed*, p. 509; Pipes, *Unknown*, p. 124.

15 *Trotsky Papers*, vol. II, pp. 579–81.

16 *Trotsky Papers*, vol. II, p. 661.

17 Pipes, *Unknown*, pp. 142, 148.

18 *Odinatsatyi s'ezd RKP (b): stenograficheskii otchet* (Moscow, 1961), pp. 132–34, 270–72, 387–89.

19 *Trotsky Papers*, vol. II, pp. 731–33.

20 Pipes, *Unknown*, pp. 166, 171; *Trotsky Papers*, vol. II, pp. 745–47.

21 Deutscher, *Unarmed*, p. 67; *Trotsky Papers*, vol. II, pp. 775, 789–801. For Lenin's relations with Trotsky at this time, see Erik van Ree, 'Lenin's Last Struggle Revisited', *Revolutionary Russia* no. 2, 2001.

22 *Trotsky Papers*, vol. II, pp. 817–33.

23 Trotsky, *My Life*, p. 179; Trotsky, *Stalin*, vol. II, p. 179; *Arkhiv Trotskogo* (Moscow: Terra, 1990), vol. I, pp. 33, 35, 40.

24 Trotsky, *My Life*, pp. 483–86.

25 *Arkhiv Trotskogo*, vol. I, p. 65; R. Service, *Lenin: A Political Life* (Basingstoke: Macmillan, 1995), vol. III, pp. 312–14.

26 *Dvenatsatyi s'ezd RKP (b): stenograficheskii otchet* (Moscow, 1923), pp. 46, 282–313.

27 For the situation in Germany, see G. R. Swain, 'Was the Profintern Really Necessary?', *European History Quarterly* no. 1, 1987, pp. 57–77.

28 For Trotsky and 'temporising', see V. Vilkova, *The Struggle for Power in Russia in 1923* (Amherst: Prometheus Books, 1996), p. 157; Leon Trotsky, *The First Five Years of the Communist International* (London: New Park Publications, 1974), vol. II, pp. 349–50.

29 Vilkova, *Struggle*, pp. 46, 58.

30 For the situation in the Politburo, see B. Bazhanov, *Bazhanov and the Damnation of Stalin* (Ohio: Ohio State University, 1990), p. 50; Vilkova, *Struggle*, pp. 37, 41, 43, 45.

31 Vilkova, *Struggle*, pp. 46–55.

32 Deutscher, *Unarmed*, pp. 14–15; Vilkova, *Struggle*, pp. 27, 75, 80, 102–21, 141.

33 Vilkova, *Struggle*, pp. 139–64, 205–06, 229–30, 322, 334, 350.

Plate 1  Leader Leon Trotsky seated with his Bolshevik Party comrades, 1920s.

Plate 2  Leon Trotsky talking to a young man, 1925.

Plate 3 Marxist revolutionary Natalia Sedova (1882–1962), the second wife of Leon Trotsky, *c.* 1910. (General Photographic Agency/Hulton Archive/Getty Images)

Plate 4 Leon Trotsky arriving for peace negotiations with the Germans, Brest-Litovsk, 27 December 1917.

(The Print Collector/Alamy)

Plate 5  Portrait of Leon Trotsky as Commissar of War, *c.* 1920.

(Popperfoto/Getty Images)

Plate 6  Leon Trotsky arrives at Petrograd (St Petersburg) railway station, 1921.

(Topical Press Agency/Getty Images)

Plate 7 Leon Trotsky addressing soldiers of the Red Army at the time of the Russian Revolution, 1917.

(Photo by Popperfoto/Getty Images)

Plate 8  Leon Trotsky with Natalia Sedova at Sukhumi on the Black Sea, 1924.

(Photo by Topical Press Agency/Hulton Archive/Getty Images)

# 6

# Combating Thermidor

## DEVIATIONIST

O nly three days after Trotsky reached an agreement with Kamenev and Stalin that would have made him head of Gosplan, he reneged on it. In the programmatic essay *The New Course*, written on 8 December 1923 and published after some haggling in *Pravda* three days later [**Document 27**], Trotsky denounced the increasingly bureaucratic leadership of the Party, asserting that the old established leaders were in conflict with a younger generation. In one of those exaggerated parallels he loved, he compared the situation among the Bolshevik leaders with the moment when the once radical allies of Marx and Engels in the German Social Democratic Party slipped almost imperceptibly into new roles as the fathers of reformism. It was a neat image, but Kamenev, Stalin and Zinoviev were hardly going to relish the implication that only Trotsky was the true revolutionary and that they were mere reformists. It remains debatable whether Trotsky's behaviour in autumn 1923 could be described as factionalist, but there is no such doubt about his actions in December. He had signed up to a compromise and then broken with it, challenging the revolutionary credentials of his Politburo comrades in the process.

So, why did Trotsky break the agreement he had so recently accepted? First, he was infuriated by the growing evidence that Stalin and Zinoviev were 'fixing' the outcome of the discussion then under way within the Party about how best to improve the way it operated. It might seem strange that what had begun as an argument about planning had ended up focusing on the Party's bureaucratic methods, but for Trotsky these two issues were intimately linked: the Party's failure to engage with Gosplan reflected its failure to produce economic managers of the right calibre, and that resulted from the Party Secretariat and its obsession with producing secretaries all of a type – loyal but incapable of running the economy. For Trotsky, 'building the Party' meant learning to operate as he had done in the Red Army, by calling conferences of experts and consulting widely. That is why his writings stressed that 'a renewal of Party staff must be carried out in order to replace old bureaucrats with fresh ones'.

There was a second reason for Trotsky's decision to break the truce. By December 1923 he had begun to worry about the danger of a Thermidor reaction, although it would be a while before he adopted this term, which was borrowed from the French Revolution. For Trotsky, three class elements operated in the Soviet Union: the workers, the peasants, and a new bourgeoisie linked to the intelligentsia. Most of the time the proletariat kept the new bourgeoisie firmly in its place, but if private capital expanded more quickly than state capital and came to satisfy the peasant market, it might become strong enough to position itself between the workers' state and the peasantry and gain enormous economic and political influence, possibly sufficient to bring about a counter-revolution. In *Results and Prospects* Trotsky had envisaged the inevitable post-revolutionary clash between workers and peasants as an open struggle. But what if this were a more gradual process? What if the counter-revolution took the form of a gradual restructuring of the state apparatus in a bourgeois direction? Party cells in the countryside were beginning to reflect ideas hostile to the Party, while the bureaucratisation of the apparatus was separating the Party from the masses. Trotsky's solution was to use Gosplan to correct the imbalance between industry and agriculture. But what if the quiet counter-revolution had already penetrated the bureaucracy, changing its nature, opposing Gosplan and opening up a gap between the Party and the workers? Bureaucratism, then, was itself an expression of negative features which could, if left to fester, lead to counter-revolution. If the country faced a quiet counter-revolution through bureaucratism, the crisis could not be solved by the Secretariat resorting to bureaucratic methods.[1]

Trotsky's *New Course* prompted an immediate response. He had broken an agreement and had written an essay appealing over the heads of the Central Committee to the rank and file, seeking to turn them, especially the Party youth, against the Party's central institutions. As such, Trotsky's views

> clearly deviate from the organisational principles on which our Party had been built for many years and undoubtedly includes elements which we are accustomed to see on the pages of newspapers which for a number of years systematically criticised 'Bolshevik centralism', 'Bolshevik committee men' and 'Bolshevik bureaucracy'.

With this none too subtle allusion to Trotsky's long association with the Mensheviks and the Interdistrict Group, the other Bolshevik leaders revealed how they planned to cope with the Trotsky problem: they would remind the Party that Trotsky's Bolshevism was, at best, skin deep.[2] When Trotsky responded, he came close to repeating some of his concerns of 1904 about the danger of substitutionism in the Bolshevik Party. The ban on factions was being used to ban debate:

> if factions are not wanted, there must not be any permanent groupings; if permanent groupings are not wanted, temporary groupings must be avoided; finally, in order that there should be no temporary groupings, there must be no differences of opinion, for where-ever there are two opinions, people inevitably group together.

Yet how, he asked, in a party of half a million members, was it possible to avoid differences of opinion? The resolution of the Tenth Party Congress could help the struggle against factionalism, which was indeed a danger, but 'it is criminal to shut your eyes to the danger represented by conservative bureaucratic factionalism'. Here was a statement his opponents, and most true Bolsheviks, could never accept: that the Party apparatus could itself be a faction – rather than what Zinoviev called 'the right hand of our Party' – was beyond Bolshevik comprehension.[3]

The Central Committee plenum on 14–15 January 1924 was dominated by the Trotsky affair. His behaviour was condemned and, ominously, the plenum agreed to establish a Military Commission to review the work of the Commissariat for War. These moves were then endorsed by the Thirteenth Party Conference, held on 16–18 January 1924, at which Trotsky and the 46 Party leaders who had signed the common platform were accused of 'a petty bourgeois deviation from Leninism'.[4]

Trotsky left Moscow on 18 January for a rest cure in the Caucasus. He was thus in Tbilisi when news came of Lenin's death on 21 January. Stalin advised that it would be difficult for him to get back for the funeral, so he should proceed to Sukhumi and look after his health. His journey to Tbilisi had taken three days, so he could have been back in Moscow by the 24th or 25th, in ample time to attend the funeral, which was first planned for the 26th but then postponed until the 27th. For whatever reason, though, he chose not to attend and did not return from the Caucasus until the eve of the Thirteenth Party Congress, which took place between 22 and 31 May.[5] There he accepted that some of his statements had been exaggerated, but stressed that he had made them because it was his Party duty to draw attention to dangers and errors. Paraphrasing the British maxim 'my country right or wrong', Trotsky declared that he believed in 'my Party right or wrong' and would accept any discipline the Party administered. The congress endorsed the Thirteenth Party Conference verdict that Trotsky had engaged in 'a petty bourgeois deviation'.[6]

In response to this humiliation, Trotsky returned to the theme of the German October. He now convinced himself that 'one could not imagine better prepared and more mature conditions for the seizure of power' than

October 1923 in Germany. Asking himself the question 'Did the communists have the majority of the working masses behind them?', he answered, 'this is a question which cannot be answered with statistics but is decided by the dynamic of the revolution – the masses were moving steadily to the communists'. Trotsky now believed any discussions about the mood of the masses merely reflected a lack of confidence among the leaders of the Party itself; 'assertions that no aggressive fighting mood was to be observed among the masses were made more than once here, too, on the eve of October'. Thus the failure of the German Revolution was linked to the near betrayal of the October Revolution by Zinoviev and Kamenev, something he had already alluded to in his letter to the Politburo of 23 October 1923.[7] In autumn 1924 these ideas were fully developed in 'Lessons of October', an essay published as the preface to that volume of his collected writings dealing with 1917.

A Central Committee plenum held on 25–27 October decided to reply to Trotsky by means of a literary debate. This focused first on Trotsky's attitude to Party organisation, and second on his disdain for the peasantry. Throughout November members of the Politburo outlined their responses. Bukharin seized on the moment Trotsky had joined the Party in summer 1917: Trotsky had still then talked of 'Bolshevik sectarianism', but this sectarianism was actually 'the organisational principle of Bolshevism'. Zinoviev pointed out that if Trotsky had had his way the Party 'would have been excluded from the immediate leadership of economic and state organs'. Kamenev thought Trotsky still believed that his 'estimate of the driving forces of the revolution was right'; he still believed in *Results and Prospects*, which 'is built entirely on an underestimation of the peasantry'.[8]

The consequences of this criticism for Trotsky were immediate. A national conference of Red Army commissars demanded that he be sacked as Commissar of War. Shortly afterwards this demand was repeated by the communist cell of the RVS. His case was to be discussed at a joint plenum of the Central Committee and Party's disciplinary body, the CCC, on 19–20 January 1925, but Trotsky felt too ill to attend. To pre-empt its decision he resigned on 15 January. His resignation letter stressed that he had stuck by the decisions of the Thirteenth Party Congress and had not used 'Lessons of October' to revive the earlier factional debates. Although Zinoviev and Kamenev called for his expulsion, he was issued with a final warning and once again left for the Caucasus to nurse his health.[9]

## PLANNING RESUMED

Trotsky returned to Moscow in May 1925, joined the Presidium of the Supreme Council of the National Economy, and took up three posts within in he would chair the Concessions Committee, the Electro-Technical Board and the Scientific–Technical Board. Within the Concessions Committee he was soon deeply involved in studying the terms of trade between the Soviet Union and the rest of the world. Trotsky was convinced that the Soviet Union could survive only if it took an active part in world trade, on terms favourable to its economic development, and therefore 'advanced the project of developing a system of comparative indices of the Soviet and world economy'. As to the two economic committees, he was especially interested in the institutes of technical science and assiduously visited many laboratories, even studying textbooks on chemistry and hydrodynamics: 'not for nothing had I planned in my youth to take university courses in physics and mathematics'.[10] Happy to associate himself with the task of building socialism in one country, an ambition announced by Stalin in May 1925, that autumn Trotsky published in *Pravda* the essay 'Towards Capitalism or Socialism'; this made very clear that the Soviet Union was on its way to socialism.

For Trotsky, there had always been a danger under NEP that state industry would develop more slowly than private agriculture, with the threat that capitalism might be restored. However, that was now unlikely since private capital's share of commerce had recently fallen by half and over 60 per cent of industrial product came from the state sector. This steady advance of socialist industry could not continue indefinitely, he warned. Industry stood in 1925 at 71 per cent of the 1913 production levels; but what would happen as it grew nearer to 100 per cent? With no new factories being brought into production the old problems of NEP could reassert themselves, if the relative weight of socialist industry began to wane and the relative weight of private trade began to increase. The logic of 'Towards Capitalism or Socialism' was a repetition of Trotsky's long-held belief that socialism in one country *could* work, but only if the correct economic policy were followed and state industrial investment gradually accelerated.[11]

Trotsky's greatest interest at this time was in the Dnieper Dam Project, a massive state investment in hydroelectricity. On 15 July 30,000 roubles had been released to start work on the technical and financial plan for this immense project. More than this, the decree announcing the project had made clear the following:

Owing to the very close connection between the proposed hydro-electric construction project on the Dnieper and the proposals for restructuring the whole economy of the southern region, it is necessary to have an overall plan for technical and economic measures in this region and a financial plan for their implementation both during construction and after the station is opened for use. The drafting of these plans is assigned to Comrade L. D. Trostky, member of the Presidium of the Supreme Council for the National Economy. Comrade Trotsky is assigned to organise an appropriate inter-departmental conference to allow the plan to be co-ordinated with the requests and needs of the Commissariat of Transport, the Commissariat of Agriculture and other offices, and to draft this overall economic, technical and financial plan.

Trotsky was not head of Gosplan, but he was Economic Plenipotentiary of the South, and hence virtual dictator of his native region. Outline plans were to be ready by mid-October, so that the loans and other funds that were needed could be incorporated into the 1925–26 budget.[12]

At this time Trotsky met his old deputy Sklyanskii, who was about to set off to America on a trade mission [**Document 28**]. During their heart to heart, Sklyanskii asked at one point: 'What is Stalin?' Trotsky responded: 'Stalin is the outstanding mediocrity of the Party.' Then, 'in that conversation I realised with absolute clarity the problem of Thermidor'. Trotsky was returning to the danger of a quiet counter-revolution he had sketched out 18 months earlier: 'a victorious counter-revolution may develop its great men; but its first stage, the Thermidor, demands mediocrities who cannot see farther than their noses – their strength lies in their political blindness, like the mill-horse who thinks that he is moving up when he is only pushing down the belt wheel'. From Trotsky's viewpoint, Stalin was soon behaving like a mill horse. Only five days after the funds for the Dnieper Dam Project had been agreed on 15 July, Stalin told Molotov: 'I do not think we can afford to take on the Dnieper Project either this year or next year, given our financial situation . . . We face the danger of squandering some of the kopecks we have managed to accumulate.' Three weeks later he let Bukharin know that the project needed to be prevented 'even if Trotsky will be some-what offended'.[13]

But Trotsky was not offended. He ran the Dnieper Dam Project in the same way that he planned the Civil War campaigns, through consultation and consensus. He accepted that the project could not be hurried and agreed that the feasibility study be extended by an extra year. 'The best personnel, nationally and internationally,' he recalled, 'were brought in to check the estimates for the project.' These working methods alarmed Stalin. They were beginning to change the Party's relationship to the economy. He told Molotov that planners were allocating funds 'while the Politburo is changing from a directing body into a court of appeals'; it was often 'Gosplan special-ists who are in charge'. By October 1925 Stalin had established a special commission to co-ordinate economic work and the Politburo was devoting at least two sessions a month to the economy.

Yet Trotsky stuck to his post. He might periodically rail against 'ignoramuses' and 'technical incompetents', but he was convinced that if schemes like the

Dnieper Dam Project came off, the socialist sector would triumph.[14] Indeed, he was so absorbed in this work that he missed the Fourteenth Party Conference in April 1925 and thus did not notice the first signs that the Zinoviev–Kamenev–Stalin triumvirate was disintegrating. Throughout April the Politburo had been discussing agrarian taxes and as part of these discussions Bukharin told a mass meeting in the Bolshoi Theatre in Moscow on 17 April that the government's policy towards peasants could be summed up in these words: 'Enrich yourselves!' When the Fourteenth Party Conference opened ten days later that phrase was condemned, but the practical result of the conference was to reduce the tax burden on wealthier peasants. For Zinoviev and Kamenev, this was a concession to the kulaks. At the Central Committee plenum in October, hard bargaining succeeded in papering over the cracks, but this did not hold. Throughout the autumn Kamenev used his influence in the Moscow Party organisation and Zinoviev his in the Leningrad Party organisation to frustrate the Politburo. At the Fourteenth Party Congress, 18–23 December 1925, Zinoviev was allowed to make a counter-report to that presented by the Politburo. He argued that, while the numerical strength of the kulaks was insignificant, their economic power was far greater and 'the kulak has his complement in the city, in the new bourgeoisie and among some of the specialists'. It was essential, therefore, to isolate the rich peasant; 'the political character of the rich peasant' could not be ignored.[15]

Despite their long history of antagonism, Trotsky's and Zinoviev's views on the kulak danger were close, and just before the congress Trotsky jotted down some notes about the possibility of forming a bloc with Zinoviev, but then rejected the idea. He felt that in essence the events of autumn 1925 were 'a ferocious apparatus struggle', since Zinoviev still had not recognised the importance of planning and in his scheme 'the planning principle is almost entirely pushed aside by credit and finance regulation'. For Trotsky, the essence of the question lay 'not in the present level of differentiation in the countryside, nor even in the rate of differentiation, but in the rate of industrial development'.[16] Despite all the frustrations of the Dnieper Dam Project, he felt progress was being made and he was prepared to work with Stalin to see it through.[17]

Things began to unravel only in the middle of March 1926 with the proposal that a loan of 300 million roubles should be used to stimulate industry. The Commissariat for Finances protested and proposed reducing the loan to 225 million; the industrialisers fought back; and eventually it was agreed on 25 March that the figure should be 240 million. Even so, some planned expenditure was going to have to be cut and Stalin insisted the axe must fall on the Dnieper Dam Project.[18] At the Central Committee plenum of 6–9 April Trotsky lost patience. He explained that it was not the cuts themselves so much as the way the decision had been reached that upset him: he had helped draft the proposed resolution on the economy three months earlier, but it had then disappeared into a commission for redrafting, from which it had emerged just days before the plenum opened. It was intolerable for Politburo members to be presented with resolutions prepared behind their backs, something which was symptomatic of the 'apparatus regime' and the stifling of necessary debate.[19]

# OPPOSITION

During the April Central Committee plenum Trotsky voted for a resolution proposed by Kamenev, and at the end of the session they and Zinoviev had their first meeting as organisers of a new United Opposition.[20] Immediately thereafter Trotsky resigned his posts linked to the Dnieper Dam Project, retaining only his job on the Concessions Committee. He then left for Germany to consult with doctors and stayed there for much of May. On his return to Moscow he persuaded Zinoviev to join him in raising the question of 'bureaucracy'; thus, during the first week of June, the Politburo was presented with a paper on the apparatus regime, warning that if the problem of bureaucracy were not seriously addressed, the Party would find itself under the rule of an autocrat. Trotsky and Zinoviev then decided to take their struggle to the rank and file, starting in the capital.[21] In response Stalin called a joint plenum of the Central Committee and the CCC for 14–23 July, and proposed removing Zinoviev from the Politburo. Trotsky would be allowed to remain as a member, 'although there are no less profound disagreements with [him]'. Trotsky and Zinoviev prepared for the joint plenum with similar care. They read out a joint statement, the *Declaration of the Thirteen* [**Document 29**], which argued that the direction of economic policy and the aspirations of the proletariat were now at variance, meaning that policies could be enforced only through 'administrative bureaucratic' repression.

As Trotsky had always feared, 'the lag of industry behind the economic development of the country' had finally begun to tell. The 'specific gravity' of the proletariat was falling and the kulaks were asserting themselves. In line with his long-term suspicion of all but the poorest of peasants, Trotsky argued, 'the fact is that under the guise of a union of the poor peasantry with the middle peasantry, we observe steadily and regularly the political sub-ordination of the poor peasantry to the middle peasantry *and through them to the kulaks*'. The *Declaration of the Thirteen* stressed the need to restore Party democracy; to end the tyranny of the apparatus; and to change economic policy in order to raise industrial wages, increase taxes on kulaks, and introduce 'a real five-year plan'.[22]

It also insisted that there was only one cause of bureaucratism and that was 'the divergence between the direction of economic policy and the direction of the feelings and thoughts of the proletarian vanguard'; any other explanation was 'secondary and did not encompass the essence of the question'. While Zinoviev and Kamenev put much of the bureaucratisation of the Party down to Stalin and his personality, Trotsky did not – how else could he have continued to work with Stalin for all this time? The emergence of Stalin was a *symptom* of bureaucratisation, and bureaucratisation was in turn the product of objective circumstances; only when those circumstances changed would the Stalin problem disappear. Bureaucracy thrived because the kulaks rather than the workers benefited from current policies. It was then 'entirely obvious that the state apparatus, in its composition and level of life, was to an overwhelming degree bourgeois and petty bourgeois . . . and favoured the land-leaser, merchant, kulak, the new bourgeoisie'.[23]

After Zinoviev's expulsion from the Politburo, both he and Trotsky organised another series of rank-and-file meetings, but, fearful of the ever more frequently heard calls for 'a new party', decided to agree a compromise with the leadership. This was hammered out at a meeting of the CCC on 11 October 1926 and formalised in a statement on the 16th. Essentially this meant an end to appeals to the rank and file. Trotsky and Zinoviev accepted that such behaviour had been factional and declared their willingness to demobilise the United Opposition as a faction and dissociate themselves from advocates of a new party; however, they would continue to stand by their principles and advance their criticisms of the leadership within the Central Committee.[24] When the *cheka* discovered that United Opposition leaflets were still circulating in Odessa, despite this agreement, Stalin used the Central Committee and CCC joint plenum on 23–26 October to demand a report be compiled on the Opposition's continued activities. Trotsky exploded, accusing Stalin of bad faith; pointing at him, he declared, 'the First Secretary poses his candidature to the post of grave-digger of the revolution'. Stalin turned pale, rose, and rushed from the hall, slamming the door behind him. After the meeting, one of Trotsky's allies arrived at Trotsky's flat shaken and at a loss for words. Trotsky's wife recalled the scene:

> He poured a glass of water, gulped it down and said: 'You know I have smelt gunpowder, but I have never seen anything like this! This was worse than anything! And why, why did he say this? Stalin will never forgive him until the third and fourth generation!'

The next day Trotsky was expelled from the Politburo.[25] A few days later, during the Fifteenth Party Conference, Kamenev suffered a similar fate.[26]

After the conference, Trotsky raised the issue of a Thermidor counter-revolution once again, this time in his private diary. On 26 November he noted that the path towards Thermidor now seemed clear as Party policy drifted to the right: 'The official adoption of the theory of socialism in one country gives sanction at the theoretical level for these moves to the Right which have already taken place and signifies the first open break with Marxism.' And yet, despite these fears, he concluded, 'to speak of Thermidor as an accomplished fact would be a crude distortion of reality', although 'the possibility of Thermidor' was clearly there. This put an enormous responsibility on the Opposition. Despite its defeat, the struggle needed to go on even if only 'Liebknecht's fate' awaited. (The German Social Democrat Karl Liebknecht, an old acquaintance from Trotsky's Vienna days, had led the German communist insurrection of January 1919 and died at the hands of the counter-revolutionary **Freikorps**.) It was a chilling analogy; clearly, Trotsky's outburst about Stalin as the grave-digger of the revolution was not an aberration.[27]

**Freikorps**: When the German Empire collapsed at the end of the First World War, in November 1918, the new government formed by the German Social Democrats called for volunteers from the defeated Imperial Army to form a 'free corps' to be used to resist the threat of communism. These volunteers were used to defeat the attempted communist insurrections in Germany of early 1919, the Spartacist Uprising in Berlin in January and the Bavarian Soviet in April. They were responsible for the brutal murder of the leaders of the Spartacist Uprising, Karl Liebknecht and Rosa Luxemburg.

The thrust of the statements made at the Fifteenth Party Conference was that the Party could work through its differences. For a while this did seem to be the case and Trotsky confined his activities in winter and spring 1927 to writing letters of protest to the Politburo about what he saw as intolerable aspects of the inner Party regime. Then, though, in April 1927, he became obsessed with the way events were unfolding in China and resolved to launch a new assault on the Stalin–Bukharin leadership. For several years the Soviet Government had been involved in the politics of nationalist China, sending both political advisers to the Nationalist Party (KMT) and the Chinese Communist Party (CCP) and military advisers to the Nationalist generals. The political advisers had come up with an unusual solution to how the KMT and CCP should relate to each other; because socialist revolution was conceivable only after a national revolution had driven the occupying imperial powers from China, the CCP should be an affiliate member of the KMT and remain within its ranks, even when, from late 1925, and more obviously throughout 1926, right-wing forces managed to gain the upper hand in the KMT leadership.

Initially China was not an issue for the Opposition. On 20 March 1926 Chiang Kai-shek established himself as virtual dictator within the KMT leadership. Trotsky, still then loyal to the leadership, suggested at a Politburo meeting that the CCP should leave the KMT. In April Zinoviev put the same proposal to the Politburo on behalf of the Opposition while Trotsky was absent in Germany, but then withdrew it when he met with overwhelming criticism. Over the summer Chiang Kai-shek began a dramatic military advance, hugely expanding the territory under his control; as he did so he established a regime which took a very negative attitude to the labour movement, particularly on the question of strikes. At the end of September Trotsky wrote an article, which he never submitted for publication, suggesting once again that the CCP should break with the KMT. He had wanted to raise the issue of China during the Fifteenth Party Conference, but Zinoviev would not agree to this.

By autumn 1926 it seemed that the situation in China was improving. In November the KMT administration carried out a reshuffle and gave two cabinet posts to communists. On 30 November, when Stalin addressed the **Comintern** Executive on the question of China, he was upbeat and urged the Chinese communists to take advantage of these favourable new circumstances to use strike action to improve the lot of workers; the time had come for a cautious revolutionary advance. To help that advance, in February 1927 Stalin arranged for one of the Left KMT leaders, then residing in France, to be transferred to China via Moscow. On 19 February the workers of Shanghai declared a strike, then returned to work a week later when they felt their demands had been met. In this newly radicalised climate the Left was able to remove some of the KMT Rightists from the leadership, and at the KMT Congress on 10–17 March limitations were imposed on Chiang Kai-shek's authority. On 21 March a second Shanghai strike overthrew the local warlord and the Nationalist Army entered the city.[28]

Trotsky had returned to the question of China early in March 1927, but his fellow Oppositionists would not support another resolution calling for the CCP to leave the KMT. He wrote on 22 March: 'I confess that at the present time the situation in China arouses in me far greater concern than does any other problem . . . the more the KMT takes on the character of a governing party, the more it becomes bourgeois'. On 31 March he wrote to the Politburo stating that while he accepted that the issue of the CCP remaining in the KMT had been settled, it was surely time to think about forming soviets in big cities like Shanghai, 'not as an instrument of proletarian dictatorship, but one of revolutionary national liberation and democratic liberation'. Certainly the situation in Shanghai seemed to be reaching a climax, with frequent clashes between Chiang's military authorities and the communist organisers of the insurrection. Stalin was optimistic that, if the right tactics were followed, Chiang could be removed from the scene: on 5 April he called a meeting of activists involved in Chinese matters and told them, 'I know Chiang Kai-shek is playing a cunning game with us, but it is he that will be crushed; we will squeeze him like a lemon and then be rid of him.'[29] It was not to be. On 12 April Chiang Kai-shek began a massacre of the Shanghai insurgents.

As reports of the deaths of thousands of communists came in, a Central Committee plenum was being held in Moscow on 13–16 April. At it Stalin and Trotsky clashed over whether soviets should have been formed in China. Stalin insisted that soviets, whatever they might have been in the past, were now organs for 'ushering in the proletarian dictatorship, a Chinese October'. Trotsky conceded that socialist revolution was not on the agenda, but stressed that soviets had existed in Russia in 1905, long before the victory of

**Communist International (Comintern):** Founded in March 1919, this was based on the theory that all the world's communist parties were elements in a single international communist party, and that therefore, notionally, the Executive of the Communist International was above the Politburo of the Russian Communist Party in terms of hierarchy. However, since in reality the Russian Communist Party had more seats on the Comintern than all the other communist parties put together, this was just an ideological fiction. However, the fiction allowed Trotsky and other dissident communists to appeal to the Comintern even after the Politburo had rejected their claims.

the socialist revolution; 'whoever opposes the formation of the soviets must say "all power to the KMT"'.[30] The debate continued in the press, with Stalin writing two articles on China and Trotsky responding with 'The Chinese Revolution and the Theses of Comrade Stalin', which *Pravda* refused to publish. It is impossible to separate Trotsky's impassioned response to the Shanghai massacre from his growing fear of Thermidor. Chiang Kai-shek's actions were a metaphor for the dangers facing the Russian Revolution. Trotsky had long accepted that, if the correct economic policy were not followed, then the sort of kulak counter-revolution envisaged in *Results and Prospects* could occur; since December 1923, he had felt that this might not be an overt clash but could take the form of a creeping counter-revolution, as the political influence of the kulaks gradually penetrated the state bureaucracy.

By April 1926, when Stalin thwarted the Dnieper Dam Project, Trotsky was openly calling this process Thermidor. Stalin and Bukharin were not 'betraying Bolshevism at its very core' because they were traitors, but because they had failed to stand up to growing class pressures from the Right. And now he suggested that the same thing had happened in China. The CCP, the party of Chinese workers and peasants, had formed a temporary NEP-style coalition with the Chinese bourgeoisie, which had allowed Chiang Kai-shek first to emerge as a 'Bonaparte' and then to carry out his own Thermidor. Trotsky wrote of Stalin's weakness in May 1927 because he felt the First Secretary would soon be replaced by a Russian Chiang Kai-shek. Yet Stalin's weakness might just provide Trotsky with the opportunity he needed to intervene, to stop the drift to the right and save the day. Victory was not certain, but he had to try. As he later recalled:'we went to meet the inevitable debacle, confident that we were paving the way for the triumph of our ideas in a more distant future . . . when the struggle is one of great principles, the revolutionary can follow one rule: *Fais ce que dois, advienne que pourra.*'[31]

## TOWARDS EXILE

Although expelled from the Politburo, Trotsky was still a member of the Executive of the Communist International (Comintern), which met on 18–30 May 1927. He sent a written statement to the meeting about the alarming drift to the right in the Bolshevik Party since the end of 1923, and when he addressed the meeting on 23 May and again on 24 May he not only repeated the points made in his unpublished *Pravda* article but noted that the demand that the Opposition be expelled from the Party came not only from the current leadership, but also from the former liberal politician and adviser to Admiral Kolchak, N. V. Ustryalov, now an émigré in Harbin, who wrote openly of the need for other former liberals to collaborate with the more sensible and nationally minded Bolsheviks. Stalin addressed the meeting shortly after Trotsky had made his speech on the 24th: he summarised the content of his published *Pravda* articles on China and then stated that Trotsky had clearly violated the terms of the compromise reached the previous October and embarked on a new factional struggle.[32]

Stalin was right. On 25 May Trotsky and his supporters published their *Declaration of the Eighty-three*, which was circulated to Comintern delegates the next day. In early June Zinoviev wrote *The Declaration of the Eighty-three and Our Tasks*, in which he asserted that the Opposition was now so strong that 'even if Stalin succeeded in cutting of its head', it would survive. The disagreements with the leadership were now so deep that the declaration had to be taken to the rank and file and used to open debate in the run-up to the Fifteenth Party Congress.[33] Called before the CCC on 24 June, Trotsky explained what he meant by the Thermidor danger. 'Every specialist, every civil servant, every "lady", whether soviet or half-soviet, knows that the workers' temperament is "no longer that of 1918"; you hear it at the stalls, on the street and in the tram.' Quietly a bourgeois ideology was seeping in, and kulaks, traders and specialists felt safe enough to build themselves ostentatious houses. A blow from the Right was imminent: 'but it would not come from the right wing of the Party, for that was only the transmission mechanism, the real danger, the core danger came from the bourgeois classes which were raising their heads'. In the French Revolution those who carried out Thermidor believed that they were just changing a few key personnel, not changing the class nature of the regime, but they had changed the class nature of the revolution in France. The logic was clear: the removal of Trotsky and Zinoviev from the Bolshevik Central Committee would change the class nature of the Soviet regime. In such circumstances, Trotsky concluded, it was the duty of the CCC not to expel people, but to 'create a more healthy and flexible regime in the Party'.[34] In a further declaration on 28 June Trotsky accused Stalin of following 'the road from the dictatorship of the proletariat to that of compromise with petty-bourgeois big-wigs, who offered a bridge to the big bourgeoisie'.[35]

During a session of the Central Committee on 27 June, Trotsky's attitude had been described as 'defeatist'. When he found out he wrote a letter of protest on 11 July, explaining that the Opposition would behave like the French Prime Minister Georges Clemenceau had in France during the First World War – that is, support the war but criticise its management.[36] At a subsequent joint plenum of the Central Committee and the CCC from 29 July to 9 August Stalin insisted, 'the Opposition must emphatically and irrevocably abandon its Thermidor twaddle and its foolish slogan of a Clemenceau experiment'. Trotsky still linked the two. Bukharin and Stalin's policy could not survive a war, for a war would bring out the underlying class contradictions, forcing 'a turn either towards Thermidor or towards the

Opposition', for he doubted 'to the highest degree' Stalin's capacity to follow the correct line in the defence of the 'socialist fatherland'.[37] As the plenum proceeded, however, Trotsky agreed to moderate his stance, at Zinoviev's suggestion. Thus, on 8 August, the Opposition issued a statement to declare that they would defend the Soviet Union unconditionally, and that, although the Thermidorian danger existed, the Party itself was not yet infected.[38]

This clarification brought another truce, but it was to last only a month. The key work of the Opposition was first to draft a 70-page platform, which it hoped would be discussed at the Fifteenth Party Congress, and then to popularise it among the rank and file. The platform was duly sent to the Politburo on 3 September, but on the 8th Stalin advised that it could not be circulated to the wider Party since it was a factional document. Trotsky and Zinoviev responded by deciding to circulate the platform themselves, but on the night of 12–13 September their printing press was seized by the *cheka*. Trotsky was summoned to the Comintern Presidium on 27 September to explain the printing press affair. In Stalin's presence he declared: 'Stalin's personal misfortune, which is fast becoming the Party's misfortune, is the colossal disparity between his intellectual resources and the power of the state and Party machine he has concentrated in his hands; [his] bureaucratic regime will lead irreversibly to one-man rule.' Stalin responded simply that 'the present regime in the Party is an exact expression of the regime that was established in the Party in Lenin's time'.[39]

Deprived of the written word, the Opposition had no choice but to organise public meetings once again, with the result that a joint plenum of the Central Committee and the CCC on 23–26 October resolved that Trotsky and Zinoviev should be expelled from the Party at the Fifteenth Party Congress. At this meeting Trotsky denounced Stalin once more, to the accompaniment of jeers, catcalls and even missiles thrown by loyal Stalinists.

> The rudeness and disloyalty, which Lenin wrote about, is no longer just a personal quality; these have become the qualities of the ruling faction, its policies, its regime . . . But the Party regime does not live for itself. In the Party regime we find an expression of all the policies of the Party leadership. This policy has, during the last years, moved its class element firmly from left to right: from the proletariat to the petty bourgeois, from the Party to the specialist, from the rank and file to the apparatus, from the landless and poor to the kulak, from Shanghai workers to Chiang Kai-shek . . . that is the very essence of Stalinism.

Stalin, he said, was 'carrying out the social order of Ustryalov' – in other words, the order of the bourgeoisie – while his call for the expulsion of the Opposition was 'the very voice of Thermidor'.[40]

On 7 November, the tenth anniversary of the October Revolution, members of the Opposition took part in the official demonstrations, but they marched separately under their own banners with such slogans as 'Down with the Kulak, the **Nepman** and the Bureaucrat' and 'Carry out Lenin's Testament'.[41] However, although Trotsky wanted to continue the struggle, Zinoviev had had enough. He had made clear to Trotsky at the outset that he would never go so far as to risk expulsion from the Party. The Central Committee and the CCC held another joint plenum on 12–14 November and Zinoviev insisted the Opposition should declare that there would be no more public meetings. It was too late to save him, though, and later that day the plenum endorsed the decision to expel both Trotsky and Zinoviev from the Party. The issue then was how they should go about gaining readmission.[42] At the Fifteenth Party Congress, 7–19 December, Zinoviev and Kamenev were ready to state that their views were 'wrong and anti-Leninist', in return for which they were put on Party probation for six months, opening the way for a full return to the Party. Trotsky would not recant, though. At their last meeting Zinoviev reminded him that Lenin had warned in his testament that the Trotsky–Stalin conflict might cause a split in the Party: 'Think of the responsibility you bear!' Zinoviev cautioned. Trotsky responded: 'Lenin also wrote in his testament that if the divergence of views inside the Party coincided with class differences, nothing would save us from a split.' For Trotsky, Thermidor had advanced to the point where the Party itself was infected. By expelling the Opposition, Stalin was acting as an agent of Thermidor, and a split in the Party was therefore inevitable. Zinoviev and Kamenev could not accept that the Party had degenerated so much and still saw its bureaucracy as recoverable, as long as the malign influence of Stalin could be removed.[43]

Trotsky's best clarification of what he meant by Thermidor had come in a letter he wrote to an old ally on 12 August 1927:

> You ask yourself: why is the regime so bad? Is it the nasty character of Stalin? No, the Party regime is a function of the political line. Namely because Stalin relies on Chiang Kai-shek . . . the civil servant, the village high-ups etc., he is forced to follow a policy not relying on the consciousness and will of the proletarian vanguard but squeezing him under the apparatus, from above, and thus reflecting and mastering the pressure of other classes on the proletariat . . . This is the road to Thermidor.

For Stalin, though, Thermidor was 'twaddle'. Trotsky was not splitting the Party to save it but merely rejecting Lenin's theory of Party organisation and proving that he was still a Menshevik. Addressing the October Central Committee and CCC plenum, the last occasion on which the two men met, Stalin concluded his speech by turning to Trotsky's 1904 pamphlet *Our*

**Nepman:** The restoration of private industry under NEP allowed for the re-emergence of small entrepreneurs, described by the Bolsheviks as Nepman.

*Political Tasks*, which Trotsky had dedicated to the Menshevik leader Pavel Akselrod: 'From Lenin to Akselrod – such is the organisational path that our opposition has travelled . . . Well, good riddance! Go to your "dear teacher Pavel Borisovich Akselrod".'[44]

On 17 January 1928 Trotsky was deported to Alma Ata. He was not downcast. For him, this was just a stage in the struggle against Thermidor. He told Natasha as they tried to sleep on the hard bunks of the train taking them east: 'I did not want to die in my bed in the Kremlin.'[45]

## FURTHER READING

As well as Trotsky's *My Life* and the Vilkova document collection (and, for readers of Russian, the four-volume *Arkhiv Trotskogo*), there is a useful document collection by Naomi Allen (ed.) – *Leon Trotsky: The Challenge of the Left Opposition (1923–25)*. On the concept of Thermidor there is a useful essay by David Law – 'Trotsky and Thermidor' – in the second volume of F. Gori's *Pensiero e Azione di Lev Troskij*. For events in China, see A. Pantsov, *The Bolsheviks and the Chinese Revolution*, while Trotsky's own writings on the Chinese question can be found in L. Evans and R. Block (eds), *Leon Trotsky on China*.

## NOTES

1  N. Allen (ed.), *Leon Trotsky: The Challenge of the Left Opposition (1923–25)* (New York: Pathfinder Press, 1975), pp. 87–92.
2  Vilkova, *Struggle*, pp. 242–45; R. Wade (ed.), *Documents in Soviet History* (New York: Academic International Press, 1995) , vol. III, pp. 96–100.
3  Allen, *Challenge*, pp. 79–84.
4  Vilkova, *Struggle*, pp. 311–28, 336; Wade, *Documents*, vol. III, p. 115; Bazhanov, *Bazhanov*, p. 62; Deutscher, *Unarmed*, pp. 132–34.
5  Trotsky, *My Life*, pp. 511–12; *Bazhanov*, p. 65. Stalin told Trotsky both the day originally planned for the funeral and 'that he could not get back in time' (Trotsky, *My Life*, p. 508). Why Trotsky accepted this when it was difficult yet patently possible to return is unclear.
6  *Trinadtsatyi s'ezd RKP (b): stenograficheskii otchet* (Moscow 1924), pp. 163–68, 211.
7  Allen, *Challenge*, pp. 165–66, 168–69.
8  Wade, *Documents*, vol. III, pp. 222–31; *International Press Correspondence*, 15 December 1924, 23 January 1925.
9  Wade, *Documents*, vol. III, pp. 291–96; Deutscher, *Unarmed*, p. 163.
10  Trotsky, *My Life*, pp. 518–19.
11  Allen, *Challenge*, pp. 322–74.

12 L. T. Lih *et al.* (eds), *Stalin's Letters to Molotov* (New Haven: Harvard University Press, 1995), pp. 86, 87 n.1

13 Trotsky, *My Life*, pp. 512–13; Lih, *Letters*, pp. 86–87, 92.

14 Allen, *Challenge*, pp. 228–29; Lih, *Letters*, p. 89; N. Valentinov, 'Dopolnenie k "Dnevniku" L Trotskogo', *Sotsialisticheskii vestnik* nos. 2–3, 1959, p. 50.

15 E. H. Carr, *Socialism in One Country* (Basingstoke: Macmillan, 1958), vol. I, pp. 274–336; Wade, *Documents*, vol. III, pp. 343–49.

16 Allen, *Challenge*, pp. 384–89, 391–92.

17 V. Serge, *Memoirs of a Revolutionary* (Oxford: Oxford University Press, 1963), p. 210; B. Souvarine, 'Pis'mo v redaktsiyu', *Sotsialisticheskii vestnik* no. 4, 1960; L. Trotsky, *The Writings of Leon Trotsky 1936–7* (New York: Pathfinder Press, 1975), p. 119.

18 A. Cummins (ed.), *Documents of Soviet History* (New York: Academic International Press, 1998), vol. IV, p. 11; Carr, *Socialism in One Country*, p. 354. Trotsky stated in July 1926 (*Arkhiv Trotskogo*, vol. II, p. 23) that Stalin began to manoeuvre against him two and a half months after the Fourteenth Party Congress, or mid-March. Letters to colleagues (*Arkhiv Trotskogo*, vol. I, pp. 187–88) show what for Trotsky was an incomprehensible row with Stalin at the very end of March.

19 *Arkhiv Trotskogo*, vol. I, pp. 207, 209–19.

20 Deutscher, *Unarmed*, pp. 262–65.

21 Trotsky's actions at this time are commented on by Molotov and Stalin; see Lih, *Letters*, pp. 100, 106, 108, 112.

22 The *Declaration of the Thirteen* is reproduced in Cummins, *Documents*, vol. IV, p. 48.

23 Cummins, *Documents*, vol. IV, pp. 50–51.

24 P. Broué, *Trotsky* (Paris: Fayard, 1988), pp 491–95; Deutscher, *Unarmed*, pp. 293–94; J. V. Stalin, *Collected Works* (Moscow, 1953), vol. VIII, p. 223.

25 Deutscher, *Unarmed*, pp. 296–97.

26 Lih, *Letters*, p. 69.

27 D. Law, 'Trotsky and Thermidor', in F. Gori (ed.), *Pensiero e Azione Politica di Lev Trockij* (Florence: Feltrinelli, 1982), vol. II, p. 443; Deutscher, *Unarmed*, p. 309.

28 For China, see A. Pantsov, *The Bolsheviks and the Chinese Revolution* (London: Curzon, 2000), pp. 84–124. Trotsky's letter of September 1926 is in L. Evans and R. Block (eds), *Leon Trotsky on China* (New York: Monad Press, 1976), pp. 113–19. Stalin's speech is in Stalin, *Works*, vol. VII, p. 389.

29 Evans and Block, *Trotsky on China*, pp. 125, 130, 133; Serge, *Memoirs*, p. 217.

30 Evans and Block, *Trotsky on China*, pp. 149–57.

31 Trotsky, *My Life*, pp. 520–21.

32 Evans and Block, *Trotsky on China*, pp. 216–38; Stalin, *Works*, vol. IX, pp. 288–311.

33 R. Daniels, *A Documentary History of Communism* (London: University Press of New England, 1985), vol. II, p. 79; *Arkhiv Trotskogo*, vol. III, pp. 382–86.

34 *Arkhiv Trotskogo*, vol. III, pp. 87–112.

35 *Arkhiv Trotskogo*, vol. III, pp. 115–26, 211–18.

36 Deutscher, *Unarmed*, pp. 349–56.

37 Stalin, *Works*, vol. X, pp. 52, 87; *Arkhiv Trotskogo*, vol. IV, pp. 32–45.

38 *Arkhiv Trotskogo*, vol. IV, pp. 67–68.

39 *Arkhiv Trotskogo*, vol. IV, pp. 68–70; Broué, *Trotsky*, pp. 521–22; Volkogonov, *Trotsky*, p. 291; Stalin, *Works*, vol. X, p. 166.

40 *Arkhiv Trotskogo*, vol. IV, pp. 218–24; Stalin, *Works*, vol. X, p. 180.

41 These events are summarised in Trotsky, *My Life*, pp. 531–32; Broué, *Trotsky*, pp. 525–28; and Volkogonov, *Trotsky*, pp. 311–21.

42 For more details, see Thatcher, *Trotsky*, p. 151; Trotsky, *Writings 1936–7*, pp. 246–47; *Arkhiv Trotskogo*, vol. IV, pp. 266, 267–69.

43 Trotsky, *Writings 1936–7*, p. 66.

44 *Arkhiv Trotskogo*, vol. IV, pp. 73–74; Stalin, *Works*, vol. X, p. 211.

45 Serge and Sedova, *Life and Death*, p. 157.

# 7

# Conclusion

It is no exaggeration to say that without Trotsky there would have been no successful Bolshevik Revolution in 1917. As the power of Kerensky and the Provisional Government visibly crumbled in September and October of that year, it was Trotsky who understood how an insurrection could be staged without provoking violent counter-measures. Both Lenin and Trotsky had been consistently calling for insurrection since the defeat of General Kornilov's attempted military coup at the end of August, but the two men had understood that insurrection differently. Lenin had in mind a classic military operation staged by the Bolshevik Party's own Military Organisation; Trotsky felt that, for all the popularity of the Bolshevik Party among workers and soldiers, they were far more responsive to what they saw as their own organisation, the Petrograd Soviet. Therefore, for the insurrection to be successful, its organiser had to be the soviet, not the Bolshevik Party. It was Trotsky, once he had become the soviet's president in September, who realised that organisation's potential for forming a Military Revolutionary Committee. Then it would be the committee's task both to organise resistance to Kerensky's orders and to start making the preparations to overthrow him. In Trotsky's own jargon, he realised that a successful revolution had to begin on the defensive and only gradually move on to the offensive.

The importance of the soviet in the success of the Bolshevik Revolution draws attention to Trotsky's second, and perhaps more contested, contribution to the revolutionary cause. Workers in 1917 not only saw the Petrograd Soviet as 'their' institution; they looked back to its origins as the Petersburg Soviet of 1905, when a working-class parliament had first been established in Russia. Back then, unlike Lenin and the Bolsheviks, who had initially kept their distance, Trotsky had thrown himself into the work of the soviet. He did so because his ideological clash with Lenin in 1903–04 had convinced him that workers, through their own actions, could acquire political consciousness and did not need to be guided by any political party. All of Trotsky's actions between 1905 and 1917 were aimed at trying to foster the development of working-class self-activity, and it is arguable that the radical stance which Russian workers adopted during the First World War had more to do with his efforts than with Lenin's repeated attempts to 'lead' the workers to the same end. The workers who carried out the February Revolution and ended the power of the Romanov dynasty knew precisely what they were doing, and immediately re-established their soviet to ensure that the gains of that revolution were not lost. Working-class self-activity aimed at the revolutionary overthrow of the established order was not solely down to Trotsky, but he certainly did much to encourage and organise it.

It is absolutely clear that without Trotsky the Bolshevik Revolution would not have survived its first year in power, and therefore would not have survived at all. In autumn 1918 British intervention forces had landed in the north of Russia and were trying to advance towards the River Volga. On the Volga itself, the Czechoslovak Legion had rebelled against Soviet power and helped the Socialist Revolutionary Party establish a rival government to Lenin's, basing itself on the authority of the Constituent Assembly. By 7 August the Bolsheviks had lost control of Kazan, yet still retained control of the railway bridge across the Volga at Sviyazhsk. If that bridge had been captured, the days of Bolshevik rule were surely numbered. Yet at Sviyazhsk Trotsky displayed the unique blend of ruthlessness, inspiration and organisational passion which turned defeat into triumph, establishing a pattern that would be repeated time and again as the Civil War continued and ended ultimately in victory for the Bolsheviks.

The methods used by Trotsky for victory in the Civil War – reliance on 'military specialists' who were officers from the old Imperial Army – taught him what he perceived to be the key to success in post-war reconstruction as well. For Trotsky, post-war recovery was not simply a matter of planning, but of basing that planning on the guidance of experts. In his view, 'bourgeois specialists' were just as essential as 'military specialists': if Gosplan were to bring about economic recovery, it had to be staffed by experts. Throughout the Civil War, Trotsky had railed against 'Party ignoramuses' who interfered in military operations. In the early 1920s he railed against the Politburo for repeatedly discussing economic matters it did not understand and therefore 'interfering' in the planning process. His stance repeatedly ruffled feathers within the hierarchy of the Bolshevik Party. During the Civil War Zinoviev had tried to ensure Party oversight of military matters, and, as economic recovery began, so Stalin joined him in insisting that the Party had an absolute right to direct the economy, rejecting as inappropriate any talk of 'interference'.

By the mid-1920s, Trotsky's response to the fact that the rest of the Bolshevik hierarchy were not only ignoring his suggestions but interpreting his admiration of non-Party specialists as an implicit rejection of Lenin's concept of the leading role of the Party was to return to the implications of *Results and Prospects*, the pamphlet he had written in 1906 and which became the credo on which he based so many of his actions. In *Results and Prospects* he had argued that, while a workers' government would initially win the support of the peasantry, this alliance would be extremely unstable and the peasantry could easily turn on the working class. His solution was to suggest that permanent salvation could be achieved only by internationalising the revolution: thus, at the time of the Brest-Litovsk Treaty he had hoped against hope that the workers of Germany and Austria-Hungary would rise up to support their Russian comrades. Throughout the Civil War, peasant disturbances had reinforced his fear that, for all Lenin's concessions to the middle peasantry, peasant loyalty was unreliable. As post-war planning began, Trotsky developed a rough and ready matrix: so long as the socialist sectors of the economy were doing better than the private peasant sector, he was optimistic that the Soviet Union was essentially socialist and, although he never used the term, socialism could be built in one country.

However, what if the matrix turned the other way, and the private peasant economy began to profit at the expense of the state sector? And what if, when people like Trotsky pointed this out to the Bolshevik hierarchy, they were not heeded but further marginalised? Did that not mean that hostile forces had somehow penetrated into the Bolshevik Party? Did that not mean that a Thermidor-style reaction had already silently begun and was using its control of the Party machinery to throttle the voice of the working class? Although Stalin thought such questions were 'twaddle', and others felt that Trotsky's identification of himself alone with the interests of the working class was to overplay his past glories, there can be no doubt of the depth of his conviction that the predictions he had made in *Results and Prospects* were coming true – the peasantry was turning on the regime. This is clear from the difficulties he faced in his alliance with Zinoviev and Kamenev against Stalin. In December 1927 Zinoviev and Kamenev were ready to recant their 'sins' and seek readmission to the Bolshevik Party. Zinoviev urged Trotsky to do the same, reminding him that Lenin's testament had urged the Party never to allow internal differences to escalate into a public split. Trotsky corrected Zinoviev and insisted that what Lenin had actually suggested was that if differences in the Party 'coincided with class differences' then a split was inevitable. Trotsky was convinced that Stalin had become the agent of Thermidor, the agent of a creeping peasant counter-revolution.

How wrong Trotsky was became clear even as he was exiled to Alma Ata. By the end of 1927 it was clear to the Soviet leadership that there were problems with the amount of grain being delivered to the state. This prompted Stalin to travel to the Urals in January 1928 and seize the grain that was needed. This was the start of a process which, by the end of 1929, had enabled Stalin to emerge as a Soviet dictator committed to policies of forced collectivisation of agriculture and rapid industrialisation. Far from being the agent of Thermidor, he had adopted Trotsky's anti-kulak rhetoric, destroyed the kulaks as a class and begun industrialising the country through a series of five-year plans. From exile, Trotsky at first doubted the seriousness of Stalin's endeavour, and then began to explain why he was doing it all wrong.

What would have been different if Trotsky had been in charge of the Soviet Union's industrialisation drive? Trotsky did not reject the notion of socialism in one country in principle, but he insisted that it was possible only if the right policies were followed and the socialist sector was never swamped by the private sector. In Stalin's five-year plans the private sector disappeared entirely. That was why Trotsky never accused Stalin of restoring capitalism in the Soviet Union; it remained a 'workers' state', although one that had degenerated from the ideal. It is clear from Trotsky's criticism of Stalin's five-year plans that he would have industrialised at a slower pace, and it can be deduced from his activities in the Civil War and his writings of the early 1920s that he would have made far more use of 'bourgeois experts' in the planning process. Trotsky's Soviet Union would thus have been more technocratic than Stalin's, and regional Party secretaries, who were so important in the Khrushchev years, would have had far less influence over economic policy. That might have led to a rather different balance of forces emerging between the Party and the state bureaucracy. It is even conceivable that this would have fostered the sort of dichotomy seen in contemporary China, with the Party controlling society and industrialists controlling the economy.

# DOCUMENTS

**Document 1**    REPORT OF THE SIBERIAN DELEGATION (1903)

We should stress one characteristic feature: the totally abstract nature of Comrade Lenin's position. Control over the members of the party is necessary. This control can only be assured if it is possible to reach each member. Now, this can only be done if all the members of the party are formally fixed, that is, registered in the appropriate manner with one of the party organizations. Then the Central Committee, present everywhere, penetrating into everything and considering everything, can reach each party member on the scene of the crime. In reality, this is a fairly innocent bureaucratic dream; if the question had remained at that level one could light-heartedly have left the partisans of Lenin's formula with the platonic satisfaction of feeling that the Second Congress of the RSDLP had discovered the surest statutory remedy for opportunism and intellectual individualism.

But, if one moves on from this sterile formalism to the real questions before the party, Comrade Lenin's formula then has certain drawbacks. It is a secret to nobody that in a whole number of towns, there is alongside the Party Committee a big organized opposition (in Petersburg, Odessa, Ekaterinoslav, and Voronezh). Comrade Lenin's formula puts the members of all these workers' organizations outside the party – while their papers still appear under its patronage. So as not to exclude these groups from the party, the Central Committee would, under Lenin's formula, have had to declare them party organizations. But it will not do so, it cannot do so because they have not been built on principles the party considers adequate. It remains to be said to the members of these organizations: if you wish, gentlemen, to stay in the party, dissolve yourselves and join the legitimate organizations of the party. 'Dissolve yourselves!' . . .

This 'centralist' solution does not seem to me to be the product of superior political wisdom. The workers' organization will worry little about whether it is a member or not, and will not dissolve itself. We think that instead of concerning itself with the verbal dissolution of opposition groups and in general instead of spending its time making 'centralizing' gestures, the Central Committee would do better to carry out serious work in the party; it would do better to re-educate, restructure and make rational use of all possible workers' organizations which have grown up during the period of decomposition of the party. For this, the way to start is not by declaring them all outlawed, as Lenin's Paragraph I would have obliged us to do. On the contrary, Martov's formula can become an excellent weapon in the hands of the Central Committee (as Martov himself indicated). 'If you want to stay in the party', it will say to the representatives of the workers' organizations, 'you must place yourself under the direction of the party organization, the local committee.' This will be enough to get the workers' organization to accept a representative of the committee, who will try to get the 'line' carried out which represents the party's general view – and do so, of course, by force of his influence alone . . .

The system of Terror is crowned by a Robespierre. Comrade Lenin reviewed the members of the party in his mind, and reached the conclusion that this iron hand could only be himself . . . The role of the Central Committee, according to Lenin . . . must be the watchdog of centralism. It dissolves oppositions and closes the gates of the party. To express to the congress the meaning of the Central Committee, Comrade Lenin held up his fist (I am not speaking metaphorically) as the political symbol of the Central Committee. We do not know if this mimicry of centralism is entered in the minutes. Let us hope so, for the fist would crown the whole construction . . .

Robespierre's dictatorship through the intermediary of the Committee of Public Safety could only hold if 'loyal' people were selected on the Committee itself, and if creatures of the Incorruptible were placed in all important state posts. Otherwise, the all-powerful dictatorship would have remained suspended in mid-air. The first condition was provided, in our caricature of Robespierre's career, by the liquidation of the old Editorial Board [of *Iskra*]. A second condition was also ensured: the appropriate selection of the members of the Central Committee, and for the rest, the establishment of the filter of 'unanimity' and 'mutual co-option' . . . Here, comrades, is the administrative apparatus which is to govern the Republic of orthodox 'Virtue' and centralist 'Terror'.

Such a régime cannot last for ever. The system of Terror ends up in reaction . . . Now, a régime which to survive begins by driving out the best members in the fields of theory and practice promises too many executions and too little bread. It will inevitably create disillusionment which may turn out to be fatal, not just for the Robespierres and the islands of centralism, but also for the idea of a single combat organization [i.e. the party] in general. It is the 'Thermidorians' of socialist opportunism who will then be masters of the situation, and the gates of the party then really will be open wide. May it not come to that.

*Source*: L. Trotsky, *The Report of the Siberian Delegation* (London: New Park Publications, 1979), pp. 21–22, 28, 36–38.

OUR POLITICAL TASKS (1904)    **Document 2**

To my dear teacher – Pavel Borisovich Axelrod . . .

The extremely primitive organisational 'plans' put forward by the author of *What is to be Done?* [Lenin] which occupied an insignificant place in the whole realm of ideas, but which, as propagated by *Iskra* and *Zarya*, were nonetheless an undeniable factor for progress, reappear three years later in the work of their 'epigone', the author of *One Step Forward, Two Steps Back* [also Lenin], as a furious attempt to prevent Social Democracy from being fully itself . . .

Against its will the Second Congress [of the Russian Social Democratic Labour Party] has become the instrument of new pretensions. It wished only to consolidate the gains of the period of 'liquidation', in fact, it has opened a new period, and has made us discover a whole universe of new tasks. And demonstrating the internal logic of the succession of these periods, the new tasks only flow specifically from our old basic problematic, which only now, thanks above all to the work of the old *Iskra*, is presented to us in a genuine, immediate form: the development of the consciousness and autonomous activity of the class of the proletariat . . .

But it should not be forgotten that the proletariat, the actual proletariat of Petersburg, remained completely outside these events, and was only afterwards able to ask the party's envoy: 'What are we going to do now?' The group of 'professional revolutionaries' was not marching at the head of the conscious proletariat, it was acting (in so far as it acted) in the place of the proletariat . . .

The task imposed on us by the new period in the party is the following: to make our propaganda lose its abstract and often scholastic nature, and give it a living political content: . . . To work then! Long live the self-activity of the proletariat! Down with political substitutionism! . . .

If we are to define the character of all work carried out by our party, in the one case we have a party which thinks for the proletariat, which substitutes itself politically for it, and in the other we have a party which politically educates and mobilises the proletariat to exercise rational pressure on the will of all political groups and parties. These two systems give objectively quite different results . . . The tactic of our committees, which consists of from time to time sending out (behind the backs of the proletariat) appeals or proclamations to the students, the *zemstvos*, the *dumas* and the various congresses, is very similar to that of the liberals in the *zemstvos* 'interceding' with the autocracy on behalf of the people. Substituting themselves for the proletariat, the leading Social Democratic groups do not understand that it is just as necessary to lead the proletariat to 'show' its class will in relation to the liberal and radical democratic movement as to lead it to demonstrate its revolutionary-democratic will against the autocracy . . .

History, having placed a definite task on the agenda, is observing us sharply. For good or ill (more for ill), we are leading the masses to revolution, awakening in them the most elementary political instincts. But in so far as we have to deal with a more complex task – transforming these 'instincts' into conscious aspirations of a working class which is determining itself politically – we tend to resort to the short-cuts and over-simplifications of 'thinking-for-others' and 'substitutionism'. In the internal politics of the party these methods lead, as we shall see below, to the party organisation 'substituting' itself for the party, the Central Committee substituting itself for the party organisation, and finally the dictator substituting himself for the Central Committee . . .

Without fear of betraying my 'bourgeois intellectual psychology', I affirm first-of-all that the conditions which impel the proletariat into concerted, collective struggle are not to be found in the factory but in the general social conditions of its existence; and further, that the objective conditions and the conscious discipline of political action, there is a long road of struggle, errors, education – not the 'school of the factory' but the school of political life, in which the Russian proletariat penetrates only under the leadership – good or bad – of the social democratic intelligentsia; and reaffirm that the Russian proletariat, in which we have barely begun to develop political self-activity, is not yet able – unfortunately for it and fortunately for Messrs. candidates for 'dictatorship' – to give lessons in discipline to its 'intelligentsia', whatever the training the factory gives him in 'common work resulting from highly developed technique'. Without the least fear of giving away my 'bourgeois intellectual psychology', I even declare my complete solidarity with the idea that 'the technical submission of the worker to the uniform rhythm of the work tool ("discipline based on work in common resulting from highly developed technique"), and the particular composition of the collective worker as individuals of both sexes and ages, creates a barracks discipline (barracks, not politically conscious discipline!) perfectly in line with the factory regime.' (Capital) . . .

Naturally, 'highly technically developed production' creates the material conditions for the political development and sense of discipline of the proletariat, just as in general capitalism creates the premises of socialism. But factory discipline is as little identical with political, revolutionary discipline of the proletariat as capitalism is to socialism . . . The barracks regime could never be the regime of our party, no more than the factory could be its model.

*Source*: L. Trotsky, *Our Political Tasks* (London: New Park Publications, 1979), pp. 50–56, 72–77, 103–04.

*RESULTS AND PROSPECTS* (1906)                     **Document 3**

In the event of a decisive victory of the revolution, power will pass into the hands of that class which plays a leading role in the struggle – in other words, into the hands of the proletariat. Let us say at once that this by no means precludes revolutionary representatives of non-proletarian social groups entering the government. They can and should be in the government: a sound policy will compel the proletariat to call to power the influential leaders of the urban petty-bourgeoisie, of the intellectuals and of the peasantry . . .

When we speak of a workers' government we have in view a government in which the working-class representatives dominate and lead. The proletariat, in order to consolidate its power, cannot but widen the base of the revolution. Many sections of the working masses, particularly in the countryside, will be drawn into the revolution and become politically organized only after the advance-guard of the revolution, the urban proletariat, stands at the helm of state. Revolutionary agitation and organization will then be conducted with the help of state resources. The legislative power itself will become a powerful instrument for revolutionizing the masses. The nature of our social-historical relations, which lays the whole burden of the bourgeois revolution upon the shoulders of the proletariat, will not only create tremendous difficulties for the workers' government but, in the first period of its existence at any rate, will also give it invaluable advantages. This will affect the relations between the proletariat and the peasantry . . .

The proletariat in power will stand before the peasants as the class which has emancipated it. The domination of the proletariat will mean not only democratic equality, free self-government, the transference of the whole burden of taxation to the rich classes, the dissolution of the standing army in the armed people and the abolition of compulsory church imposts, but also recognition of all revolutionary changes (expropriations) in land relationships carried out by the peasants. The proletariat will make these changes the starting-point for further state measures in agriculture . . .

The proletariat can only achieve power by relying upon a national upsurge and national enthusiasm. The proletariat will enter the government as the revolutionary representative of the nation, as the recognized national leader in the struggle against absolutism and feudal barbarism . . . [However,] every passing day will deepen the policy of the proletariat in power, and more and more define its class character. Side by side with that, the revolutionary ties between the proletariat and the nation will be broken, the class disintegration of the peasantry will assume political form, and the antagonism between the component sections will grow in proportion as the policy of the workers' government defines itself, ceasing to be a general-democratic and becoming a class policy . . . The proletariat will find itself compelled to carry the class struggle into the villages and in this manner destroy that community of interest which is undoubtedly to be found among all peasants . . . From the very first moment after its taking power, the proletariat will have to find support in the antagonisms between the village poor and the village rich . . . The cooling-off of the peasantry, its political passivity, and all the more the active opposition of its upper sections, cannot but have an influence on a section of intellectuals and the petty-bourgeoisie of the towns. Thus the more definite and determined the policy of the proletariat in power becomes, the narrower and more shaky does the ground beneath its feet become . . . [creating] terrible difficulties for the consolidation of the revolutionary policy of the proletariat in power . . .

Without the direct State support of the European proletariat the working class of Russia cannot remain in power and convert its temporary domination into a lasting socialistic dictatorship. Of this there cannot for one moment be any doubt. But on the other hand there cannot be any doubt that a socialist revolution in the West will enable us directly to convert the temporary domination of the working class into a socialist dictatorship.

If the Russian proletariat, having temporarily obtained power, does not on its own initiative carry the revolution on to European soil, it will be compelled to do so by the forces of European feudal-bourgeois reaction. Of course it would be idle at this moment to determine the methods by which the Russian revolution will throw itself against old capitalist Europe. These methods may reveal themselves quite unexpectedly. Let us take the example of Poland as a link between the revolutionary East and the revolutionary West, although we take this as an illustration of our idea rather than as an actual prediction.

The triumph of the revolution in Russia will mean the inevitable victory of the revolution in Poland. It is not difficult to imagine that the existence of a revolutionary regime in the ten provinces of Russian Poland must lead to the revolt of Galicia and Poznan. The Hohenzollern and Habsburg Governments will reply to this by sending military forces to the Polish frontier in order then to cross it for the purpose of crushing their enemy at his very centre – Warsaw. It is quite clear that the Russian revolution cannot leave its Western advance-guard in the hands of the Prusso-Austrian soldiery. War against the governments of Wilhelm II and Franz Josef under such circumstances would become an act of self-defence on the part of the revolutionary government of Russia . . .

Left to its own resources, the working class of Russia will inevitably be crushed by the counter-revolution the moment the peasantry turns its back on it. It will have no alternative but to link the fate of its political rule, and, hence, the fate of the whole Russian revolution, with the fate of the socialist revolution in Europe.

*Source*: L. Trotsky, *The Permanent Revolution and Results and Prospects* (New York: Pathfinder Press, 1969), pp. 69–77, 105–15.

**Document 4**   *PRAVDA* NO. 2 (17–30 DECEMBER 1908)

For the Struggle with Unemployment and Hunger:

In the complex and stubborn struggle with the calamities produced by the crisis and unemployment, Social Democrat workers are called to stand in the first ranks. They must comprise the heart and the brain of every proletarian organisation. At the most difficult and dangerous post, where the onslaught of the enemy is most ferocious, that is where the proletarian Social Democrat should stand. He who gives most will be rewarded most. Stand by us, comrades! In the trade unions, the co-operatives and the Social Democratic Party organisations.

Collect detailed information about unemployment, about the needs of workers and peasants, publish them in proclamations and legal and illegal newspapers. Send them to *Pravda*. Inform your workers' deputies in the State Duma.

And, in the face of the Tsar's government and Stolypin's Duma, allow the Workers' Social Democrat Group to push through the urgent demands of the working masses in both town and countryside. Let the ears of the black Duma's struggle resound to the threatening voice of the hungry millions.

**Document 5**   *PRAVDA* NO. 16 (24 SEPTEMBER 1910)

Towards Recovery

The first stage of industrial recovery is when workers are presented with the greatest opportunity to make the broadest conquests, everything is still before them. It should become, it will become, a period for planned economic struggle, for the persistent organisation of trade unions and the trade union press. Follow the state of industry and the mood of the masses closely; don't allow burgeoning energy to be dissipated in wildcat strikes; formulate demands carefully; choose the moment for open struggle; lead those strikes; organise mutual support and sympathy actions from other factories, towns, people and professionals; unite the trade unions and the party – these are the vital tasks of worker Social Democrats in the coming period. Relying on the strengthening consciousness of the masses and the growth of the trade unions, we can develop widespread agitation around the demand for the legal protection of labour – and in the centre of that agitation, led jointly by the party and the trade unions, will be, quite naturally, the Duma Group.

*PRAVDA* NOS. 18–19 (29 JANUARY/11 FEBRUARY 1911)          **Document 6**

The Situation in the Country and Our Tasks:

For us, the elections [to the Fourth State Duma] are above all a unique opportunity to mobilise all the conscious workers in the country . . . The elections are not a local, but an all-Russian concern. It is essential to strain every sinew to create an all-party apparatus. There is just one path to this, the one indicated by the last general meeting of the Central Committee of our party one year ago: to call a party conference. Serious preparatory work for a conference will link together the scattered parts into a new whole, and formulate a general programme of action acceptable to all tendencies of party thought, it will work out the slogans for the electoral campaign and strengthen our organisational apparatus. We cannot delay the elections to the Fourth Duma, they are fixed and they impose on our party a serious political challenge. It is impossible, therefore, to kick into the long grass the work on preparing a conference. Work must begin at once, from every angle at the same time.

*HISTORY OF THE RUSSIAN REVOLUTION* (1932)          **Document 7**

No practical plan of insurrection, even tentative, was sketched out in the session of the 10th. But without introducing the fact into the resolution, it was agreed that the insurrection should precede the Congress of Soviets and begin, if possible, not later than 15 October . . . Lenin was alarmed by the delay, and insisted upon the calling of a new meeting of the Central Committee with representatives from the more important branches of party work in the capital. It was at this conference, held on the 16th in the outskirts of the city, in Lesnoi, that Zinoviev and Kamenev advanced the arguments for revoking the old date [agreed on the 10th] and against naming a new [date for the insurrection] . . .

Trotsky was not present at this meeting. During those same hours he was carrying through the Soviet the resolution on the Military Revolutionary Committee. But the point of view which had firmly crystallised in Smolny during the past days was defended by Krylenko, who had just been conducting hand in hand with Trotsky and Antonov-Ovseenko the Northern Regional Congress of Soviets. Krylenko had no doubt that 'the water is boiling hard enough'. To take back the resolution in favour of insurrection 'would be the greatest possible mistake'. He disagreed with Lenin, however, 'on the question who shall begin it and how it shall begin'. To set the date of the insurrection definitely now is still inexpedient. 'But the question of the removal of the troops is just that fighting issue upon which the struggle is taking place . . . The attack upon us is thus already a fact, and this we make use of . . . It is not necessary to worry about who shall begin, for the thing is already begun.' Krylenko was expounding and defending the policy laid down by the Military Revolutionary Committee and the Garrison Conference. It was along this road that the insurrection continued to develop . . .

Within the general frame of Lenin's formula, which united the majority of the Central Committee, there arose subordinate, but very important, questions: How on the basis of the ripened political situation are we to approach the insurrection? How to find a bridge from the politics to the technique of revolution? And how to lead the masses along that bridge?

*Source*: L. Trotsky, *History of the Russian Revolution* (London: Sphere, 1965), vol. III, pp. 148–49.

**Document 8**     SPEECH TO THE SOVIET EXECUTIVE (8 DECEMBER 1917)

The armistice has made a breach in the war. The gunfire has ceased and everyone is nervously waiting to see how the Soviet Government will deal with the Hohenzollern and Habsburg imperialists. You must support us in treating them as foes of freedom, in ensuring that not one iota of this freedom is sacrificed to imperialism . . . We are becoming more and more convinced that peace talks will be a powerful weapon in the hands of other peoples in their struggle for peace.

If we are mistaken, if Europe continues to be silent as the grave, and if this silence gives Wilhelm the chance to attack us and to dictate his terms to us, terms which would insult the revolutionary dignity of our country, then I am not sure whether, given our shattered economy and the general chaos (the result of the war and internal strife), we could fight.

I think, however, that we could do so. For our lives, for our revolutionary honour, we would fight to the last drop of our blood . . . [raising] an army of soldiers and Red Guardsmen, strong in its revolutionary enthusiasm.

*Source*: J. L. H. Keep (ed.), *The Debate on Soviet Power* (Oxford: Oxford University Press, 1979) p. 187.

**Document 9**     STATEMENT BY TROTSKY AT THE BREST-LITOVSK PEACE CONFERENCE ON RUSSIA'S WITHDRAWAL FROM THE WAR (28 JANUARY 1918)

We have heard the reports of our representatives on the territorial sub-commission and, after prolonged discussion and a thorough examination of the question, we have come to the conclusion that the hour of decision has struck. The peoples are impatiently awaiting the results of the peace negotiations at Brest-Litovsk. They are asking, when will there be an end to this unparalleled self-destruction of humanity provoked by the selfish and ambitious ruling classes of all countries? If ever the war was being fought in self-defence, that has long ceased to be true for either side. When Great Britain seizes African colonies, Baghdad and Jerusalem, that is no longer a war of self-defence; when Germany occupies Serbia, Belgium, Poland, Lithuania and Romania, and seizes the Moon Islands, that too is not a war of defence. That is a struggle for the partition of the world. Now it is clear, clearer than ever before.

We do not wish to take part any longer in this purely imperialist war, in which the claims of the propertied classes are being paid in blood. We are as implacably opposed to the imperialism of one camp as to the other, and we are no longer willing to shed the blood of our soldiers to defend the interests of one imperialist side against the other.

While awaiting the time, which we hope is not far off, when the oppressed working classes of all countries will take power into their own hands, as the working people of Russia have done, we are withdrawing our army and our people from the war. Our peasant-soldiers must return to their land, so that they can this spring cultivate the soil which the revolution took from the landlords and gave to the peasants. Our workmen-soldiers must return to the workshops to produce there not weapons of destruction, but tools for creative labour, and together with the peasants build a new socialist economy.

We are withdrawing from the war. We are informing all peoples and all governments of this. We are issuing orders for the complete demobilization of our armies now confronting the German, Austro-Hungarian, Turkish and Bulgarian troops. We expect and firmly believe that other peoples will soon follow our example. At the same time we declare that the terms of peace proposed by the governments of Germany and Austria-Hungary are basically opposed to the interests of all peoples. These terms will be rejected by the working masses of all countries, including even the peoples of Austria-Hungary and Germany. The peoples of Poland, Ukraine, Lithuania, Courland [Latvia] and Estonia regard these conditions as a violation of their will, while for the Russian people themselves they represent a permanent threat. The popular masses of the entire world, guided by political consciousness or by moral instinct, reject these conditions, in expectation of the day when the working classes of all countries will establish their own standards of peaceful coexistence and friendly co-operation of peoples. We refuse to give our sanction to the conditions which German and Austro-Hungarian imperialism writes with the sword on the body of living peoples. We cannot put the signature of the Russian revolution to conditions which carry with them oppression, misfortune, and misery to millions of human beings.

The Governments of Germany and Austria-Hungary want to rule over lands and peoples by the right of armed conquest. Let them do their work openly. We cannot approve violence. We are withdrawing from the war but we are compelled to refuse to sign the treaty of peace. In connection with this statement, I am handing to the joint delegations the following written and signed declaration:

> In the name of the Council of People's Commissars, the Government of the Russian Federative Republic informs the Governments and peoples of the countries at war with us, and of the Allied and neutral countries that, while refusing to sign an annexationist peace, Russia, for its part, declares the state of war with Germany, Austria-Hungary, Bulgaria and Turkey at an end. At the same time, an order is being given for the complete demobilization of the Russian troops along the entire front.

*Source*: E. Acton and T. Stableford (eds), *The Soviet Union: A Documentary History* (Exeter: University of Exeter Press, 1988), vol. I, pp. 78–79.

**Document 10**    TROTSKY TO LENIN AND SKLYANSKII (TROTSKY'S DEPUTY) (7–9 AUGUST 1918)

The slow rate of arrival of reinforcements constituted the principal, direct cause of the Kazan catastrophe. We promised to supply reinforcements. They were expected to be forthcoming. Those concerned put their hope not so much in their own forces as in the reinforcements that had been promised them. The reinforcements did not get there in time for the decisive moment, and this created a state of psychological collapse.

It is essential to redouble efforts towards assuring the onward transit of units to this area. They should be routed to Nizhnyi Novgorod and steps taken to ensure against any hold up in Moscow.

It is essential to mobilise gunners, engineers and non-commissioned officers as quickly as possible. Make it clear that non-commissioned officers will receive not only pay, but also the full soldier's issue.

Vācietis demands that a strategic reserve be created in Vyatka. Please take action.

The lack of revolvers creates an impossible state of affairs at the front. There is no hope of maintaining discipline without having revolvers.

The sort of Communists that need to be sent here are those who know how to obey orders and are prepared to undergo deprivations and ready to lay down their lives. Lightweight agitators are not needed here.

Dispatch one good band to Sviyazhsk.

*Source*: J. M. Meijer (ed.), *The Trotsky Papers* (The Hague: Mouton and Co., 1964), vol. I, pp. 69–71.

TROTSKY TO LENIN (13 AUGUST 1918)                    **Document 11**

Stubborn fighting is in progress here. To date the numbers of those killed are to be counted in tens, those wounded in hundreds. On our side we have a certain numerical preponderance in artillery. On his side the enemy is superior in organisation and in the accuracy of his fire. The allegation that our men do not want to fight is a lie. Wherever there is a good or tolerably good commander and good commissars, the soldiers fight. The presence of workers who are Communists is most beneficial. There are many supremely devoted and courageous men among them. When the Commander wants to say that such and such a post is occupied by a reliable person, he says: I have got a Communist there. I am not going to attempt to predict what tomorrow may bring. But I have no doubt of victory.

*Source*: J. M. Meijer (ed.), *The Trotsky Papers*, vol. I, p. 81.

TROTSKY TO LENIN (23 AUGUST 1918)                    **Document 12**

As far as Larin's proposal to replace General Staff officers by Communists is concerned, in the first place it runs counter to the first proposal you put forward [to make Vācietis Commander-in-Chief], since your candidate is not a Communist and those whom he selects to be at his side are not Communists, but men with military training and combat experience. Many of them commit acts of treachery. But on the railways, too, instances of sabotage are in evidence in the routing of troop trains. Yet nobody suggests replacing railway engineers by Communists. I consider Larin's proposal as being utterly worthless.

The conditions are now being created whereby we can carry out a radical weeding-out among officers: on the one hand concentration camps, and, on the other, active service on the Eastern Front. Catastrophic measures such as that suggested by Larin can only be dictated by panic . . . It is essential to make the entire military hierarchy more compact and get rid of the ballast by means of extracting those General Staff officers that are efficient and loyal to us and not on any account by means of replacing them with Party ignoramuses.

*Source*: J. M. Meijer (ed.), *The Trotsky Papers*, vol. I, p. 107.

TROTSKY TO SVERDLOV AND LENIN (4 OCTOBER 1918)                    **Document 13**

I categorically insist on Stalin's recall. Things are going from bad to worse on the Tsaritsyn Front, despite the superabundance of military forces. Voroshilov is able to command a regiment, but not an army of 50,000 men. Nonetheless I will retain him as commander of the 10th Tsaritsyn Army on condition that he places himself under the orders of the Commander of the Southern Front, Sytin. Right up to this day the Tsaritsyn people have failed to send even operational reports to Kozlov. I had required them to submit operational and intelligence reports twice daily. If this is not carried out tomorrow I shall commit Voroshilov and Minin for trial and announce this in an army order. So long as Stalin and Minin remain in Tsaritsyn, according to the constitution of the Military Revolutionary Council they merely enjoy the rights of members of the Military Revolutionary Council of the 10th Army. For the purpose of launching an attack there remains only a short while before the autumn weather makes the roads impassable, when there will be no through road here either on foot or on horseback. Operations in strength are impossible without coordination of operations with Tsaritsyn. There is no time for diplomatic negotiations. Tsaritsyn must either obey orders or get out of the way. We have a colossal superiority of forces but total anarchy at the top. This can be put right within 24 hours given firm and resolute support your end. In any event this is the only course of action that I can envisage.

*Source*: J. M. Meijer (ed.), *The Trotsky Papers*, vol. I, pp. 135–37.

**Document 14**　　TROTSKY TO LENIN (13 OCTOBER 1918)

In view of changed circumstances, a certain section of the officer class is displaying its readiness to work in the service of the Soviets. On this I propose the following: in those cases where there are no direct, serious charges against the arrested officers, that the question be put to them: do they agree to serve the Red Army and the Red Fleet. That, in the event of an affirmative answer, they be put at my disposal. That, at the same time, their family position be ascertained and they be warned that, in the event of treachery or desertion to the enemy's camp on their part their families will be arrested.

*Source*: J. M. Meijer (ed.), *The Trotsky Papers*, vol. I, p. 149.

**Document 15**　　TROTSKY TO THE CENTRAL COMMITTEE (25 DECEMBER 1918)

Dear Comrades,

The discontent of certain elements in the Party with the general policy of the War Department has found expression in an article by a member of the Central

Executive Committee, Comrade A. Kamenskii in issue No. 281 of the central organ of our Party, *Pravda*. The article contains a wholesale denunciation of the use of military specialists . . . [It is true] I sent off a telegram to Comrades Lashevich and Smilga in which I drew their attention to the desertion of officers and to the total absence of any reports on this subject from the commissars concerned, who had failed to keep any check or to administer punishment, and I concluded the telegram with a phrase to the effect that commissars who let White Guard supporters slip through their hands should be shot. It stands to reason that this was not an order for the shooting of Zalutskii and Bakaev . . . It could never have occurred to me that a legend might arise out of this to the effect that only the steadfastness of Smilga had saved two of the best comrades from the shooting I had decreed for them, 'as had happened to Panteleev'. Panteleev was shot in accordance with the court's findings, and I had appointed the court not for the purpose of trying Panteleev – I did not know of his presence among the deserters, nor his name – but to try the deserters who had been captured aboard the steamship, and the court sentenced Panteleev to be shot along with the others. As far as I remember, there have been no other cases of commissars being shot . . .

In view of the foregoing, I ask the Central Committee:

To declare publicly as to whether the policy of the War Department is my personal policy, the policy of some group or other, or the policy of our Party as a whole.

To establish for the benefit of the public opinion of the entire Party the grounds which Comrade Kamenskii had for his assertion about the shooting of the best comrades without trial.

*Source*: J. M. Meijer (ed.), *The Trotsky Papers*, vol. I, p. 155.

TROTSKY TO THE CENTRAL COMMITTEE (AFTER 25 MARCH 1919)          **Document 16**

Dear Comrades,

I have received the Central Committee decree of 25 March based on the written report of Comrade Zinoviev. I consider it essential to set out the following observations on this subject.

For practical purposes, the principles formulated by the Commission of the Congress do not contain anything that contradicts the policy of the War Department, such as it has been carried out to date with the approval of the CC. It is necessary merely to say that these principles are formulated in supremely general and vague terms, and part of them are based on a misunderstanding.

1) Absolutely no indication is given as to the direction in which the reorganisation of Field Headquarters is to be carried out and in what sense closer contact with the fronts is postulated. Up to now the burden of the remonstrances coming from the front has, on the contrary, been predominantly that the central command interferes in too detailed a fashion in the operations of the fronts.

2) The regularisation of the work of the Military Revolutionary Council of the Republic, which is what the following clause demands, is also vague. The comrades who promoted remonstrances to this effect have demanded on more than one occasion that I personally, as Chairman of the Military Revolutionary Council, should not tour the fronts but sit at the centre. Has the Congress Commission this form of regularisation in mind? Is this the CC's understanding of this question?

3) The proper ordering of the work of the All-Russian General Staff and the strengthening of Party representation on it is unquestionably a desirable measure. I have talked this subject over with Comrade Sverdlov more than once. We were, regrettably, unable to select suitable Party workers for this work. On certain occasions Comrade Sverdlov put forward the names of Comrade Smilga and Comrade Lashevich as candidates.

4) The summoning of periodic conferences of responsible Party representatives working at the front is, of course, a useful measure, though it is precisely the simultaneous recall from the front of the most responsible Party workers that is scarcely possible; yet such conferences presuppose the simultaneous recall of the most responsible Party workers – conferences of any other type would hardly yield any practical result.

5) 'A general enquiry of Party workers at the front as to how far the question of the uniform and insignia for commander personnel has been satisfactorily settled.' This clause is based on a misunderstanding. We have no commander personnel insignia. We do have insignia as such. One and the same insignia for the Red Army private, the Commissar and the Commander. Is clause 5 meant to be understood in the sense that insignia are from now on to be retained only for commander personnel, or did the Commission simply lack information on the subject of the awarding of insignia?

Despite the obscurities and evident misunderstandings noted above, the five clauses I have listed do not contain anything which would run counter to military policy as it has taken shape. The same has to be said with regard to the twelve clauses contained in the supplementary resolution of the Congress that deal with practical measures. All these clauses amount either to merely underlining measures that either have long since been or are being taken, or to proposals for organisational changes that in no way constitute matters of principle.

But all these practical proposals are set out by the CC in the light of Comrade Zinoviev's report. This report lays down a special point of view on the practical proposals mentioned above and has, as it were, to fix some sort of new line of conduct.

Comrade Zinoviev, in his assessment of the opposition, gives it as consisting of two groups; the first group being a body of offended gentry who count for little; the second being a very important and solid group which is wholly in agreement with us on the questions of the partisan movement and military specialists but extremely dissatisfied with my attitude towards Communists working in the army. Comrade Zinoviev demands some sort of radical change in attitude towards Communists working in the army and says straight out that 'without this no progress will be made'. He ends his report with the words: 'the support with which my report has met in the CC gives me the assurance that we shall rapidly put this matter right'.

I regard Comrade Zinoviev's report as entirely incorrect and, if it is really to be the foundation for a new line of conduct, I am obliged to qualify Comrade Zinoviev's trend as being an extremely dangerous one, one that simply amounts to a modified reflection of that very same opposition, the meaning and composition of which Comrade Zinoviev has wrongly assessed.

*Source*: J. M. Meijer (ed.), *The Trotsky Papers*, vol. I, pp. 328–30.

*A LETTER TO THE MIDDLE PEASANTS* (6 FEBRUARY 1919)        **Document 17**

An agitation is being carried on among the peasants and in the Red Army, against the Soviet power and its policy in respect of food and of military affairs. This is quite natural, because the Soviet power has deprived all exploiters and, in particular, the village kulaks, of their former extensive privileges. It is also not surprising if counter-revolutionary agitators resort to all sorts of tricks and stratagems, trying to confuse the more backward, less informed peasants and Red Army men. Recently, counter-revolutionary agitators have widely circulated among the masses a rumour to the effect that there are very big disagreements among the central Soviet authorities: Comrade Lenin, they say, is for the middle peasants, whereas Trotsky, according to this story, is an irreconcilable enemy of the middle peasants, and even incites the army against them! Any worker who is at all serious-minded and politically experienced, any thinking peasant, cannot but realise that this rumour is a monstrous lie . . .

I have no differences with Comrade Lenin where the middle peasants are concerned. Our Communist Party is the party of the proletariat and the village labourers, the poor peasants. The rural kulaks are, for us, enemies just like the town bourgeoisie. The middle peasants stand between the rural proletariat, on the one side, and the kulaks, on the other. One wing of the middle peasants is close to the proletariat while the other one passes over imperceptibly into kulak status. Is the peasant of middling status our enemy or our friend? By virtue of his whole situation and all his interests, the middle peasant, provided he has not been duped by kulaks' lies, ought to be our friend. Only the Soviet power finally did away with the landlords' yoke and gave the land to the peasants, among whom middle peasants predominate. Only the Soviet power is conducting and will continue to conduct a war of extermination against the kulaks, who are trying to get into their clutches the land and the means of agricultural production, robbing the middle peasants and depriving them completely of their share . . .

Only fools or scoundrels can say that the Red Army has been formed to oppose the middle peasants . . .

Being unready to appear with their true face, the White Guards, the enemies of the working people, have repainted themselves as Left SRs, or else they incite Left SR idiots and hysterical women against the Soviet power. The wretched clique of adventurers and political rogues who call themselves the Left SR party are now the principal centre from which come lies and slanders for duping the more backward sections of the population. It is mainly Left SR agitators who are spreading the false story about the Red Army being formed to fight the middle peasants.

*Source*: J. M. Meijer (ed.), *The Trotsky Papers*, vol. I, pp. 314–17.

**Document 18**   *CRIMINAL DEMAGOGY* (17 JULY 1919)

In the town of Sumy, that is, in the zone adjacent to the front, a newspaper called *Krasnaya Zvezda* is published, declaring itself to be the organ of the Kharkov Committee of the Bolshevik-Communists and of the political administration of the Kharkov Military District. There appeared in this paper's issue of 10 July 1919 a criminally demagogic article entitled: *Military specialists – or Red commanders?*

'We must consider as one of the main causes of the break-up of the Southern front,' says the article, 'the treachery of the commanding personnel, who went over in whole "packs" from the Red Army to Denikin.' This entire sentence is a monstrous lie . . .

The Southern front has suffered big defeats as a result of the twofold and threefold superiority of numbers on the part of the enemy . . . The writer alleges that commanders in all parts of the Southern front went over to Denikin in packs, whereas in fact, commanders went over to Denikin only on these very small sectors of the Southern front where the entire organisation was worthless, where there was no order among the political workers, but instead confusion and demagogy reigned . . .

Towards the end of this article it is said: 'We must understand the lesson given to us by the catastrophe (and how else can one describe the break-up of the Southern front?) which has befallen us in the struggle against Denikin! We must have the courage to recognise our previous mistakes. Our immediate slogan must be: "Long Live the Red Commander!"' Here again we see a criminally demagogic distortion of the facts in the interests of a lying argument . . . It is true that in the Kharkov sector a considerable number of betrayals occurred. But we have often observed on other fronts as well, during their infancy, how the work of sham-revolutionary demagogues has been complemented by treachery on the part of commanders. The overwhelming majority of the officers of the old army lacked even elementary political education. They easily lost their bearings when the slightest change occurred in the political situation. The prejudices of the petty-bourgeois milieu were strong among them. But at the same time our Party programme, which is opposed by the demagogues of *Krasnaya Zvezda*, speaks clearly and precisely of the methods by which the working class can and must make use of the experience of the military specialists: (1) general leadership of the life of the army and supervision of loyal specialists to be concentrated in the hands of organised representatives of the working masses: (2) relations of comradely collaboration to be established with the military specialists, creating conditions for them in which they can develop their powers.

There are Communists of a poor sort who treat military specialists as though they were accused persons, or simply persons under arrest, imagining that this is how to safeguard the interests of the revolution. Actually, in this way they impel unstable, wavering members of the commanding personnel to seek safety in Denikin's camp.

Posts of command in parts of the Kharkov sector and other administrative positions were given to military specialists whose families were resident in Kharkov. When Kharkov was captured, these 'specialists' preferred to remain with their families . . . How prudent was it to put them in a situation where the place of residence of their own families would incline them towards going over to the enemy's camp? Whose fault was that? The fault of the local Soviet military organisation . . .

We must and will keep a sharp look-out for the activity of counter-revolutionary scoundrels who have penetrated our ranks. But at the same time we shall not allow unbalanced windbags and demagogues to hinder serious Party workers in their task of building a properly organised army, especially by employing qualified commanders on a wide scale . . . The army needs serious, responsible political workers. There is no place among them for demagogues.

*Source*: J. M. Meijer (ed.), *The Trotsky Papers*, vol. I, p. 597.

**Document 19**    TROTSKY TO THE CENTRAL COMMITTEE (TELEGRAM, 17 FEBRUARY 1920)

I consider it essential to proclaim martial law in the Ural coal-mines. At the Chelyabinsk mines out of 3,500 fewer than 2,000 are turning up for work. The effort they put into the work is negligible. At other mines the situation is about the same. On this question the opposition of local 'trade-unionists', and indeed of those at the centre too, must be overcome.

TROTSKY TO THE CENTRAL COMMITTEE (A FURTHER TELEGRAM, ALSO 17 FEBRUARY 1920)

The People's Commissariat of Supply must be compelled, no later than to-day, to rescind the ban on moving consignments of provisions and fodder from one province to another within the zone of operations of the First Army. Provisions and fodder which are not brought out cannot even be used to meet the needs of the Urals. A stop must be put to this monstrous bureaucracy. The Council of the Labour Army consists of sufficiently senior Party workers for it not to start indulging in experiments.

*Source*: J. M. Meijer (ed.), *The Trotsky Papers*, vol. II, pp. 47, 75.

**Document 20**    REPORT TO THE THIRD CONGRESS OF TRADE UNIONS (9 APRIL 1920)

Comrades! The internal civil war is coming to an end . . . History is bringing us face to face in real earnest with our fundamental task – organising labour on new social foundations. The organisation of labour is, in its essence, the organisation of the new society: every form of society known to history is basically a particular organisation of labour. Whereas every past society was an organisation of labour in the interests of a minority, which organised its own state coercion of the overwhelming majority of the working people, we are making the first attempt in world history to organise labour in the interests of the working majority itself. This, however, does not rule out the element of compulsion in all its forms, from the most gentle to the extremely severe. The element of obligation, of state compulsion, not only does not disappear from the historical scene, but, on the contrary, will still play, for a consider-able period, an extremely big role . . . Labour service is inscribed in our Constitution and in our Labour Code. But hitherto it has remained only a principle. Its application has always had a casual, partial, episodic character. Only now, when we have been brought right up against the problems of reviving the country economically, have the problems of labour service confronted us in full concreteness. The only solution to our economic difficulties which is correct both from the standpoint of principle and also in practice is to see the entire population of the country as a reservoir of the labour-power we need – an almost inexhaustible reservoir – and to introduce strict order into the work of registering, mobilising and utilising it.

How, in practice, are we to set about getting hold of labour power on the basis of labour service?

Hitherto, only the War Commissariat has had experience in the sphere of the registration, mobilisation, formation and transference from one place to another of large masses of people. These technical methods and practices were, to a considerable extent, inherited by our War Commissariat from the past. In the economic sphere there is no such heritage, since what operated previously in that sphere was the principle of private rights, and labour-power made its way from the market to each enterprise separately. It is consequently natural that, if so obliged, we should, at least during the initial period, make extensive use of the apparatus of the War Commissariat for labour mobilisation.

We have set up special organs for the implementation of labour service at the centre and in the localities: in the provinces, districts and parishes we already have labour service committees at work. They rely, for the most part, on the central and local organs of the War Commissariat. Our economic centres – the Supreme Economic Council, the People's Commissariat of Agriculture, the People's Commissariat of Transport, the People's Commissariat of Food – draw up estimates of the amount of labour-power they require. The Chief Committee on Labour Service receives these estimates, co-ordinates them, relates them to the local sources of labour-power, gives corresponding directions to its local organs, and through these organs carries out labour mobilisations. Within the boundaries of regions, provinces and districts, the local organs perform this work independently, so as to satisfy local economic requirements.

All this organisation exists at present only in outline. It is still extremely imperfect. But the course we have adopted is unquestionably the right one . . .

The militarisation of labour

The introduction of labour service is inconceivable without the application, to a greater or less degree, of methods of militarising labour. This term brings us at once into the realm of the biggest superstitions and outcries from the opposition.

To understand what militarisation of labour means in a workers' state, and what its methods are, one needs to appreciate how it was that the army itself was militarised, for, as we all remember, in its early days the army did not at all possess the necessary 'military' qualities. During these two years we mobilised for the Red Army nearly as many soldiers as there are members in our trade unions. But the members of the trade unions are workers, whereas in the army workers constitute about 15 per cent, the rest being a mass of peasants. And yet we can have no doubt that the real builders and 'militarisers' of the Red Army have been the advanced workers, brought forward by the Party and the trade-union organisation. Whenever the situation at the front was difficult, whenever the freshly mobilised mass of peasants failed to display sufficient staunchness, we turned, on the one hand, to the Central Committee of the Communist Party, and, on the other, to the Presidium of the All-Russia Trade-Union Council. From both of these sources advanced workers were sent to the front, and there they built the Red Army after their own image and likeness-educating, tempering and militarising the peasant mass. This fact must be kept in mind today, with all possible clearness, because it throws the proper light on the very meaning of militarisation under the conditions of a workers' and peasants' state. The militarisation of labour has more than once been proclaimed as a watchword, and realised in particular branches of the economy, in bourgeois countries both in the West and here, under Tsardom. But our militarisation differs from those experiments by its aims and its methods, just as the conscious proletariat, organised for emancipation, differs from the conscious bourgeoisie, organised for exploitation.

From the confusion, half-conscious and half-intentional, between the historical forms of proletarian, socialist militarisation and bourgeois militarisation spring most of the prejudices, mistakes, protests and outcries on this subject. It is on such a confusion that the whole position of the Mensheviks, our Russian Kautskyites, is based, as it was expressed in their resolution on matters of principle that was moved at the current [Third All-Russian] Trade Union Congress . . .

History has known slave labour. History has known serf labour. History has known the regulated labour of the mediaeval guilds. Throughout the world there now prevails wage-labour, which the yellow journalists of all countries counterpoise, as the highest form of freedom, to Soviet 'slavery'. We, on the contrary, counterpoise to the capitalist slavery socially regulated labour on the basis of an economic plan, obligatory for the whole people and, therefore, compulsory for every worker in the country. Without this we cannot even think of the transition to socialism. The element of material, physical compulsion may be greater or less: that depends on many conditions – on the level of wealth or poverty of a given country, on its heritage from the past, on its cultural level, on the state of transport and the administrative apparatus, and so on. But obligation, and, consequently, compulsion, is a necessary condition for bridling bourgeois anarchy, socialising the means of production and labour, and reconstructing the economy on the basis of a single plan . . .

Why do we speak of militarisation? This is, of course, only an analogy, but an analogy very rich in content. No social organisation except the army has ever considered itself justified in subjecting citizens to itself to such a degree, and controlling them by its will in every aspect, as the state of the proletarian dictatorship considers itself justified in doing, and does. Only the army – just because it used to decide, in its own way, questions of the life or death of nations, states and ruling classes – was endowed with the power to demand from each and everyone complete submission to its tasks, purposes, regulations and orders. And it achieved this the more completely the more the tasks of military organisation coincided with the requirements of social development . . .

While a planned economy is inconceivable without labour service, the latter is unrealisable without eliminating the fiction of freedom of labour, without substituting for this the principle of obligation, which is reinforced by actual compulsion . . . Without labour service, without the power to give orders and demand that they be carried out, the trade unions will be transformed into a mere form without content, for the socialist state which is being built needs trade unions not for a struggle for better conditions of labour – that is a task for the social and state organisation as a whole – but in order to organise the working class for production.

*Source*: L. Trotsky, *How the Revolution Armed* (London: New Park Publications, 1979–81), vol. III, pp. 98–108.

TROTSKY TO THE CENTRAL COMMITTEE PLENUM (7 AUGUST 1921)     **Document 21**

New economic policy guidelines have been laid down at the tenth Party Congress and at the All-Russian Party Conference. It must, however, be stated that the carrying out of the directives laid down in the sphere of direct economic activity on the part of Soviet organs, the adoption of appropriate decrees and the mastering of the new premises of economic policy on the part of Party and Soviet workers at large is being achieved too slowly and is not proceeding at the pace required by the fearful state of the economy. One of the main reasons for the slow implementation of the new policy and also for the practical muddle and ideological confusion evoked by it is the extremely unsystematic way in which the premises laid down are being worked out. In the field of the economy a policy of major switches, and all the more so where they lack interco-ordination, is totally inadmissible. The lack of a real economic centre to watch over economic activity, conduct experiments in that field, record and disseminate results and co-ordinate in practice all sides of economic activity and thus actually work at a co-ordinated economic plan – the absence of a real economic centre of this sort not only inflicts the severest shocks on the economy, such as fuel and food crises, but also excludes the possibility of the planned and co-ordinated elaboration of new premises of economic policy . . .

Given such a conception – the only correct one – of the task of Gosplan, its total reorganisation is incumbent as regards its make-up and its methods of work. An economic plan cannot be worked out theoretically, its working out must develop in the course of its practical implementation. This means that the economic plan must be worked out solely by whoever implements it. In this respect the present situation of Gosplan excludes any possibility of achieving real planned direction of the economy. It is wholly evident that the Council of Labour and Defence does not and will not exercise real, constant direction of industry. The task of the Council of Labour and Defence consists of drawing up the bases of economic policy, of general supervision of economic work, and of finding a practical settlement of those special situations which prove insoluble at other levels of the economic organisation.

The economic plan must essentially be put together around large-scale nationalised industry, as a pivot. Gosplan likewise must be fitted in around this pivot. Whoever is in practical charge of economic life must also direct ideologically and organisationally the elaboration, verification and regulation of the implementation of the economic plan, day in day out and hour by hour. In the event of Gosplan being unable to reach agreement, the matter would be referred to the Council of Labour and Defence. But as a general rule co-ordination of the economic plan is to be worked out and ensured by Gosplan in the course of its daily work from the angle of large-scale nationalised industry being the governing economic factor.

*Source*: J. M. Meijer (ed.), *The Trotsky Papers*, vol. II, 579–81.

**Document 22**    MEMORANDUM TO THE POLITBURO ON THE PARTY'S INVOLVEMENT IN THE ECONOMY (10 MARCH 1922)

One of the most important questions, both for the party itself and for Soviet work, is the relation between the party and the state apparatus. In fact, this question is passed over in the theses (for the Eleventh Party Congress), and to the extent that it is touched on (in regard to economic training, and so on) nudges in the right direction.

Without freeing the party as a party from the functions of direct administration and management, it is impossible to cleanse the party of bureaucratism and the economy of indiscipline. This is the fundamental question. It is a ruinous 'policy' when meetings of the provincial [party] committee decide, in passing, questions concerning the province's sowing campaign or whether or not to lease a factory. And it is in no wise better in the district committee or the central one. Such a method is propaganda in deed against serious specialization, against responsibility, against study of the matter in practice, against respect for specialized knowledge, against serious, unremitting, properly organized work.

When the Central Committee encountered, in different questions, the most egregious instances of direct interference by the provincial committees in judiciary matters, it fought such tendencies. But in all its practice, unconsciously, it has de facto instilled such a manner of acting, depriving all government organs of personal responsibility, removing responsibility for actual work, undermining self-confidence, and at the same time fostering the party's extreme bureaucratization.

We have now passed a resolution that will finally free the trade unions from the functions of economic management. With the change in economic policy, this is unquestionably correct. But for the sake of efficiency, i.e., for actual success, it makes no difference whether the interference comes from the trade unions or from the Central Committee, provincial committees, district committees, or party cells. If the New Economic Policy requires that trade unions be trade unions, then this same policy requires that the Party be a party. Training for the correct implementation of commercial functions and economic functions in general is not the task of the party, but the task of the appropriate economic organs for which the party ensures solid leadership and provides the opportunity to select employees and train them without sporadic and incompetent outside interference. The party explains to the working masses the importance and significance of commercial operations as a method of socialist construction. The party combats prejudices that hinder the proper development of economic activity. The party fights attempts to use the New Economic Policy as a device for instilling bourgeois morals in the Communist Party itself. The party firmly establishes what is allowed and what is forbidden. But the party does not direct commercial operations, because it is incapable of doing that. The party does not train people for economic activity, and, in particular, commercial activity, because it is not capable of that.

The party has power in its hands, but it governs only through the properly functioning state apparatus. It sends back 99 percent of the matters submitted to it for decision, on the grounds that they contain nothing of concern to the party.

At the same time, the party concentrates its attention on the theoretical education of party youth to a far greater extent than in the past.

*Source*: R. Pipes, *The Unknown Lenin* (New Haven: Yale University Press, 1998), p. 148.

**Document 23**     TROTSKY TO THE POLITBURO OF THE CENTRAL COMMITTEE
(21 APRIL 1922)

*Concerning the Conclusions of the Members of the Politburo on Comrade Lenin's proposal concerning the Work of Assistant Heads, issued 18 April 1922.*

1) The problems posed are so general that this is tantamount to posing no problems at all. The Deputies must strive to ensure that all is well in every field and in every connection – that is what the draft of the regulatory order boils down to. The paragraphs present, as it were, a certain appearance of providing instructions on how to contrive matters so that all is well in all quarters – even down to the proper editing of '*Ekonomicheskaya Zhizn*'.

2) The People's Commissariat of Workers' and Peasants' Inspection is designated as the apparatus for performing these general tasks. Yet the People's Commissariat of Workers' and Peasants' Inspection of its essence is not suited for this and cannot become so. One must not shut one's eyes to the fact that the People's Commissariat of Workers' and Peasants' Inspection is staffed chiefly by officials who have come to grief in various fields of activity. Hence, among other things, the extraordinary growth of intrigue in the organs of the People's Commissariat of Workers' and Peasants' Inspection, which has long become proverbial throughout the country. There is absolutely no basis for the idea that this apparatus (not its small group of leaders but the organisation as a whole) can be revitalised and strengthened, for the decent officials will still continue to be posted to jobs of basic importance and not to jobs of inspectors. The plan to pull up the Soviet apparatus of State by using the People's Commissariat of Workers' and Peasants' Inspection as a lever is therefore plainly make believe.

3) Likewise I simply do not believe in the possibility of educating administrators and economic executives from among non-Party workers and peasants through the medium of the People's Commissariat of Workers' and Peasants' Inspection. For this we must have a system of schools and training courses – particularly training courses connected with specific branches of economics and State activity. We must start, as is proper, with the young, and teach them properly and not merely notionally through the People's Commissariat of Workers' and Peasants' Inspection.

4) I have great misgivings lest the mutual relationship of the Deputies become a source of difficulties. Here the dictaphone will not help. Once there are two Deputies their mutual relationship must be on an absolutely correct basis.

5) The main thing is that I still cannot envisage the sort of organ which will in practice be able to control economic work on a day-to-day basis.

If it is a bad thing that the Central Statistical Administration is an academic institution, it is a hundred times worse, and absolutely catastrophic, that the State Planning Commission is academic. At the beginning of last year it was already plain that there was no organ for co-ordinating and actually controlling economic matters. The present organisation of the State Planning Commission approximates outwardly to what I proposed last year, but only outwardly. In essence the parcelling out of responsibility remains a fact, and it is absolutely unknown who in practice controls the indents for fuel, transport, raw materials or money. As a matter of inter-departmental controversy these questions are put before the Council of Labour and Defence or the Politburo and are solved by rule of thumb, and that at the moment when the water is reaching our throats. There should be an establishment with an economic calendar for a year ahead hanging on the wall; an establishment that anticipates and, in the light of its foresight, co-ordinates. The State Planning Commission should be such an establishment. In my opinion the chairmanship of the State Planning Commission would be for one of the Deputies a much more realistic task than anything that is spoken of in the resolution.

*Source*: J. M. Meijer (ed.), *The Trotsky Papers*, vol. II, pp. 731–33.

TROTSKY TO THE DEPUTY CHAIRMAN OF THE COUNCIL OF PEOPLE'S COMMISSARS AND POLITBURO (23 AUGUST 1922)                     **Document 24**

[Lenin, the Chairman of the Council of People's Commissars was at this time too ill to take part in affairs of state.] The most vital and urgent administrative-organisational economic measures are adopted by us with, what I estimate to be on an average, a delay of a year and a half to two years. It may be that the moment for serious discussion and settlement of the question of a planning organ is not yet. Nevertheless, I consider I do not have the right to refrain from putting forward preliminary observations about how it is to be settled. With the change-over to the new economic policy State funds are a vital lever in the economic plan. Their allocation is predetermined by the economic plan. Outside of fixing the volume of monetary issues and allocating financial resources between departments there is not and cannot be any economic plan at the moment. Yet, as far as I can judge, Gosplan has no concern with these fundamental questions. Is this because Gosplan's plan is not related to the current year's economic tasks? Is it because Gosplan can have nothing to contribute to the discussion and solution of these questions? Whichever of these explanations one adopts it is perfectly obvious that here we have a radically wrong organisation . . . How can it have happened that when discussing the question of the allocation of funds and the volume of money in circulation no one in the Politburo called Gosplan to mind? . . . How can one require efficiency and proper accountability from individual departments and organs if they do not have the slightest certainty as to what to-morrow will look like? . . . It may very well be that the present Gosplan is performing very valuable work. But this work is not the work of Gosplan.

*Source*: J. M. Meijer (ed.), *The Trotsky Papers*, vol. II, pp. 745–47.

**Document 25**    TROTSKY TO THE POLITBURO CONCERNING STALIN'S LETTER ABOUT GOSPLAN AND THE COUNCIL OF LABOUR AND DEFENCE (15 JANUARY 1923)

1) At the centre of a number of my written recommendations submitted to the Central Committee stood the question of the need to ensure the correct planned direction on a day to day basis of the State economy – from the standpoint, in the first place, of the re-establishment and development of State industry. I sought to establish the point that we did not have an organ directly responsible for the planned direction of the State economy or capable in terms of its rights, duties and composition of exercising such direction. I sought to show that this was precisely the cause behind the urge to accumulate more and more directing and coordinating organs which in the final resort only get in one another's way. Apart from the Council of People's Commissars and the Presidium of the All-Russian Executive Committee we have at the moment: the Collegium of Assistant Heads (the three-man body), the Council of Labour and Defence, the Financial Committee, the Lesser Council of People's Commissars and Gosplan. Yet questions time and again get referred to the Central Committee (Secretariat, Orgburo and Politburo). I considered that this multiplicity of directing establishments with undefined mutual relationships and fragmented responsibilities generated chaos from the top downwards.

Comrade Stalin recommends that we now merge the Council of Labour and Defence, the Collegium of Assistant Heads and the Financial Committee. This proposal, irrespective of its immediate practical value, is in any case a token of the inexpediency of having a self-contained Collegium of Assistant Heads and a self-contained Financial Committee. When I first put forward my recommendation for having a co-ordinating economic organ in Gosplan I was, of course, unable to evaluate Comrade Stalin's proposal since this was submitted two years later than my proposal. Moreover Comrade Stalin's exceptionally important proposal, as regards its substance, for the reorganisation of the central organs is being put forward by Comrade Stalin *inter alia* as a criticism of my repeated proposals.

2) I judged the mistake in our economic policy of the most recent period to be the primacy accorded to financial questions. A galloping rouble cannot be the regulator of the economy, and therefore the financial dictatorship time and again degenerates into a betting venture at the expense of the State economy. For a time such a policy can yield fictitious successes. But it inevitably begets its own collapse.

I considered and consider the essential corner-stone to be the postulate of the interests of the State economy – with all necessary reservations – and the need to take one's cue from these interests. This prompted my recommendation to have the Chairman of the Supreme Council of the National Economy as the Chairman of Gosplan so that the elaboration of all planning questions should be undertaken above all from the viewpoints of the interests of industry. If long term planning under this system were violated, adjustments could be made from above by the Council of Labour and Defence. Comrade Stalin's project eliminates all the departments, including the Supreme Council of the National Economy, from the Council of Labour and Defence but leaves it with the People's Commissariat of Finance. In so doing the mistaken inter-relationship between finance and industry receives in Comrade Stalin's project new organisational expression . . .

5) Without a co-ordinating plan and a co-ordinated direction no economic work is possible. The plan must be not an academic one but a practical one. It is impossible to segregate the plan from the supervision of its realisation. Our planning organ is Gosplan; the higher organs (the Council of Labour and Defence, the Council of People's Commissars, the Financial Committee, the Collegium of Deputy Chairmen, the Central Committee) are compelled either to rely on Gosplan or else to improvise and set up innumerable commissions. The only way out of this situation is to take Gosplan in hand, i.e. to equip it with senior officials for its regular current work, combining them with specialists in the appropriate proportions . . . By way of analogy I would say that Gosplan would discharge the role of staff headquarters and the Council of Labour and Defence that of the Military Revolutionary Council.

*Source*: J. M. Meijer (ed.), *The Trotsky Papers*, vol. II, pp. 817–33.

TROTSKY'S REPORT TO THE TWELFTH CONGRESS OF THE RUSSIAN COMMUNIST PARTY (17–25 APRIL 1923)  **Document 26**

In view of the general economic structure of our country, the restoration of State industry is narrowly bound up with the development of agriculture. The necessary means for circulation must be created by agriculture in the form of a surplus of agricultural products over and above the village consumption before industry will be able to make a decisive step forwards. But it is equally important for the State industry not to lag behind agriculture, otherwise private industry would be created on the basis of the latter, and this private industry would in the long run swallow up or absorb State industry.

Only such industry can prove victorious which renders more than it swallows up. Industry which lives at the expense of the budget, i.e., at the expense of agriculture, could not possibly be a firm and lasting support for the dictatorship of the proletariat. The question of creating surplus value in State industry is the fateful question for the Soviet power, i.e., for the proletariat.

An expanded reproduction of State industry, which is unthinkable without the accumulation of surplus value by the State, forms in its turn the condition for the development of our agriculture in a socialist and not in a capitalist direction.

It is therefore through State industry that the road lies which leads to the socialist order of society. . . .

The attainment of a price regulation, on the basis of the market, better corresponding with the needs of industrial development, the establishment of more normal correlations between the branches of the light industry and those branches of industry and agriculture which provide it with its raw materials, and finally the straightening out of the front of the heavy and light industry – these are the root problems of the State in the sphere of industrial activity in the second period of the new economic policy now beginning. These problems can only be solved by a correct correlation between the market and the State industrial plan.

In Soviet Russia, where the chief means of industry and transport belong to one owner, the State, the active interference of the latter in industry must of necessity take the form of a State industrial plan. In view of the predominating rôle of the State as an owner and a master, the principle of a uniform plan acquires at the very outset an exceptional importance.

The whole of previous experience has shown, however, that a plan of Socialist economy cannot be established *a priori* in a theoretical or bureaucratic manner. A real Socialist economic plan embracing all branches of industry in their relations to one another, and in the relation of industry as a whole to agriculture, is possible only as a result of a prolonged, preparatory economic experience on the basis of nationalisation, and as the result of continuous efforts to bring into practical accord the work of different branches of industry, and to correctly estimate the results achieved.

Thus for the coming period our task is to determine the general direction, and is, to a considerable extent, of a preparatory character. It cannot be defined by any single formula, but presupposes a constant and vigilant adaptation of the guiding economic apparatus, of its basic tasks, methods and practice to the phenomena and conditions of the market. Only at the final stage of their development can and must the methods of planned industry subordinate the market to themselves, and by this very fact abolish it.

Hence we can perceive quite clearly two dangers accompanying the application of State methods of planned industry during the present epoch, viz., (a) If we try to outstrip economic development by means of our planned interference, and to replace the regulating function of the market by administrative measures which have no basis in actual experience, then partial or general economic crises are inevitable, such as occurred in the epoch of military communism; (b) If centralised regulation lags behind the clearly matured need for it, we shall have to solve economic questions by the wasteful methods of the market in cases where timely economic-administrative interference could obtain the same results in a shorter space of time and with a smaller expenditure of effort and resources. . . .

It is quite evident that the fundamental planning of industry cannot be attained within the industry itself, i.e., by way of strengthening its guiding administrative organ (the Supreme Council of National Economy), but must form the task of a separate organisation which stands above the organisation of industry, and which connects the latter with finance, transport, etc. This is the function of the State Planning Commission. It is necessary, however, to define more clearly its position, to organise it more strongly, to give it more definite and incontestable rights and, especially, duties. It ought to be established as an immovable principle that not a single economic question which concerns the State as a whole may be dealt with in the higher organs of the Republic without consulting the State Planning Commission. . . . the State Planning Commission [is] the general staff of the State economy . . .

The Party will accomplish its historic mission only if the economic experience of the whole Party grows together with the growth in size and complexity of the economic problems which the Soviet power has to face. Therefore the Twelfth Congress is of the opinion that not only a proper distribution of workers, but also the function of supervising every important branch of economic administration must be considered by the Party as its bounden duty, especially in view of the New Economic Policy, which creates the danger of degeneration for a part of the managing staffs and of perverting the proletarian line of policy in the process of economic reconstruction. Under no circumstances whatever should this guidance turn, in practice and as a matter of course, into frequent dismissals or transference of managers, into a meddling in the current every-day work of the administration, or into attempts at their direction . . . The Twelfth Congress especially calls to mind that in accordance with the resolution of the Eleventh Congress, the Party organisations 'solve economic questions independently only in those cases and in so far as the questions imperatively demand a solution according to Party principles'.

*Source*: *Labour Monthly* vol. 5, no. 1, July 1923 (also at http://www.marxists.org/archive/trotsky).

**Document 27**    *THE NEW COURSE – BUREAUCRATISM AND THE REVOLUTION* (DECEMBER 1923)

The essential conditions which not only prevent the realization of the socialist ideal but are, in addition, sometimes a source of painful tests and grave dangers to the revolution are well enough known. They are: a) the internal social contradictions of the revolution which were automatically compressed under War Communism but which, under the NEP, unfold unfailingly and seek to find political expression; b) the protracted counter-revolutionary threat to the Soviet republic represented by the imperialist states.

The social contradictions of the revolution are class contradictions. What are the fundamental classes of our country? a) the proletariat, b) the peasantry, c) the new bourgeoisie with the layer of bourgeois intellectuals that covers it.

From the standpoint of economic role and political significance first place belongs to the proletariat organized in the state and to the peasantry which provides the agricultural products that are dominant in our economy. The new bourgeoisie plays principally the role of intermediary between Soviet industry and agriculture as well as between the different parts of Soviet industry and the different spheres of rural economy. But it does not confine itself to being a commercial intermediary; in part, it also assumes the role of organizer of production.

Putting aside for the moment the question of the tempo of the development of the proletarian revolution in the West, the course of our revolution will be determined by the comparative growth of the three fundamental elements of our economy: state industry, agriculture, and private commercial-industrial capital . . .

Let us take the historical hypothesis more unfavourable to us. The rapid development of private capital, if it should take place, would signify that Soviet industry and commerce, including the cooperatives, do not assure the satisfaction of the needs of peasant economy. In addition it would show that private capital is interposing itself more and more between the workers' state and the peasantry, is acquiring an economic and therefore a political influence over the latter. It goes without saying that such a rupture between Soviet industry and agriculture, between the proletariat and the peasantry, would constitute a grave danger for the proletarian revolution, a symptom of the possibility of the triumph of the counter-revolution.

What are the political paths by which the victory of the counter-revolution might come if the economic hypothesis just set forth were to be realized? There could be many: either the direct overthrow of the workers' party, or its progressive degeneration, or finally, the conjunction of a partial degeneration, splits, and counter-revolutionary upheavals. The realization of one or the other of these eventualities would depend above all on the tempo of the economic development. In case private capital succeeded, little by little, slowly, in dominating state capital, the political process would assume in the main the character of the degeneration of the state apparatus in a bourgeois direction, with the consequences that this would involve for the party. If private capital increased rapidly and succeeded in fusing with the peasantry, the active counter-revolutionary tendencies directed against the Communist Party would then probably prevail.

If we set forth these hypotheses bluntly, it is of course not because we consider them historically probable (on the contrary, their probability is at a minimum), but because only such a way of putting the question makes possible a more correct and all sided historical orientation and, consequently, the adoption of all possible preventive measures . . .

That is why, on the basis of the economic policy indicated above, we must have a definite state and party policy (including a definite policy inside the party), aimed at counteracting the accumulation and consolidation of the tendencies directed against the dictatorship of the working class . . . It is beyond doubt that through the medium of the rural and military [party] cells, tendencies reflecting more or less the countryside, with the special traits that distinguish it from the town, filter and will continue to filter into the party . . .

The state apparatus is the most important source of bureaucratism . . . [and] the bureaucratization of the apparatus threatens to separate the party from the masses. This is precisely the danger that is now most obvious and direct. The struggle against the other dangers must under present conditions begin with the struggle against bureaucratism.

It is unworthy of a Marxist to consider that bureaucratism is only the aggregate of the bad habits of office holders. Bureaucratism is a social phenomenon in that it is a definite system of administration of men and things. Its profound causes lie in the heterogeneity of society, the difference between the daily and the fundamental interests of various groups of the population. Bureaucratism is complicated by the fact of the lack of culture of the broad masses. With us, the essential source of bureaucratism resides in the necessity of creating and sustaining a state apparatus that unites the interests of the proletariat and those of the peasantry in a perfect economic harmony, from which we are still far removed. The necessity of maintaining a permanent army is likewise another important source of bureaucratism.

It is quite plain that precisely the negative social phenomena we have just enumerated and which now nurture bureaucratism could place the revolution in peril should they continue to develop. We have mentioned above this hypothesis: the growing discord between state and peasant economy, the growth of the kulaks in the country, their alliance with private commercial industrial capital, these would be given the low cultural level of the toiling masses of the countryside and in part of the towns the causes of the eventual counter-revolutionary dangers.

*Source*: L. Trotsky, *The New Course* (New York: New International Publishing Company, 1943), pp. 39–46.

**Document 28**     *MY LIFE* (1930)

But I must finish Sklyanskii's story. With that rudeness characteristic of Stalin, without even being consulted about it, he was transferred to economic work. Dzerzhinskii, who was glad to get rid of Unschlicht, his deputy at the GPU, and secure for industry such a first-class administrator as Sklyanskii, put him in charge of the cloth trust. With a shrug of his shoulders, Sklyanskii plunged into his new work. A few months later he decided to visit the United States, to look about, study, and buy machinery. Before he left he called on me to say good-by and to ask my advice. We had worked hand in hand during the years of civil war. But our talk had usually been about troop units, military rules, speeding up the graduation of officers, supplies of copper and aluminium for military plants, uniforms and food, rather than about the party. We were both too busy for that. After Lenin was taken ill, when the plots of the epigones began to force their way into the war commissariat, I refrained from discussing party matters, particularly with the military staff. The situation was very indefinite, the differences were then only beginning to crop up, and the forming of factions in the army concealed many dangers. Later on I was ill myself. At that meeting with Sklyanskii in the summer of 1925, when I was no longer in charge of the war commissariat, we talked over almost everything.

'Tell me,' Sklyanskii asked, 'what is Stalin?'

Sklyanskii knew Stalin well enough himself. He wanted my definition of Stalin and my explanation of his success. I thought for a minute.

'Stalin', I said, 'is the outstanding mediocrity of the party.' This definition then shaped itself for me for the first time in its full import, psychological as well as social. By the expression on Sklyanskii's face, I saw at once that I had helped my questioner to touch on something significant.

'You know,' he said, 'it is amazing how, during this last period, the mean, the self-satisfied mediocrity is pushing itself into every sphere. And all of it finds in Stalin its leader. Where does it all come from?'

'This is the reaction after the great social and psychological strain of the first years of revolution. A victorious counter-revolution may develop its great men. But its first stage, the Thermidor, demands mediocrities who can't see farther than their noses. Their strength lies in their political blindness, like the mill-horse that thinks that he is moving up when really he is only pushing down the belt-wheel. A horse that sees is incapable of doing the work.'

In that conversation I realized for the first time with absolute clarity the problem of the Thermidor – with, I might even say, a sort of physical conviction. I agreed with Sklyanskii to return to the subject after he got back from America. Not many weeks later a cable informed us that Sklyanskii had been drowned in some American lake while boating. Life is inexhaustible in its cruel inventions.

*Source*: L. Trotsky, *My Life* (London: Pathfinder, 1970), pp. 512–13.

*DECLARATION OF THE THIRTEEN* (14 JULY 1926)

**Document 29**

It is completely obvious that the more difficult it is for the ruling centres to carry through their decisions by the methods of party democracy, the less the vanguard of the working class sees their policy as its own. The divergence between the direction of economic policy and the direction of the feelings and thoughts of the proletarian vanguard inevitably strengthens the need for repression and gives all policy an administrative-bureaucratic character. Any other explanation of the growth of bureaucratism is secondary and does not encompass the essence of the question.

The lag of industry behind the economic development of the country as a whole signifies, in spite of the growth in the number of workers, a lowering of the specific gravity of the proletariat in the society. The lag in the influence of industry on agriculture and the rapid growth of the kulaks lower in the village the specific gravity of the hired workers and poor peasants and their trust in the state and in themselves. The lag of wage raises behind the rising living standard of the non-proletarian elements of the city and the upper groups of the village inevitably signifies the lowering of the political and cultural self-esteem of the proletariat as the ruling class. From this, in particular, comes the clear decrease in the activity of the workers and poor peasants in the elections to the soviets, which is a most serious warning for our Party . . . In questions of agricultural policy in the village the danger of shifts to the side of the upper groups in the village is all the more clearly defined . . . The fact is that under the guise of a union of the poor peasantry with the middle peasant, we observe steadily and regularly the political subordination of the poor peasantry to the middle peasants, and through them to the kulaks . . . The number of workers in our state industry does not now reach two million; together with transport, it is less than three million. The soviet, trade-union, cooperative and all other employees certainly do not number less than that figure, and this comparison alone testifies to the colossal political and economic role of the bureaucracy; it is entirely obvious that the state apparatus, in its composition and level of life, is to an overwhelming degree bourgeois and petty-bourgeois, and inclines away from the proletariat and the village poor, on the one hand, toward the displaced intelligentsia, and on the other toward the landleaser, the merchant, the kulak, the new bourgeois.

*Source*: L. Trotsky, *The Challenge of the Left Opposition (1926–27)* (New York: Pathfinder Press, 1980), pp. 76–77, 80–81.

# Bibliography

Acton, E. and Stableford, T. (eds) *The Soviet Union: A Documentary History* (Exeter: University of Exeter Press, 1988)

Allen, N. (ed.) *Leon Trotsky: The Challenge of the Left Opposition (1923–25)* (New York: Pathfinder Press, 1975)

Argenbright, R. 'Red Tsaritsyn: Precursor of Stalinist Terror', *Revolutionary Russia* no. 2, 1991

*Arkhiv Trotskogo* (Moscow: Terra, 1990)

Bazhanov, B. *Bazhanov and the Damnation of Stalin* (Ohio: Ohio State University, 1990)

*The Bolsheviks and the October Revolution: Central Committee Minutes* (London: Pluto Press, 1974)

*Bolshevitskoe rukovosdstvo: perepiska, 1912–27* (Moscow: ROSSPEN, 1996)

Broué, P. *Trotsky* (Paris: Fayard, 1988)

Browder, R. P. and Kerensky, A. F. *The Russian Provisional Government 1917: Documents* (Stanford: Stanford University Press, 1961)

Butt, V. P., Murphy, A. B., Myshov, N. A. and Swain, G. R. (eds) *The Russian Civil War: Documents from the Soviet Archives* (Basingstoke: Macmillan, 1996)

Carr, E. H. *Socialism in One Country* (Basingstoke: Macmillan, 1958)

Cummins, A. (ed.) *Documents of Soviet History* (New York: Academic International Press, 1998)

Daniels, R. *A Documentary History of Communism* (London: University Press of New England, 1985)

Day, R. B. *Leon Trotsky and the Politics of Economic Isolation* (Cambridge: Cambridge University Press, 1973).

Deutscher, I. *The Prophet Armed, The Prophet Unarmed, The Prophet Outcast* (Oxford: Oxford University Press, 1970)

*Devyatyi s'ezd RKP: stenograficheskii otchet* (Moscow, 1920)

*Dvenatsatyi s'ezd RKP (b): stenograficheskii otchet* (Moscow, 1923)

Eastman, M. *Leon Trotsky: Portrait of a Youth* (London: Faber and Gwyer, 1926)

Evans, L. and Block, R. (eds) *Leon Trotsky on China* (New York: Monad Press, 1976)

Heywood, A. J. *Modernising Lenin's Russia* (Cambridge: Cambridge University Press, 1999)

*Istoriya soveta rabochikh deputatov* (Petersburg, 1906)

Keep, J. H. (ed.) *The Debate on Soviet Power* (Oxford: Oxford University Press, 1979)

Knei-Paz, B. *The Social and Political Thought of Leon Trotsky* (Oxford: Clarendon Press, 1978)

Law, D. 'Trotsky and Thermidor', in F. Gori (ed.), *Pensiero e Azione Politica di Lev Trockij* (Florence: Feltrinelli, 1982)

Lenin, V. I. *On the Revolution of 1905* (Moscow, 1955)

Lih, L. T., Naumov, O. V. and Khlevniuk, O. V. (eds) *Stalin's Letters to Molotov* (New Haven: Harvard University Press, 1995)

Lunacharskii, A. *Revolutionary Silhouettes* (Harmondsworth: Penguin, 1967)

McCullough, F. 'Trotsky in Ekaterinburg', *Fortnightly Review* vol. 108, 1920

Meijer, J. M. (ed.) *The Trotsky Papers* (The Hague: Mouton and Co., 1964)

*The Military Papers of Leon Trotsky, 1918–24* (Microfilms from the Russian State Military Archive filmed by Research Publications, an imprint of Primary Source Media)

*Odinatsatyi s'ezd RKP (b): stenograficheskii otchet* (Moscow, 1961)

Pantsov, A. *The Bolsheviks and the Chinese Revolution* (London: Curzon, 2000)

Patanaude, B. *Trotsky: Downfall of a Revolutionary* (New York: HarperCollins, 2009)

Pearce, B. 'Lenin versus Trotsky on "Revolutionary Defeatism"', *Sbornik* no. 7, 1987

Pearce, B. (ed.) *1903: Second Congress of the Russian Social Democratic Labour Party: Minutes* (London: Pluto Press, 1978)

Pipes, R. *The Unknown Lenin* (New Haven: Yale University Press, 1998)

Rabinowitch, A. *Prelude to Revolution* (Bloomington: Indiana University Press, 1968)

Ree, E. van 'Lenin's Last Struggle Revisited', *Revolutionary Russia* no. 2, 2001

Reissner, L. 'Sviyazhsk', in J. Hansen *et al.* (eds), *Leon Trotsky: The Man and his Work* (New York: Merit, 1969)

Rosenberg, W. G. 'The Social Background to Tsektran', in D. Koenker *et al.* (eds), *Party, State and Society in the Russian Civil War* (Bloomington: Indiana University Press, 1989)

Rubinstein, J. *Leon Trotsky: A Revolutionary's Life* (New Haven: Yale University Press, 2011)

Schapiro, L. *The Origin of the Communist Autocracy* (London: Macmillan, 1977)

Serge, V. *Memoirs of a Revolutionary* (Oxford: Oxford University Press, 1963)

Serge, V. and Sedova-Trotsky, N. *The Life and Death of Leon Trotsky* (London: Wildwood House, 1975)

Service, R. *Lenin: A Political Life* (Basingstoke: Macmillan, 1995)

—— *Stalin* (Basingstoke: Macmillan, 2004)

—— *Trotsky: A Biography* (Basingstoke: Pan, 2009)

Souvarine, B. 'Pis'mo v redaktsiyu', *Sotsialisticheskii vestnik* no. 4, 1960

Stalin, J. V. *Collected Works*, vols. VII, VIII, IX and X (Moscow, 1953)

*Stenograficheskii otchet X s'ezda RKP* (Petrograd, 1921)

Sukhanov, N. *The Russian Revolution: A Personal Record* (Princeton: Princeton University Press, 1984)

Surh, G. D. *1905 in St Petersburg* (Stanford: Stanford University Press, 1989)

Sverchkov, D. *Na zare revolyutsii* (Leningrad, 1925)

Swain, G. R. *Russian Social Democracy and the Legal Labour Movement, 1906– 14* (Basingstoke: Macmillan, 1983)

—— 'Was the Profintern Really Necessary?', *European History Quarterly* no. 1, 1987

—— 'Freedom of Association and the Trade Unions, 1906–14', in O. Crisp and L. Edmondson (eds), *Civil Rights in Imperial Russia* (Oxford: Oxford University Press, 1989)

—— 'Before the Fighting Started: A Discussion on the Theme of the "Third Way"', *Revolutionary Russia* no. 2, 1991

—— *The Origins of the Russian Civil War* (London: Longman, 1996)

—— 'Russia's Garibaldi: The Revolutionary Life of Mikhail Artemovich Muraviev', *Revolutionary Russia* no. 2, 1998

—— *Russia's Civil War* (Stroud: Tempus, 2000)

—— 'Vācietis: The Enigma of the Red Army's First Commander', *Revolutionary Russia* no. 1, 2003

—— 'Late Imperial Revolutionaries', in I. D. Thatcher (ed.), *Late Imperial Russia: Problems and Prospects* (Manchester: Manchester University Press, 2005)

—— *Trotsky* (Harlow: Pearson Longman, 2006)

—— 'Trotsky and the Russian Civil War', in I. D. Thatcher (ed.), *Reinterpreting Revolutionary Russia* (Basingstoke: Macmillan, 2006)

Thatcher, I. D. '*Bor'ba*: A Workers' Journal in St Petersburg on the Eve of the First World War', *English Historical Review* no. 113, 1998

—— *Leon Trotsky and World War One* (Basingstoke: Palgrave Macmillan, 2000)

—— *Trotsky* (London: Routledge, 2003)

—— 'The St Petersburg/Petrograd Mezhraionka, 1913–17: The Rise and Fall of a Russian Social Democratic Workers' Party Unity Faction', *Slavonic and East European Review* no. 2, 2009

*Trinadtsatyi s'ezd RKP (b): stenograficheskii otchet* (Moscow, 1924)

Trotsky, L. *The New Course* (New York: New International Publishing Company, 1943)

—— *Trotsky's Diary in Exile* (London: Faber, 1959)

—— *Terrorism and Communism* (Ann Arbor: University of Michigan Press, 1961)

—— *Results and Prospects* (London: New Park Publications, 1962)

—— *History of the Russian Revolution* (London: Sphere, 1965)

—— *Stalin: An Appraisal of the Man and his Influence* (London: Panther, 1969)

—— *The Permanent Revolution and Results and Prospects* (New York: Pathfinder Press, 1969)

—— *My Life* (London: Pathfinder, 1970)

—— *1905* (Harmondsworth: Penguin, 1973)

—— *The First Five Years of the Communist International* (London: New Park Publications, 1974)

—— *The Writings of Leon Trotsky 1936–7* (New York: Pathfinder Press, 1975)

—— *How the Revolution Armed* (London: New Park Publications, 1979–81)

—— *Our Political Tasks* (London: New Park Publications, 1979)

—— *The Report of the Siberian Delegation* (London: New Park Publications, 1979)

—— *The Challenge of the Left Opposition (1926–27)* (New York: Pathfinder Press, 1980)

—— *The War Correspondence of Leon Trotsky: The Balkan Wars, 1912–13* (New York: Monad Press, 1980)

Valentinov, N. 'Dopolnenie k "Dnevniku" L Trotskogo', *Sotsialisticheskii vestnik* nos. 2–3, 1959

Vilkova, V. *The Struggle for Power in Russia in 1923* (Amherst: Prometheus Books, 1996)

Volkogonov, D. *Trotsky: The Eternal Revolutionary* (London: HarperCollins, 1997)

Wade, R. (ed.) *Documents in Soviet History* (New York: Academic International Press, 1995)

White, J. D. 'Lenin, Trotsky and the Arts of Insurrection: The Congress of Soviets of the Northern Region, 11–13 October 1917', *Slavonic and East European Review* no. 1, 1999

Yurenev, I. 'Mezhraionka, 1911–17', *Proletarskaya revolyutsiya* no. 1, 1924

Ziv, G. *Trotskii: kharakteristika po lichnym vospominaniem* (New York: Narondnopravstvo, 1921)

# Index